Ferrets For Dummies

DISCARD Cheat Sheet

P9-CMX-267

Important Numbers to Have

Your vet's number: _____

24-hour emergency clinic: _____

National Animal Poison Control Center;
800-548-2423 ($30 per case, credit cards only)
900-680-0000 ($20 for the first 5 minutes, $2.95 for
each additional minute, applied to your phone bill)

For a pet sitter referral   800-296-PETS

Signs of a Healthy Ferret

Take this list with you when you go to pick out
your fuzzy:

- Fur is soft and shiny, and there are no patches
  of missing fur.
- Eyes are clear and bright.
- Eyes, ears, and nose free from any discharge.
- Underside of the ferret is clean and healthy
  looking and has no signs of diarrhea or bloating.
- The ferret is inquisitive when you approach and
  may be jumpy and playful. He does not cower
  or run to a hiding place.

A Few Fun Definitions

Bottom dwellers Ferts sleeping on the bottom of
the fuzzy pile.

Cat nip The little warning bite a cat receives to
remind him of the fert's superiority.

Curtain call The unmistakable shriek made by
humans when they discover that the fert reached
the top of the curtains.

Delayed gratification When a ferret waits
patiently for you to return the freshly cleaned litter
box so he can christen it.

Flatliner A ferret imitating a speed bump.

Fuzzy reception line The streak you see out the
corner of your eye when a group of ferrets have
joined in a high-speed chase.

Hostile takeover When a ferret claims another
ferret's hidey-hole and/or treasures.

Mind over matter The ferret human contemplating
cleaning up all the fuzzy mess.

Nonobadferret A common ferret nickname.

Yikes A word that is preferable to the one usually
said when stepping in ferret poopie.

Info to Provide a Ferret Sitter

The list explains the basics you should leave for
a sitter who's watching your ferret while you're
gone. Chapter 12 has more info on traveling without
your fuzzy.

- The phone number where you can be reached
  and the name of the people you're staying with.
- An emergency phone number (or two) of some-
  one close to home, such as a friend or relative.
- Your veterinarian's phone number and address
- The emergency clinic's phone number and
  address.
- A supply of necessary medication and instruc-
  tions on how to medicate your ferret.
- Written description of each ferret and each
  ferret's personality (attach a photo next to each
  description to be extra helpful).
- A list of do's and don'ts.
- An adequate supply of food.
- Written instructions on feeding
- Instructions on how to clean up after your ferts,
  supervise safe playtime, and watch for signs of
  illness or injury.

First-Aid Kit Checklist

Keep this list handy with your first-aid kit and use it to keep track of the supplies you need to replace or update. For convenience, this list is arranged alphabetically. For complete information on the first-aid kit, see Chapter 13.

___Adhesive bandage tape

___Antibiotic ointment (such as Neosporin)

___Baby wipes

___Bene-Bac

___Betadine solution

___Can of prescription feline A/D

___Can of strawberry or vanilla Ensure

___Canola or olive oil

___Chemical heating pack (portable heat for the young or sick ferret)

___Chicken or lamb baby food

___Cotton balls and cotton swabs

___Desitin

___Ear cleanser

___Eye wash/rinse

___Ferretone/Linatone

___Gauze pads

___Gauze wrap

___Hairball preventative (Petromalt or Laxatone)

___Health records

___Heating pad

___Hydrogen peroxide

___Ice pack

___Immodium liquid

___Kaopectate or Pepto Bismol

___Light Karo syrup or NutriCal

___List of any medications your ferret is currently taking

___Nail clippers

___Pedialyte or Gatorade

___Pediatric Liquid Benadryl

___Pen light

___Petroleum jelly (such as Vaseline)

___Pill crusher

___Rabies certificates

___Rectal thermometer

___Rubber or latex gloves

___Scissors

___Small plastic atomizer

___Styptic powder or bee's wax

___Tongue depressors

___Tweezers

___Washcloths

For Dummies: Bestselling Book Series for Beginners

Praise for Ferrets For Dummies

"*Ferrets For Dummies* is a very enjoyable presentation of the care and feeding of our ferret friends, with excellent guidelines and recommendations. The information is valuable for everyone from the least experienced to the veteran shelter operator."

— Karen Purcell, DVM, Author of Essentials of Ferrets: A

"A m⋯ ⋯every sea-
son⋯ ⋯elf as we
spea⋯ ⋯ven the
mos⋯ ⋯ice to hope-
fully⋯ ⋯ws up!"

⋯ret
⋯r,

"Kim⋯ ⋯ical issues.
She⋯ ⋯r can follow
with⋯

⋯l Hospital,

"An i⋯ ⋯best friend
for ⋯

⋯arms

"*Feri*⋯ ⋯ng a ferret
as ⋯ ⋯of sea-
son⋯ ⋯us and
fun⋯ ⋯*Dummies*
ser⋯ ⋯yable.
Wa⋯

⋯elter &
⋯American

"I am honored to have been asked to review *Ferrets For Dummies*. Kim is a very eloquent writer who educates in a light hearted, yet persuasive manner. Ferrets should travel with this instruction manual! I thoroughly enjoyed previewing her book and look forward to recommending her book to my friends and supporters."

> — Hildy A. Langewis, Rescue Coordinator, California Domestic Ferret Association, and Founder, Ferret Hotline Founder

"I would recommend all potential and current ferret owners read the chapter on ferret psychology. Ferrets are not like any other animal, and by giving their owners a greater understanding of them and what makes them tick, they'll be happier, healthier, and less likely to end up in shelters."

> — Kim Rushing, Director, KiSta Ferret Shelter (New Jersey)

"Ferret culture, like cat and dog cultures, have a language of their own. This book not only explains what it is to have to care for a ferret, but how to "speak" the ferret community language. After reading this book, novice ferret owners can communicate like they've owned ferrets for years. By the way, this book should be mandatory reading for people considering buying or adopting a ferret. It should be stocked in every library, book shop, animal rescue, and pet shop. After reading it, you won't be a dummy about ferrets any longer."

> — Pam Troutman, Director, Shelters That Adopt & Rescue (STAR) Ferrets(Virginia)

"Excellent introductory guide to the ferret world for the first time ferret owner — entertaining and easy to read, yet filled with solid facts. Five paws up from this shelter!"

> — Mary McCarty-Houser, Director, Pennsylvania Ferret Rescue Assoc. of Centre County

"Ms. Shilling has captured the effervescent spirit of our beloved ferrets in catchy titles and brought their charm and unique needs to light in her easy-to-read chapters. *Ferrets For Dummies* is a wonderful addition to any ferret lover's library, and a 'must have' for every new ferret parent."

> — Julie Fossa, West Central Ohio Ferret Shelter

"*Ferrets For Dummies* is an informative and entertaining guide for prospective, novice, and experienced ferret owners alike. Using a breezy style that reflects the ferret's breezy personality, Kim Schilling covers all aspects of the planning and implementation of ferret parenthood. Besides the usual pet care advice, diverse topics include how and where to find the perfect ferret, legal issues, traveling with a ferret, and alternatives to the store-bought diet. Ms. Schilling also deals thoughtfully with more serious issues such as how to avoid becoming part of the pet overpopulation problem and how to deal with the loss of a beloved fuzzy. *Ferrets For Dummies* is a complete, clever, and clearly written guide to ferret care."

— Linda Iroff, Co-founder, Ohio Ferret Shelter
Association, and Director, Ohio Ferret Coalition

"Everyone should own this book — it's something that every ferret caretaker should have — from novice to shelter to breeder to veterinarian that treats them. The book is thorough and concise and contains various levels of ferret knowledge in an easy-to-read-and-understand format. It dispels many ferret myths and misunderstandings and will be a valuable part of my ferret reference library."

— Lisa Leidig, Director, The Ferret Haven
"By-the-Sea" (shelter) (Virginia)

"Easy to read, pertinent facts, a truly "ferret-icious" adventure! If you're considering a ferret as a companion, then this book is for you! If you're thinking of breeding ferrets for the first time or the 50th time, you'll find out what people DON'T tell you in here. All potential and existing ferret owners should have this book somewhere in their bookcase."

— Emma-Jane Stretton, Secretary,
Heart of Ohio Ferret Association

"A wonderful book written by a special person, *Ferrets For Dummies* opens the world of ferrets to anyone wishing to know more!"

— Michael J. Miller, DVM, Owner,
Roberts Road Animal Clinic, Palos Hills, IL

"What an awesome book! Kim provides inclusive and accurate information with a wonderful touch of humor and common sense. If you are owned by ferret(s) or are considering being owned by ferret(s), you need this book. Our ferrets give it 5 raisins!"

— Mike and Denise Orlowski, Furry O's Ferrets
(Pennsylvania)

"*Ferrets For Dummies* is a wonderful book that all ferret owners and per-spective owners should have on their shelves. It's written in a precise and easy-to-understand manner for the beginners, yet is packed with information even the experienced ferret lovers will find valuable. As the operator of a ferret shelter, I believe Kim did an outstanding job getting the word out on ferret shelters and the lovable ferrets waiting for homes. You can bet I'll have a copy on hand to recommend and even encourage all ferret enthusiasts to buy!"

— CJ Jones, Founder and Director, 24 Carat Ferret
Rescue and Shelter, Las Vegas, NV

"This book is the only ferret book I have ever read that I feel can be benefi-cial to both new and old ferret owners. It hits not only on how to care for ferrets in general, but is very factual in letting new ferret owners know what to expect when bringing a new ferret into their home. I strongly believe that any ferret owner who reads this book will be able to care for their ferrets better and in the long run will have a happier, healthier ferret. It is a must-have for both new and experienced ferret owners. I would highly recommend it to anyone with an interest in ferrets."

— Samantha Pfaffinger, Veterinary Technician and
Founder, Club Ferret Las Vegas

"We really enjoyed the chapter 'On the Trail of a New Fuzzy.' Kim has done a great job in explaining the possible sources for a new ferret and the pros and cons of each."

— Kurt and Sara Petersen, Directors, FURRY (Ferrets
Underfoot Running Round You), Shelter (Missouri)

Ferrets FOR DUMMIES®

by Kim Schilling

Foreword by Kate Ball, DVM

Wiley Publishing, Inc.

Ferrets For Dummies®

Published by
Wiley Publishing, Inc.
111 River Street
Hoboken, NJ 07030
www.wiley.com

Copyright © 2000 by Wiley Publishing, Inc., Indianapolis, Indiana

Published by Wiley Publishing, Inc., Indianapolis, Indiana

Published simultaneously in Canada

For general information on our other products and services or to obtain technical support, please contact our Customer Care Department within the U.S. at 800-762-2974, outside the U.S. at 317-572-3993, or fax 317-572-4002.

Wiley also publishes its books in a variety of electronic formats. Some content that appears in print may not be available in electronic books.

Library of Congress Cataloging-in-Publication Data:

Library of Congress Control Number: 00-104230

ISBN: 0-7645-5259-7

Manufactured in the United States of America

10 9 8 7

3B/RV/QU/QU/IN

About the Author

Not too many years ago, the state of Massachusetts was graced with **Kim Schilling's** presence when her young biological mother was rushed to the hospital for what was thought to be acute appendicitis. Kim, undoubtedly, was much cuter than the inflamed organ the astounded doctors had expected to find. As a toddler, she was adopted by her Chicago parents and moved to Illinois where she's remained firmly planted ever since. From the get go, she related much better to animals than humans and spent her entire adolescence and teenage years caring for every sick, injured, stray, exotic, and wild animal that happened her way (either by accident or on purpose), whether they liked it or not. Her calling in life appeared clear and early: She wanted to become a veterinarian before she could even pronounce the word. To prepare herself for the medical terms she'd encounter in veterinary school, she even took four years of Latin in high school. Although she had the grades and ambition, she never made it to veterinary school. Instead, her life took her down a different path toward helping and saving animals. In 1989, she began taking in various animals, mostly exotic and difficult critters, that had been abused, neglected, or abandoned. At the same time, she fell head over heels in love with ferrets and their endearing antics. These lovable creatures quickly filled her life, her heart, and her home. In 1993, she also adopted her husband David, an addictions specialist no less, who supported her in her passion. That same year, Kim became USDA licensed, obtained various conservation permits, and formed Animals for Awareness, a no-kill organization dedicated to taking in unwanted, abused, confiscated, or abandoned exotic and domestic critters. News of Animals for Awareness spread quickly. From unwanted bear and cougar cubs to stray parrots and neglected ferrets, their home sometimes overflows. While Animals for Awareness doesn't adopt out exotic animals to the general public, they do find permanent USDA facilities for the bigger exotics and always have domestic critters such as ferrets up for adoption. Kim and many of her critters frequently hit the road to educate as many people as possible — their main goal to promote responsible pet ownership and discourage the keeping of exotic, dangerous, or wild animals. The future for Animals for Awareness looks bright. Animals for Awareness obtained non-profit status in 1999 and continues to search for that perfect piece of land to build a dream sanctuary, where even the fuzzies can have their own large rooms filled with toys and snooze sacks. As Kim proudly states, ferrets are one of her favorite residents. When she began writing this book, she had 23 ferrets of her own. When she completed the book, she had over 30.

About Howell Book House
Committed to the Human/Companion Animal Bond

Thank you for choosing a book brought to you by the pet experts at Howell Book House, a division of Wiley Publishing, Inc. And welcome to the family of pet owners who've put their trust in Howell books for nearly 40 years!

Pet ownership is about relationships — the bonds people form with their dogs, cats, horses, birds, fish, small mammals, reptiles, and other animals. Howell Book House/Wiley understands that these are some of the most important relationships in life, and that it's vital to nurture them through enjoyment and education. The happiest pet owners are those who know they're taking the best care of their pets — and with Howell books owners have this satisfaction. They're happy, educated owners, and as a result, they have happy pets, and that enriches the bond they share.

Howell Book House was established in 1961 by Mr. Elsworth S. Howell, an active and proactive dog fancier who showed English Setters and judged at the prestigious Westminster Kennel Club show in New York. Mr. Howell based his publishing program on strength of content, and his passion for books written by experienced and knowledgeable owners defined Howell Book House and has remained true over the years. Howell's reputation as the premier pet book publisher is supported by the distinction of having won more awards from the Dog Writers Association of America than any other publisher. Howell Book House/Wiley has over 400 titles in publication, including such classics as The American Kennel Club's *Complete Dog Book,* the *Dog Owner's Home Veterinary Handbook, Blessed Are the Brood Mares,* and *Mother Knows Best: The Natural Way to Train Your Dog.*

When you need answers to questions you have about any aspect of raising or training your companion animals, trust that Howell Book House/Wiley has the answers. We welcome your comments and suggestions, and we look forward to helping you maximize your relationships with your pets throughout the years.

The Howell Book House Staff

Dedication

This book is dedicated to all the uniquely wonderful fuzzballs that have stolen my heart and greatly enriched my life with their playful antics, endless affection, and thieving ways. To Ron Collier, my dearest recently departed friend and mentor who always believed in me no matter what — you will always live in my heart! Special dedication to Norm and Mary Stilson who, along with the Greater Chicago Ferret Association, have truly inspired me through their difficult work and undying devotion to ferrets.

To my husband, David Schilling, who supports my often outlandish dreams and who married me despite my animal fanaticism. Without him, I couldn't do this. To my parents, Carol and Gerard Meyer, and my big brother, Gerry, for providing me with an education of a lifetime. And finally, to all my little ones who have passed on to a better place, especially ferrets Simon, Oscar, and Scooter, and my 16½ year old wolfdog, Ara Glen.

Author's Acknowledgments

A big, big thanks to Bob Church, a true gentleman and ferret expert extraordinaire, for taking many precious hours out of his busy schedule to proofread, check for ferretical correctness, and also throw in more than his two dooks worth! I treasure his friendship! What a guy! I can't begin to express enough gratitude to our veterinarians Dr. Mike Miller and Dr. Kate Ball who proofed the health sections, made suggestions and corrections, and kept me from making any major medical blunders in front of the world. Extra thanks to Mike for consistently helping with general critter upkeep and vet work. His talents, generosity, and friendship are immeasurable. More thanks also to Kate for her friendship and for writing a wonderful foreword. She is always ready to voluntarily jump in when additional help is needed with the critters, and her enthusiasm and bubbly personality keep our spirits high! We're so lucky to have both of you on the AFA team!

This book has been three long years in the making. I know I drove many people crazy in that time! Thanks to my friends and coworkers at Ferrara Pan Candy, especially Liz Ahern, who were supportive and understanding (and glad it's over). I know I owe my Project Editor Tracy Barr a few nights on the town. She remained gracious and steady despite my severe mood swings and frustration during the final months. She did a fantastic job! And my husband David! Wow. He was able to live with me and remain smiling almost the entire time. Thank you! To my volunteers: Lizzie, Lauren, and, especially, Sally Hines (who is an absolute angel for putting in so many hours here and getting the job done!): You guys make my life easier and afforded me the time needed to write this book! A major BLESS YOU to Renee and Jon Park for finding a way around that obnoxious quirk in my Word document so that I didn't have a massive coronary when I thought I had to start to book all over for the second time.

Finally, many other people generously helped bring this project together and contribute to its success. Thank you to my reviewers: Lisa Leidig, Linda Iroff, Mary McCarty-Houser, Norm Stilson, Julie Fossa, Kim Rushing, Denise and Mike Orlowski, Hildy Langewis, Faith Hood, Pam Troutman, Kurt and Sara Petersen, Emma Stretton, Amy Flemming, CJ Jones, Dr. Karen Purcell, Vickie McKimmey, Dr. Deborah Kemmerer, and Samantha Pfaffinger. All of you provided essential feedback and positive support in many ways. Whether your material was used in the end or not — THANK YOU!

Thanks to the following people who supported me through the anxious times or contributed some other great tidbits to this book: Hildy Langewis, Margie Szelmeczka, Sandy Repper, Sherri-Lynn White, Isabelle Doiron, Debbie Hunton, Sukie Crandall, Nancy Sanders, Jean Caputo-Lee, Rebecca McFarlane, Jen Taylor, and Bob Martin. Their contributions — from e-mailing greatly needed information to providing quirky definitions and pictures to keeping me relatively sane and grounded — mean more to me than I can express. I know some of your contributions were deleted in the end, and I apologize for that! My paws were tied! The Appendix "Definitions Only a Ferret Owner Can Appreciate" is on my web site! It was tooooo good not to mention somewhere!

Ferret nips on that little piece of skin between my nostrils if I forgot anyone!

Publisher's Acknowledgments

We're proud of this book; please send us your comments through our online registration form located at www.dummies.com/register.

Some of the people who helped bring this book to market include the following:

Acquisitions, Editorial, and Media Development

Project Editor: Tracy Barr

Acquisitions Editor: Scott Prentzas, Senior Editor

Copy Editor: Sandra Blackthorn

Technical Editor: Bob Church

Editorial Manager: Pamela Mourouzis

Editorial Administrator: Michelle Hacker

Cover Credit: © Eric Ilasenko Photography

Interior Photos: David and Kim Schilling

Production

Project Coordinator: Regina Snyder

Layout and Graphics: Jackie Bennett, Brian Drumm, Jason Guy, Tracy K. Oliver, Kristin Pickett, Rashell Smith, Jacque Schneider,

Proofreaders: Vickie Broyles, Chris Collins, John Greenough, Linda Quigley, Marianne Santy

Indexer: Joan Griffitts

Publishing and Editorial for Consumer Dummies

Diane Graves Steele, Vice President and Publisher, Consumer Dummies

Joyce Pepple, Acquisitions Director, Consumer Dummies

Kristin A. Cocks, Product Development Director, Consumer Dummies

Michael Spring, Vice President and Publisher, Travel

Brice Gosnell, Associate Publisher, Travel

Suzanne Jannetta, Editorial Director, Travel

Publishing for Technology Dummies

Richard Swadley, Vice President and Executive Group Publisher

Andy Cummings, Vice President and Publisher

Composition Services

Gerry Fahey, Vice President of Production Services

Debbie Stailey, Director of Composition Services

Contents at a Glance

Cartoons at a Glance

By Rich Tennant

"As you can see, this breed comes with a mask, although the big floppy shoes were our idea."

page 7

"We keep her diet high in protein, high in nutrients and high off the floor behind a locked door."

page 97

"Give it up. You're never going to train that thing to lie on your neck and act like a collar."

page 307

SLOTH/FERRET PROJECT

"We figure if they mate it will either result in a sloth that's interesting to watch or a ferret that's easy to catch."

page 275

"Hey—that's a record! Honey, I just clocked the ferret at 28 mph coming through the living room!"

page 35

"Let me guess—the vet's analysis of the ferret's fleas showed them to be of the 100 percent fresh ground Colombian decaf variety."

page 157

"What I don't understand is how you could put the entire costume on without knowing the ferret was inside."

page 321

"Mary, go ahead and pet the ferret. Mark, why don't you hold off until we're sure we've got her biting habit under control."

page 243

Fax: 978-546-7747
E-mail: richtennant@the5thwave.com
World Wide Web: www.the5thwave.com

Table of Contents

Foreword

⬤ ⬤

My first encounter with a ferret was not until veterinary school. My roommate had two of them scampering about. Needless to say, I was absolutely delighted by them! My very first ferret, Rosie, bounced into my life about 2 months after I graduated vet school. Quite the graduation present to myself! Rosie was 2 years old and needed a home, so I became her mom. A few months later, I purchased an 8-week-old kit to keep her company. I named our new baby Tess. My home has never been the same since. Ferrets instantly find their way into your heart with their adorable little faces and comical antics!

It was during my second year out of vet school when I met Kim Schilling and discovered her organization, Animals for Awareness. Since knowing her, it's become apparent that not only is she one of the most caring people I've ever met, but her love for ferrets overflows. Kim takes in and cares for many different animals — nursing any that need it back to health and then finding good homes for as many possible, or keeping them safe, happy, and healthy for the rest of their lives. Kim loves and enjoys each and every one of her animals, but ferrets hold a special and dear place in her heart. Her knowledge and years of experience make her the perfect author for this book.

A complete and updated comprehensive guide to ferrets and ferret care is something that, in my opinion, has been long overdue. Most of the ferret handbooks available to pet owners are relatively old and not nearly as complete as *Ferrets For Dummies.* Also, there is still a tremendous amount of misinformation about ferrets circulating in the general public. *Ferrets For Dummies* takes a comprehensive look at the ferret: Where it came from and its personality, care, and health. This book touches on every imaginable subject relating to keeping ferrets in your home.

Kim has written this book so that it is easy to read and understand — even the more complicated subjects. And Kim has even managed to add quite a bit of humor throughout! One of the neatest things about *Ferrets For Dummies* is Kim's ability to touch on difficult, or generally hands-off, topics. Her well-written section on the oh-so-hard topic of when to say goodbye to our little loved ones is one subject that nobody likes to think about, but is so necessary for the well-being of both pets and their caretakers. I believe this book is highly informative and a must for the new or potential ferret owner. But do not be mistaken by the title, as *Ferrets For Dummies* will also greatly add to the knowledge of current, more experienced ferret owners.

Kate Ball, DVM

Introduction

· ·

*N*umerous people have told me that a true love for animals may be genetically predisposed. Maybe this is true. Or maybe some animals just tug
at our heartstrings a little harder than others do. I believe both statements to
be the case for me. While this condition may be termed *genetics* by the white-
coated scientists in those sterile laboratories, I prefer to call what was passed
on to me *a blessing.* I knew the moment my eyes locked onto those of a bouncing, chattering ferret that I'd been hooked by something mysteriously fascinating. Each one of my ferrets has provided me with much happiness and joy
over the years. Even though all of them, young and old, share in common the
ability to make me break out in laughter with their habitual silliness, each one
is a unique little fuzzball. They continuously amaze me with their intelligence
and social play.

Ferrets are fun and mischievous. They are cunning looters. They can steal
your heart as well as break your heart. They come in all sorts of colors and
sizes. Ferrets can get into the littlest cracks and holes, both in your home and
in your soul. They are bound to make you break out in uncontrollable laughter at least once a day. They steal any chance they can to dance and dook
and chatter about. And when they're all through amazing you with their
antics, most ferrets love nothing more than to curl up somewhere warm with
you and snooze the rest of the day away.

Sound like the perfect pet? Not necessarily. As a shelter director, my motto is
always "Not all animals make good pets for people, and not all people make
good parents for pets." No two households, people, or lifestyles are the
same. In addition to all the joy they bring, ferrets can also be quite
challenging at times.

That's why I wrote this book about these amazing creatures. For those of you
who don't yet have a ferret, this book can help you decide whether a ferret
is for you. And for those of you who already have a ferret, this book can help
you give him the best possible care. To boot, this book offers practical health
and medical information. And everything in here is in cut-to-the-chase
format — only what you need to know, in good ol' plain English.

About This Book

There's a lot to know about — and a lot of responsibility that comes with — being owned by a ferret. Pet ownership is never to be taken lightly. You should always make a *lifetime commitment* when deciding to bring any pet into your home. This book helps you gain better insight into what's required of you so that you can make the right choice for your lifestyle. If you already have a ferret, this book gives you all the information you need to help keep your ferret happy and healthy.

This book isn't meant to be read from cover to cover (of course, you can read it that way if you want to). Instead, this book is a reference. If you have a particular topic in mind, you can turn right to the chapter that covers the topic.

Each chapter is divided into sections, and each section contains a piece of info about some part of ferret keeping — things like this:

- Is a ferret the right pet for you?
- Picking a healthy ferret
- Ferret-proofing your home
- Setting up your ferret's cage
- What medical conditions require a vet's care

Conventions Used in This Book

Ferrets For Dummies makes information easy to find and use. To help you make sense of the information and instructions in this book, I've used certain conventions:

- *Italics* is used for emphasis and to highlight new words or terms that are defined.
- **Boldfaced** text is used to indicate the action part of numbered steps.
- `Monofont` is used for Web and e-mail addresses.

Foolish Assumptions

In writing this book, I made some assumptions about you:

- ✔ You're one of thousands and thousands of people out there who has a nagging child or spouse, or both, whining daily about wanting to have a ferret. Or maybe you've simply had your own emotions kidnapped by a ferret you just happened to see, and you want to make sure that a ferret is the pet for you *before* you get one.

- ✔ Perhaps you're one of those lucky folks who already owns a ferret(s) and wants to know how to properly care for him.

- ✔ You might be a volunteer or employee at a ferret shelter, humane society, veterinarian clinic, or pet shop who's been given (or volunteered for) the task of ferret-keeper, and you want to know about the fantastic furballs.

- ✔ You may fall into the category of "seasoned" ferret owner and discovered that *Ferrets For Dummies* covers topics that aren't found in other ferret books, such as the behavior challenges, alternative diet, and saying goodbye.

- ✔ You may be a veterinarian who wants to know as much about the ferrets you treat, including basic history, as you do about the people who bring them in.

Whatever reason made you buy this book, hold onto your hat, 'cuz you're in for the thrill of a lifetime.

How This Book Is Organized

To help you find the information you're looking for, this book is divided into eight parts. Each part includes several chapters relating to that part.

Part I: Is a Ferret the Pet for You?

This is probably the most important part for people who are still in the "considering" stage. Ferrets are not cats. They are certainly not dogs. And heaven knows they're not for everyone! This part tells you what you can expect from a ferret and what a ferret will expect (and need) from you. For those of you who are absolutely set on being owned by a ferret, or those of you who are still unsure, you need to check this part out to brush up on the legalities of owning a ferret where you live.

Part II: Finding Your Ferret and Hanging Up the Welcome Hammock

So many ferrets, so little time! This part gives you detailed steps on what to look for in a new ferret and how to go about finding him. Young or old? Single, pair, or trio? Shelter, breeder, or pet shop? Once you decide on the right ferret, there's important stuff to do before he comes home, like setting up his cage properly and getting all the ferret supplies. This part gives you solid tips on interacting with your new ferret and safely introducing him to other family members.

Part III: Basic Care and Feeding

More decisions — what kinds of foods and treats are good for your ferret? How do I keep him from getting bored? This part gives you suggestions for how to be creative and stay safe in the ferret kitchen and the ferret playground. But having a ferret isn't not all fun and games. You'll also find out how and when to clean up your ferret and his cage. This part also has great tips and guidance that can help you make decisions on whether or not to travel (and how to travel) with your ferret.

Part IV: Health Issues, Concerns, and Treatments

From the must-have first-aid kit to knowing first aid to more serious health issues, this part covers all aspects of health care right down to knowing when to say goodbye to your dearly loved ferret. In addition, this part helps you find the best vet for your ferret and gives you a basic overview of illnesses and diseases so that you'll know when you need to head off to the vet.

Part V: Ferret Psychology and Sociology 101

So you think your ferret's crazy? What's your ferret saying? And what does he mean when he moves in all directions at one time? This part clues you in to ferret communication and behavior. And knowing a little more about that will help you with basic training such as nip training, litter box training, and using a leash and harness. But just as important as all these things is getting step-by-step instructions on dealing with the behaviorally challenged ferret, such as the aggressive or biting ferret.

Part VI: If You're Thinking about Breeding

This part offers a brief introduction on ferret reproduction and growth, from the breeding pair to birth to preparing the kit for his new home. It touches on medical issues related to breeding and also explains what's required from you to be a responsible breeder. But most importantly, this part gets you to think about the whole picture! Why breed? What are the problems associated with breeding? Do you have what it really takes, or are you just creating more need for ferret shelters?

Part VII: Ferrets: Past and Future

So where did our domesticated ferret really come from and when did he get here? This part talks about the history of the ferret, both historically and in theory. A good deal of this part also talks about the endangered black-footed ferret. How closely related is it to our domestic ferret? What caused the black-footed ferret to be titled one of the world's most endangered mammals? This part offers some insightful information on man's heavy involvement in the uprising of the domestic ferret and the downfall of his relative, the black-footed ferret.

Part VIII: The Part of Tens

Some of the best has been saved for last! Thinking of trying that alternative diet? Read about some great recipes to try at home. And no one could ever get enough ferret resources. This part lists books, magazines, Web sites, and more, so that you can always be sure you've got the latest ferret stuff at your fingertips.

Icons Used in This Book

To help you navigate through all this great information, I've included icons that point out helpful hints and fun facts and things you'd be wise to keep in mind. In a nutshell, they are the following:

This icon points to tidbits that will make your life as a ferret mom or dad a little easier. Many of these tips were discovered by people, including myself, who learned some things the hard way.

This icon points out interesting and sometimes technical ferret facts, some of which I stumbled on while doing researching for this book. Not all of this stuff makes good dinner conversation, but you're never too old to learn. Consider this information interesting but nonessential. You can skip it at will.

Don't miss the information accompanying this icon. Paying attention to what's here can save your ferret's life or prevent injury and illness — and perhaps even major vet bills.

The information accompanying this icon points out important stuff that you'll want to store in an easily accessed part of your brain.

This icon highlights terms that may be new to you and that you may encounter or need to know as a ferret owner.

Where to Go from Here

If you're thinking about getting a ferret or want to know how to get a healthy one, start at the beginning with Parts I and II. If you already have a ferret, you can delve in wherever you want, hopping around as issues or problems arise or time permits.

Bottom line? Enjoy the book as it was meant to be enjoyed and remember: New things are learned everyday about ferrets. And the best teachers are our ferrets themselves. Don't be afraid to ask questions from the experts out there. Doing so is well worth the time, and it makes ferret parenting a much more pleasant experience. Besides, asking is the only way we learn.

Part I
Is a Ferret the Pet for You?

The 5th Wave   By Rich Tennant

"As you can see, this breed comes with a mask, although the big floppy shoes were our idea."

In this part . . .

Every animal has a beast within that takes a little getting used to. Even humans do. Because you're reading this book, it's probably safe to assume that you're thinking of adding a ferret to your family. The world, it seems, has been bombarded with dogs and cats, and maybe you've decided you're up for something a smidgen more exciting to spice up your life. What's wrong with a ferret? Maybe nothing at all. A ferret may be the perfect pet for you. Or maybe not. The answer to the question "Can't we all just get along?" is never cut and dried. That goes for us as well as pets. It's important to know what you're dealing with before taking on any pet. And this part helps you sort out exactly what you're dealing with.

Chapter 1

Things to Know about Ferrets

In This Chapter

▶ Knowing what a ferret is and what other animals he's related to

▶ Basic ferret info: colors, claws, weight, and more

▶ The truth about the smell

To the undiscerning eye, he looks a little rat-like. But look at his body movements: He acts more like a cat than a rat. Sometimes he fools us and becomes quite dog-like. He resembles some animals we see in our own backyard or those curious critters featured on an afternoon nature television show. And at some point, you'll undoubtedly witness some people pointing at a cage full of them, inquiring, "Good heavens, what in the world are those?"

Why they're ferrets, of course. Belonging to such a colorful clan of creatures, it's no wonder they resemble so many different animals. This chapter is about the ferret's vast family, his close and distant relatives, and his interesting history. (And for you technical readers, I've thrown in all sorts of Latin lingo that may confuse even the professionals out there.)

First Question: What Is a Ferret?

While ferrets may look slightly rodent-like with their long, pointed snouts and ticklish whiskers (see Figure 1-1), they are not rodents at all. Ferrets come from the Order Carnivora, which simply means "meat or flesh eating." This order encompasses a huge group of animals, from Fifi the common lap dog to the mighty African lion. Ferrets are further broken down into the Family Mustelidae, which they proudly share with such bold critters as the badger, wolverine, pine marten, sea otter, and skunk. Included in that family are domesticated ferrets and ferret-like animals such as the weasel, European polecat, steppe polecat, black-footed ferret, and mink.

Figure 1-1: Although they may look like rodents, ferrets aren't rodents at all.

Will the real daddy please stand up?

A huge amount of mystery and controversy surrounds our little ferret friends. The fact of the matter is that all polecats are very closely related and can interbreed among themselves successfully. That is, they can produce viable offspring. Nobody really knows exactly how the ferret is related to the rest of the polecats. Several theories exist, but the most commonly accepted one points toward the European polecat *Mustela putorius* as having likely claims to ferret ancestry. While there has been little archeological evidence found to support this idea, genetically speaking, the European polecat and today's modern ferret are practically twins. It's possible that our domestic ferret is a polecat hybrid. The domestic ferret's genetic makeup may be more of one polecat, probably the European, than another polecat. One of his grandparents may even no longer exist. But even a seemingly insignificant genetic difference can mean the difference between a horse and a zebra or a dog and a coyote.

Genetic differences, however slight, can be highly significant. So the studies move forward. Researchers continue to compare our domestic ferret to other potential ancestors. However, it's quite possible that we may never know the real answer in our own lifetime. For our own purposes, all we truly need to know is that we are dealing with a unique little creature — more affectionate than ferocious and so easy to fall in love with.

Ferret Latin

The ferret's current scientific name, preferred mostly by North American scientists, is *Mustela putorius furo* because of original beliefs concerning the relationship between our domesticated ferret and the rest of the polecats. These beliefs are now being challenged, particularly some of the DNA evidence, as used in some paternity tests. The white coats doing most of the ancestral and DNA research on the ferret are Europeans who — along with a handful of others, including myself — prefer to call the ferret *Mustela furo*. Currently, several papers exist that support *Mustela furo*, and it's possible the scientific name of our domestic ferret may actually be changed in the near future.

For those of you who don't speak Latin, *Mustela* means "weasel" or "mouse killer." *Putorius* is derived from the Latin word *putoris*, meaning "stench," and *furo* is derived from the Latin word *furis*, meaning "thief." The word *ferret* itself is derived from the Latin word *furonem*, which also means "thief." Put this all together, and you have one little "stinky mouse killing thief." While the historical ferret may have lived up to this name, today's ferret is more often than not a cuddly little furball. For all practical purposes, I fondly refer to my ferrets as *Ferretus majorus pleasorus* in the comfort of my nonscientific home.

The word *ferret* is appropriately derived from the Latin word *Furonem*, which also means "thief." Most ferret owners will quickly come to realize just how thieving their new family members are. As cute as this endearing trait may be at times, it once took me over a day to find the entire contents of my purse, which I foolishly left open in the presence of roving ferrets.

A lot of ferret owners call their furballs a variety of nicknames. Some that I use throughout this book are *fert, fuzzy, carpet shark, snorkeler, furball,* and *fuzzbutt,* so don't get confused.

Seeing the resemblance between the skunk, wolverine, and ferret is difficult. However, all members of this family have scent glands located on both sides of the anus. While ferrets that have not been descented are capable of expelling an offensive musky odor through these glands when they're feeling threatened or overstimulated, the smell dissipates rapidly and washes away with soap and water. As for his distant cousin the skunk, we know his reputation as being the worst offender in the stink department and also the most difficult to clean up after.

JARGON ALERT

The name game

What's long and furry and capable of moving in several different directions at one time? You guessed it. We ferret parents fondly refer to them as ferts, furballs, fuzzies, fuzzballs, fuzz-busters, and even carpet sharks. I know that many more terms of enfertment exist out there. But to the technical community, male ferrets are called *hobs* until that wonderful day of neuter-ing, when they officially become known as *gibs.* Female ferrets are called *jills,* unless they're spayed, at which time they become *sprites.* (The terms gib and sprite are North American terms. In other places around the world, they may refer to altered male ferrets as castrated, neutered, or vasectomized hobs. Altered females may be referred to as neutered or spayed jills.) Baby ferts are simply called *kits* either way until they are about 6 months old. Put a whole group of ferrets together, and you get a *business* of fer-rets, in addition to a heap of fun.

Taking Physical Inventory

When I say physical, I pretty much mean all the general stuff regarding the physical characteristics of the fert, from his paws and claws to his remark-able as well as not-so-remarkable senses. My version of physical also covers other tidbits you should know, like color combos and life span, since knowing how long you'll be caring for your fuzzy is important.

Life span of a fuzzy

The average life span of a well-cared-for fert is between 6–8 years, but I hear many, many stories of ferrets living for up to 11 and 12 years, barring any unforeseen mishaps. At 1 year old, they're full grown. At 4 to 5 years old, they're considered geriatrics, or old ferts. At this time, they may also begin to slowly lose weight and start encountering debilitating illnesses.

As heartbreaking as it is, ferrets are prone to many diseases and cancers. It's not so much that they're genetically or medically flawed. Like most compan-ion pets whose life spans are short compared to humans, ferrets have their lives compacted into only 7 or 8 oh-so-short years. The average human has 65–70 years to experience what a ferret experiences in only 7 to 8 years. My oldest ferret, Scooter, was almost 12 years old when I chose to put him at rest, and he'd been living with cardiomyopathy, lymphoma, and insulinoma for 4 of those final years. The ferret is an amazing trooper with a tremendous fight for life.

In this corner, weighing in at . . .

The carpet shark's size makes him an ideal pet for both the apartment dweller and the homeowner. As is the case with most other mammal species, male ferrets are typically up to two times larger than females. This is called *sexual dimorphism*. You can see the weight difference in the head and torso, the male being wider and less rodent-like.

A typical female ferret weighs between a mere ¾ pound (0.3 kg) to a whopping 2 ½ pounds (1.1 kg) — and that's a big girl. Neutered males are normally 2 to 3 ½ pounds (0.9–1.6 kg), and unaltered males have been known to weigh in at 4 to 6 pounds (1.8–2.7 kg) or more. In tape measure terms, without the tail, females are between 13 and 14 inches (33–35.5 cm) long, and males are generally between 15 and 16 inches (38–40.6 cm) long. The tail is 3–4 inches (7.6–10 cm) long.

Ferts are kind of like humans in that they bulk up quite a bit in the winter. Sometimes they gain 40 percent of their weight at this time and then lose it in the spring. This isn't always the rule because some ferts always seem skinny, and others are belly draggers all year round. Could it have something to do with health and or exercise? Better check it out. (Parts III and IV of this book cover various issues related to exercise and health.)

So when do they come out to play?

If you let them, a healthy ferret will sleep 18 to 20 hours a day. Does this make them nocturnal or diurnal? Neither. I think they should get a category all by themselves. How about ferturnal? Actually, most weasels are considered nocturnal, although they may change their sleeping patterns depending on habitat, competition, and food availability. Ferrets, on the other hand, tend to be *crepuscular*, which means they usually come out at dusk and dawn, similar to deer. However, if you haven't noticed already, ferrets change their activity levels to meet their humans' schedules. Therefore, just as weasels will adapt to best suit their survival needs, ferrets will be diurnal, nocturnal, or crepuscular. What they are probably is up to you!

They look so angelic curled up in their ferret sacks and piled on each other. They look lazy and innocent in their dozing states, legs sprawled out on all sides or smooshed up under their bellies. It's a sight to behold. But don't be fooled by their short, stubby legs because they are strong and powerful and are capable of hoisting the entire body up to get a closer look at the treats in your hand. The legs can propel the ferret effortlessly across floors, counters, and tabletops. Ferrets can do the tango and scoot backward while juggling a plastic ball. And that's just the first minute after waking. Ferret legs are amazing things. Ferrets would be speed bumps for sure without them.

Points about claws and teeth

On each soft paw is a set of five nonretractable claws that were designed for digging and grasping (see Figure 1-2). The claws were designed to stay there, so please don't ever remove them. Frequent clipping does just fine.

Declawing your ferret is a Big Fat No No. For a fuzzball, declawing is a painful, mutilating surgery that carries way more risks than benefits. Ferrets need their claws for digging, grasping, walking, and playing. In addition, the base of the claw gives the foot added strength to support the ferret's weight. Removing the claws will only cause foot problems and/or pain when walking. If you're too lazy to clip nails, then a ferret isn't for you.

Like all carnivores, ferrets have large canine teeth that can be rather intimidating because they usually hang lower than the lip flap and are in view. While anything with a mouth can and will bite under certain circumstances, I've found the biting ferret to be the exception rather than the rule. Most ferrets only use their canine teeth to show off to their friends or to eat, whichever they happen to be doing at the time. Sometimes ferrets nip out of fear or play. And an occasional warning nip may be a sign of the fert's disapproval of one thing or another. Make no doubt about it, though, the bite of a disgruntled ferret is painful and can draw blood. Unless medically warranted for the ferret's health, the canine teeth should be left unaltered in the ferret's mouth where they belong.

Figure 1-2:
Ferrets need their claws for everything from climbing and walking to just hanging around.

Making sense of senses

The ferret's senses vary in degree of acuteness. Like human infants, their eyesight is poor, and their ability to distinguish color is limited. Ferrets do see some reds and blues. Make no mistake about it, though: The most restricted ferret can and will find anything he was not intended to find (and his stubby little legs will help steal it back to the hidey-hole).

His sense of smell is far superior to ours, and his little paw pads are sensitive to the touch. In a sense, all ferrets have sticky fingers: If they find it, it belongs to them. If they want it, it's theirs. If they think it's theirs, it is. You get the idea.

A fuzzy's sense of hearing is remarkable. If you open a bag of raisins from across the house, be assured your ferret will hear the bag opening and come a-begging. So remember to whisper when discussing sensitive issues such as neutering or going on vacation.

Have I mentioned that they have another sense? They seem to understand us humans. Scary.

All about colors and patterns

These long, slender beauties come in a variety of colors, from the easily recognized albino with his white fur and pink eyes and the dark-eyed white (DEW) with his white coat and dark eyes to the darker sables and all shades in between. Although ferret people are coming up with more and more definitions of coat colors and patterns just to confuse the general public, many basic colors and patterns are already defined out there.

Colors

Groups of ferret experts argue over the names of shades of sables and silvers. So you may find that one group calls one shade a fancy name and another group calls it something different. No matter how many names the experts come up with, you'll always be able to come across a fert that is lighter or darker than what they've already defined. So it seems the definitions may never end. Every ferret has a color, and in that color is a pattern. And remember, colors and patterns sometimes change from season to season, so unless you bought a neon ferret, your ferret will most likely fall into one of these simple color categories that most ferret experts seem to agree on.

✔ **Sable:** This is probably the most common color. Guardhairs are dark in color, ranging from the darkest brown to black. These guardhairs are evenly and densely dispersed. The undercoat on the neck, back, and belly is cream colored. The undercoat may show through quite a bit. The legs and tail are the same color as the body but solid with no undercoat. The mask is a full band across dark brown or black eyes, giving the ferret a true raccoon-like appearance (unless he's a panda or blaze). The sable's nose is pink, patchy brown, or sometimes black. If your baby has white feet, then he's a "sable mitt." If the fert's mask extends all the way up over his head, then he's a "hooded sable" or "hooded sable mitt." If he has a white blaze, he's a sable blaze, and so on.

Guard hairs are simply the stiffer, more prominent and longer fur that covers the shorter and softer undercoat. Guard hairs provide the critter's coloration or camouflage and, in many mammals, also aid in waterproofing the fur. The undercoat's job is to act as insulation and also to provide a water resistant barrier.

✔ **Silver:** There are several different types of silver-colored patterns. The darkest, or pewter, is often mistaken for a standard sable, but the hairs are charcoal gray. Other variations include coats that are mostly light with the tail being heavily littered with silvery gray hairs. Often, the coat is also marked with gray fur on the head, saddle, and legs, but the silver ferret can also be solid white with silver color only on his tail. Silver markings can be heavy or light. The eyes are dark brown or black. Silver ferrets' noses can be pink, patched, or black. The silver ferret usually lacks a full mask but rather has a couple of smudges of silver color around the eyes.

✔ **Black sable:** The fert in this category is so dark that he actually appears black from the tip of the nose to the tip of the tail. He has a white or cream undercoat that barely shows through the dark guardhairs. The black sable should have a black hooded mask that not only extends up and over the ears but also down to the nose leather. The hooded mask is preferred in the show ring, and at least 50 percent of the nose should also be black.

✔ **Albino:** This color is the most easily recognized in any animal. Resulting from a lack of pigment in the skin and eyes, albino ferrets range from a yellowish white to a snow-white color. All have light to medium pink eyes and pink noses.

✔ **Dark-eyed white (DEW):** This category is one of my favorites. These beauties resemble albinos with their white coats and pink noses — with the exception of eye color, which can vary from burgundy to brown or black. Many of these ferrets are actually silver ferrets that have lost most or all of their silver markings. Occasionally, a few dark hairs reside along the back. This color of ferret is prone to deafness.

Waardensburg Syndrome is a ferret condition that genetically links the white fur on the head to deafness (similar to the condition of deafness in many blue-eyed white cats). In addition to dark-eyed whites, pandas and shetlands/blazes (other ferret pattern types; see the following section) are often prone to this deafness, though this isn't always the case. I know of many unimpaired shetlands/blazes and pandas out there. However, the incidence or deafness is frequent. ***Note:*** Deaf ferrets make fine pets when you take extra care to properly train them and be careful not to startle them.

✔ **Cinnamon:** Many experts argue that true red cinnamons don't exist any longer. So many people interchange champagne with cinnamon. The cinnamon's coat is a very beautiful shade of reddish brown but can range from strawberry blonde to blonde to dishwater blonde. The legs and tail are slightly darker, while the mask color is a shade lighter. A full mask is not always present in the cinnamon, especially in the lighter shades. The nose should be pink, and his eyes can be black, red, or ruby.

✔ **Chocolate:** The chocolate ferret's coat is just another shade variation of sable but in a unique shade of chocolate brown with no hints of red. The chocolate ferret should also have a mask (see Figure 1-3). Lighter colors may resemble milk chocolate or that yummy chocolate powder you sprinkle on cappuccino, or they can be dark chocolate. The undercoat is cream or yellow colored. The eyes are almost always black. The chocolate's nose can be pink, patchy, or brown.

Figure 1-3:
Bernie is a handsome chocolate-hooded sable.

Other funky specialty colors include dalmation, striped white, light and medium patterned (roan), chocolate shaded silver, platinum, and a few others that make my head spin. Again, don't get too excited over coat color and patterns. Some ferrets (albinos and DEWs excluded) can change colors and/or patterns in a blink of a season, even if only slightly. Most fuzzies also get lighter in color as they age. Coat density varies depending on season and the age and health of your fuzzy.

Ferrets come in basically four colors: sable (including the black sable and chocolate), DEW, albino, and silver. All ferrets, no matter what fancy name they're called, fall into one of these four colors.

Patterns

Variations in pattern can include *mitts, hoodeds* (also known as the *T-bar* or *self* pattern), and *roan.* Ferrets with the mitts pattern look like their paws have mysteriously been dipped in white marshmallow fluff. These ferts also have white bibs. Hoodeds refers to ferrets with the raccoony facemask extending up and over the head and joining the rest of the coat down the back. The roan pattern describes ferrets whose color has a mixture of white guardhairs sprinkled in the dark guardhairs.

With patterns, the main discriminating factors are the legs and tail, or *points,* and how the point color or mask shape relates to the rest of the body color.

- **Siamese, or point patterned:** These are ferrets of any color that have much darker points than the body color. Their mask is shaped like the letter V and is also darker than the body. Or the Siamese may only have eye rings. When the points are only slightly darker, the pattern is considered a standard pattern. If you examine a Siamese's belly, you'll also notice a line of color running the length of the underside — a feature called a *zipper.*

- **Pandas:** These are ferrets of any color that have white heads reaching all the way down to the shoulders. Pandas also have white bibs, bellies, and feet. Their body color should form the shape of a saddle on the back.

- **Shetlands, badgers, or blazes:** These ferrets are quite unique because they usually have smudges or rings of color around their eyes instead of a mask. The white blaze extends from the face up over the head and hopefully down the neck a tad. All four feet and the bib are also white. Sometimes the knees (yes, ferrets have knees) are also white.

  Pandas, blazes, shetlands, and badgers are also prone to deafness.

Smell this, man!

All ferrets come standard equipped with a really neat scenting mechanism. It's quite different from the human scenting mechanism, which is more often than not triggered by disagreeable food or the simple desire to offend. Located just inside the ferret's anus on both sides are anal sacs filled with a foul-smelling fluid. All carnivores have these sacs, including the beloved canine. When excited, overstimulated, scared, or angry, your angel will, without aim, discharge the secret weapon. Unlike the skunk's odor, the ferret's odor, while intentionally disturbing, is temporary and rapidly dispels.

The majority of ferrets I've run across have been descented at a very early age before they reach the pet trade. That's because most ferts are commercially raised in fuzzy farms where neutering and descenting occur before they're shipped out. There's no real way to tell whether a ferret has been descented, however. The moment of truth comes at the moment of nasal impact.

If you should happen upon an undescented ferret, take note: Descenting is not necessary for living happily with a ferret. Unless medically necessitated, leave the fert be and pay more heed to his emotional state. Some people actually like the smell. I find myself to be neutral to it. Those living with other people will surely agree that ferret odor is more often the lesser of the two evils.

Chapter 2

Is a Ferret for You?

. . . .

In This Chapter

▶ Knowing what having a ferret means by way of time commitment and financial obligations

▶ Deciding whether you'd make a good ferret parent

. . . .

*B*efore you actually run out and get your new family member, you must take into consideration all the things that'll be required of you by a ferret. After all, how can you promise to be a good fuzzy mom or dad if you don't even know all the stuff that's involved? Taking an honest look at the requirements can mean the difference between living happily with a new family member or taking on a major, unwelcome chore.

This chapter deals with all the things that most people fail to consider when committing to the lifelong care of a ferret — or any pet for that matter. The fert's odor is special and requires regular maintenance for odor control. So you need to change his oil and rotate his tires every 3,000 miles. And these are not hamsters we're talking about. They need daily exercise and attention outside of their cages. Fuzzies can require substantial veterinary care over the years. You need to get out of certain lifestyle habits and rearrange your house to make it safe for ferrets.

If you read through this chapter and think you can handle a ferret, you'll be ready to move on to the next part. Good luck.

The Time Consideration

Whether or not a ferret is the perfect pet for you depends on you and your lifestyle. Ferrets are interactive pets. If you're looking for a pet to keep in a cage and look at every once in a while, then a ferret most definitely isn't for you. Fish are good when left in their cages. Ferrets are exploratory characters who aim to please their humans. Okay, they really aim to please themselves but tickle us pink in the process.

They need a lot of exercise and attention to be happy (see Figure 2-1). No less than two hours a day of playtime in a safe, enriched, ferret-proof environment will do. It will do you a world of good to get right down there on the floor with your fert and let your inner ferret out. (For more information about enriching your ferret's life, check out Chapter 10.)

If for some reason you can't provide your ferret with the proper amount of exercise and attention, and that's your only ferret hang-up, perhaps you should consider two ferrets. They live to play and they play to live, so if you can't be an interactive human, get your fuzzy a playmate. Besides, while one furball is intensely amusing, two (or more) are downright hysterical.

Ferrets are highly intelligent animals that need a lot of attention. In terms of owner interaction, they are high-maintenance pets — if you want to keep them happy and healthy. They require at least two hours of playtime each day in a safe and stimulating environment. If you can't or won't take the time to let them play and explore, consider a hamster instead.

Figure 2-1: Ferrets, like Buster here, require lots of playtime out of the cage.

The Odor Factor

This topic appears throughout the book because so many people give up ferrets due to their odor. It's often the fault of the human, who fails to do what's needed to keep the fert smelling fresh.

Someone you should know

I don't know which ships sailed the first ferrets to the United States 300 years ago, so I don't know exactly where the credit lies. However, the late Dr. Wendy Winsted, author of *Ferrets in Your Home* (published by TFH Publications), was herself the leading expert in ferret care 30 or so years ago when owning a pet ferret was almost unheard of. As a singer-songwriter in the late 1960s, Wendy grew lonely during long road trips. One friend suggested an armadillo to keep her company. Another suggested a pet skunk. Wendy ended up with two skunks, Eli and Sally-Michael, which she found both fascinating and wonderful company.

When Sally-Michael died, Wendy again found herself longing for a new companion. A friend suggested that she purchase a ferret kit, although the friend had never seen one and Wendy hadn't even heard of a ferret. And this is where it all began.

Wendy's first ferret was a dark sable female named McGuinn, who actully came by mail order. Wendy later added two more females, Melinda and Sally, to her furry family.

The ferrets accompanied Wendy almost everywhere she went, from shopping and school to movie theaters and restaurants. They fit nicely in her oversized handbag and sometimes even slept on her lap as she took notes during college lectures. People who did notice the extra baggage were pleasantly surprised to find how friendly and charming ferrets really were.

Wendy was so taken with ferrets that she wanted McGuinn to have ferret babies of her own; however, she knew that unneutered males were notoriously stinky and that she wouldn't be able to find homes for the boys. Wendy didn't want to put them to sleep just because they stunk. Eli the skunk had the perfect answer for her.

A quick phone call to her friend and veterinarian, Dr. Paul Cavanaugh, who had descented several skunks, proved priceless. Although he'd never heard of it being done before, he agreed to descent a young ferret. Shortly after the successful procedure, Wendy, an experienced vet tech, descented McGuinn with a little guidance from the good doctor. The amount of stink coming from the females was greatly reduced. (When the stud ferret arrived and was descented, Wendy found only a little difference in odor.) Neutering became the key to reducing the male's smell.

Over the years, Wendy taught her descenting techniques to major ferret breeders all over the United States. With the onset of altered and descented ferret kits hitting the pet trade, ferret popularity dramatically increased. It had been the odor of the ferret that had been keeping these lovable fuzzies out of most homes. The fact that ferrets are popular companion pets today is due in great part to Dr. Wendy Winsted's love of ferrets and her strong desire to show the world what wonderful companion pets ferrets can make.

Frequently changing the litter and bedding is the best way to control odor. Bathing a ferret too often results in a stinkier ferret because the oil glands go into overdrive to replace the oils you've been working so hard at washing down the drain.

If you're one of those people who can barely tolerate the musk, but you really want a ferret as a pet, avoid an unneutered male. Also, try to find a fuzzy that's already been descented so you won't have to put up with the occasional anal explosion. But don't forget that even that smell doesn't last long. It's more of an annoyance than anything else.

There's always some odor involved with ferrets. Even the most well-cared-for ferret will have a slight musky smell. On average, the odor is no worse than a dog's smell, but people's tolerances for smell are different. Obviously, if you let a ferret go for very long periods without a bath or if you become too lax with changing his litter box and bedding, the smell will be stronger.

Financial Matters

Ferrets can be expensive pets. Whether you purchase your baby at a pet store, adopt him from a shelter, or have a neighbor leave him on your doorstep, you need to fork over not only emotion but money as well.

Basic expenses include such things as cages and accessories, toys, and treats. Ferrets need a high-quality kitten food or ferret food, which is more costly than low-quality foods. The more ferrets you have, the more they eat. Are you willing to pay more for a high-quality food to keep your ferrets as healthy as possible?

And don't forget the routine trips to the vet. Besides checkups, your ferret should receive annual rabies and distemper vaccinations, as well as heartworm preventives. If you're one of those people who saves money by not vaccinating your pets and rationalizes it by saying that your pet never goes outside or comes in contact with sick animals, please think twice about your justification. The inevitable can and does happen. Heartworm is spread by mosquitoes. And you yourself can bring disease into the house on clothing and shoes just from a chance encounter with a sick animal. Don't let your pet suffer at your expense.

As your ferret ages, the chances of him developing an illness or disease also increases. Often, this means more frequent trips to the vet, special tests, and/or medication. Remember that you owe it to any pet you have to provide quality medical care at all times. A pet should never suffer because you don't want to or can't pay for the cost of treating the illness.

Investing in a ferret family member has many intangible rewards, but you must be willing to put out the cash when necessary to keep him safe and sound. The dollars can add up. Think about starting a pet fund on a weekly basis, putting aside a few dollars in case an emergency comes up and you fall a little short financially. This way, you'll be able to handle most emergencies without your fert having to suffer.

A fuzzy should be looked at as an investment, more emotional than anything else. A ferret will give 150 percent back to any loving human who treats him kindly and takes the time to interact with him. Ferrets deserve the best care possible, and you need to be willing to commit to that care if you're to have a ferret for a pet.

The Space They Need

No pet should be brought home before his house has been completely and adequately set up. Even though ferts make great pets for both the house and apartment, the cage should be roomy, and adequate room must be made for it (see Figure 2-2).

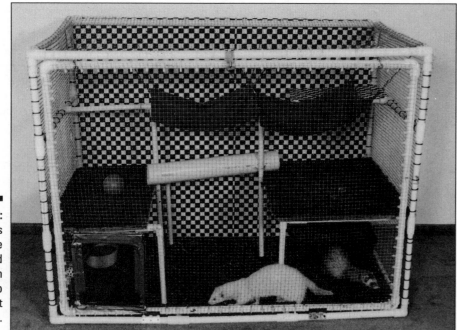

Figure 2-2: Spacious cages are required and can take up quite a bit of room.

If your only available space is the wall that's supporting the world's largest beer can collection, then consider parting with the cans or packing them up. Even if you could squeeze in both the ferret and the beer cans, doing so wouldn't be a good idea. The inevitable noise of the cans crashing to the ground could hurt the little carpet shark's ears. But the thief would still manage to drag a can or two back to his secret hidey-hole.

The Challenges of Ferret-Proofing Your Home

Ferrets get into every little thing they can. They are trouble magnets. From digging up the plants and carpeting to terrorizing the cats and dogs, if something can be messed with, a fert *will* mess with it.

I compare this vigorous playtime madness to a human toddler on a double espresso. You need to ferret-proof your home or at least the areas the little buggers have access to. It may be as simple as moving the houseplants, or it may be more involved, like boarding up the cracks and crevices under your cabinets.

A ferret is designed to search out your ferret-proofing failures. You'll probably find that ferret-proofing is a continuous activity as more and more flaws are pointed out to you by your curious fert.

Ferret-proofing your home can be quite challenging. Rarely is this process ever complete. If you even question whether or not something is unsafe, it probably is unsafe. Otherwise, you wouldn't give it a second thought. Expect the impossible. Prepare for the worst. Hope for the best. What actually happens will probably be somewhere in between. For tips on how to make your home safe for a ferret, head to Chapter 7.

Experience doesn't guarantee safety

I remember sitting outside on my back porch one summer day when a ferret walked right up to me. "Wow," I thought. "This looks just like my Tank." I was excited that I might have a new addition to the family if no one claimed this poor stray. Just then another ferret went bouncing by. She looked just like my little Jasmine. A sense of panic swept over me as the light finally went on in my thick skull. I rushed inside to find that one of the dogs had opened the door to the laundry room to get at the dog treats. Two of my beloved little furballs grabbed the opportunity to navigate through a hole in the dryer vent tubing, which led them up and out to the scary world. Fortunately, the other eight fuzzies hadn't followed them. I had known the hole was there and figured I'd have time to fix it later. That was before I was acutely aware of the dangers a house presents to a ferret looking for trouble. Expect the unexpected and prepare for it.

Ferrets and Kids

Ferrets can make good pets for the single person or the family. I don't like to stereotype human children as a whole by saying this pet or that pet isn't good with kids. Usually, it's the other way around. A lot of kids aren't good around some types of pets. There are exceptions. I was taking care of many pets before I was even 10 years old, and I did so with great pleasure and responsibility. I didn't mind getting scratched or bitten. I didn't mind the cage cleaning. I was an exception to most kids.

Ferrets can be playfully nippy and squirmy. Most young children can and will instantly activate the hyper switch in ferrets. And don't be fooled by your kid promising to be 100 percent responsible for any new pet. Evaluate your family members honestly before bringing a ferret home. Expect that you'll be the main caretaker.

Legal Aspects

Be aware of the legal aspects of owning a ferret. If you think you've passed the time, cost, adjustment, and olfactory considerations discussed briefly in this chapter, do a little more digging to be sure ferrets are legal where you live. What permits might you need?

It is truly heartbreaking to lose your ferret to legal snags after having invested so much time and love for your little fert. Fortunately, I have not experienced the pain firsthand, but I do shed tears when I read the emotional testimonies of those who've lost the legal battle and ultimately their beloved fuzzy. For more information about the legal issues surrounding owning a ferret, head to Chapter 3.

A few fun definitions

Here are a few definitions that only ferret owners can appreciate. For a complete list of these fun definitions, go to my Website at www.animalsforawareness.org.

- **A-bomb:** The act of a ferret emptying its anal glands.

- **Cache and carry:** The action of carrying toys to the hidey-hole.

- **Cache flow:** Moving toys from one hidey hole to another.

- **Cute:** Anything a ferret does that would get a dog in trouble.

- **Divorce:** Preferable to losing a ferret.

- **Freckle face:** A ferret with a spotted or incomplete mask.

- **High and dry:** The goal of a ferret as it races up your arm during bath time.

- **Houseguest:** The ferret caretaker living in the same dwelling as their ferrets.

- **Loco-motion:** Dancing, bumping into things, falling over, and generally looking silly.

- **No:** A word without meaning in Ferretese.

- **Over and out:** What happens to a ferret when it encounters an inadequate barrier.

- **Pushing up daisies:** What happens when a ferret encounters a live potted plant.

- **Speedbump:** The ability of a ferret to suddenly collapse motionlessly and remain in that position for several seconds before returning to normal hyperactivity.

- **Stamped:** When a ferret leaves a nose print on your glasses.

- **Tear jerker:** What happens to your nose should you move when a ferret clamps on.

- **Throwing stones:** 1) A fuzzy digging out all the litter in the litter box. 2) The fert catapulting the ferret-proof rocks out of your floor plant.

- **Toe hold:** When a ferret attempts to drag you under the couch by you toes.

- **Wayward weasel:** A lost ferret.

(Thanks to Bob Church for his contributions!)

Chapter 3

Ferrets and the Law

Some of you may be leaning toward mild adoration of the fuzzy that has melted the hearts of millions. So you may be surprised to learn that ferrets are actually illegal in some cities and even some states as a whole. Places where ferrets are not welcome or are downright illegal are called *ferret-free zones*. Likewise, *ferret-friendly zones* are places where your fert is usually safe from the politicians. Whether your area is a ferret-free or ferret-friendly zone has to do with how your local government classifies the ferret.

This chapter explains how to find out whether having a fuzzy is illegal where you live. Obviously, you should find out before you take one into your heart and home. I show you the rationale behind outlawing these critters and the ramifications of being caught red-handed with a fugitive furball. I hate that a chapter like this needs to be written in the first place. Hopefully, someday understanding and reasoning will be gained by the currently intolerant.

Why Ferret-Free Zones Exist

Although the United States Department of Agriculture classifies ferrets as domesticated critters, some state agencies still insist that the domestic ferret is actually a wild animal. A few say it is not a wild animal but rather an exotic animal. Others believe it is domesticated but still hold firmly to the belief that ferrets are dangerous. Technically, the ferret is domesticated. But because many states regulate wild and exotic animals to some degree, and the poor ferret gets lumped in where it just doesn't belong, ferrets end up getting regulated or discriminated against unjustly in some places.

At the time of this writing (summer 2000), California and Hawaii remain the only states that continue to outlaw ferrets. However, just because your state may have ferrets listed as legal doesn't mean your city does. Many major and some small cities still remain non-ferret-friendly. Check it out. See the section "Know the Law" to find out where to get this information.

While our lovable ferret continues to get wrapped up in the political crapola of our governmental bureaucracy, dedicated ferret freedom fighters continue to mow down untruths and misconceptions in the hopes of protecting and legalizing ferrets everywhere.

You may wonder how captivating bundles of energy and joy can be such a source of controversy. It all lies in the myths and misconceptions department, as the following sections explain.

What's it gonna be? Wild, domestic, or exotic?

Perhaps the biggest misconception is that ferrets are wild or nondomesticated animals, no different from the neighborhood skunks and raccoons. The truth is that ferrets are domesticated animals and have been for thousands of years. Ferrets depend on their humans for survival. So how can the government classify them as wildlife? The answer probably lies in how scientists named them way back when.

Depending on your school of belief, the ferret is either a species all to itself (*Mustela furo*) or a variation of the wild European polecat (*Mustela putorius furo*). Since the ferret is scientifically known as the latter, it's the legal glitch some have used to classify the fuzzy as wildlife. And a whole lot of stuff comes with being classified as wildlife — such as wildlife can be dangerous, unpredictable, and a disease risk. Wildlife is also either illegal to keep or requires a special permit in most cities and states. Another reason ferrets may be considered wild is because they look so much like their cousins the minks, weasels, and polecats. Or consider the fact that one of the world's most endangered wildlife, the black-footed ferret, happens to have *ferret* in its name. And yet, some places (including Hawaii) recognize ferrets as domestic animals but lump them in the exotic category and proceed to ban certain exotic animals. Often, the ferret is included on the prohibited list.

Feral ferts in my neighborhood?

Perhaps the most outrageous misconception — or, better yet, unfounded paranoia — is the fear that escapee ferrets will unite together in the wild, form large *feral* (wild) colonies, and develop their own organized crime ring.

Okay. Some governmental suits actually believe the part about the development of feral colonies. And they preach the idea that native wildlife and livestock will be destroyed by these make-believe colonies of roving feral ferrets. Here are some reasons why this scenario is very unlikely:

✔ Ferrets are domestic animals, and they rely on us humans for survival (see Figure 3-1).

✔ The majority of ferrets entering the pet trade are already spayed or neutered.

✔ Ferrets are indoor pets.

Most species of domestic animals are capable of going feral. But for a colony of these feral animals to be formed, the environment has to be just perfect for them. There must be several feral breeders around to make more animals. There must be an open environmental niche. There are few open niches left in North America for small predatory mammals such as the ferret. They're already filled with other, more competitive mustelids, such as the American mink and long-tailed weasel. The animal must also know how to escape predators and find food. And these are just a few of the *many* reasons why the likelihood of ferrets taking over the environment is very small. In fact, the California Department of Fish and Game did a survey of all 50 states — "1996-97 Nationwide Ferret Survey of State Wildlife Agencies" — and found no documented cases of feral ferrets in any state. (For more information on this survey, go to www.dfg.ca.gov/new.html.)

Figure 3-1:
Jayme shows how vicious fuzzies really can be. *Not.*

The unfounded fear of rabies

Zero reports have been made of rabies being transmitted from a ferret to a human, and only a small handful of rabies in ferrets have ever been documented. In fact, dogs and cats, while incidences are low, are at much greater risk of being exposed to rabies, thus putting you at greater risk.

> ✔ Ferrets have little opportunity to come in contact with a rabies-infected animal in the first place.
>
> ✔ Infected ferrets are thought to contract *dumb rabies* and die quickly after being infected. (To find out what dumb rabies is, compared to furious rabies, see Chapter 15.)
>
> ✔ Researchers are in the early stages of proving that the ferret doesn't even pass the virus through his saliva. (Chapter 15 has the full scoop on rabies.)

An approved rabies vaccine is available for ferrets. Part of being a responsible ferret owner is having your lovable fuzzball vaccinated on a yearly basis. Most cities and states recognize the rabies vaccine developed for the ferret, so for your sake and your ferret's, keep proof on hand.

A License? But He Can't Even Reach the Pedals

Some cities/states require licenses or permits. They can be free (such as in my state of Illinois) or cost as much as $100 per year. Some fees are per ferret, so double-check. Not all permits come free of strings. For example, some require that you don't have children under a certain age in the household if you want to keep a ferret. Some require proof of vaccinations and or neutering/spaying.

Some states/cities don't regulate ferrets at all, but at the same time, ferrets are not looked upon as welcome guests. Where ferret tolerance is low, confiscation or fines may be imposed routinely or randomly. Some cities are very confused; they say that permits are necessary to breed and or sell ferrets but that it's illegal to own them. Huh? And many military bases, depending on the base commander, ban the ownership of ferrets. It can seem at times to be a conspiracy on the part of a few against the masses of ferret lovers.

Know the Law

The only possible way to know whether your ferret is welcome for sure is to call your local Fish and Game Department, Department of Conservation, or Wildlife Department. Another good source is the local humane society. It's their business to know the laws pertaining to animals. But perhaps the best source of ferret law is the local ferret club or shelter. The latter source is probably the safest and gives the most accurate information. After all, ferret people have the most invested in keeping their ferts safe.

Do not, do not, do not rely solely on the advice or opinion of a pet shop employee or breeder when it comes to ferret law. If these folks even know your local law at all, they may not be forthcoming in providing accurate information to a potential buyer. This isn't true with all pet shop employees or breeders, but why risk it? If you must ask, get a second opinion also.

Ferrets are not legal or tolerated everywhere. Check with an appropriate and knowledgeable agency before obtaining a ferret to find out exact details pertaining to ferret ownership where you live. Doing so can save your ferret's life in the long run.

If You Break the Law

So I get caught red-handed. So what?

So what? First of all, the danger to your fuzzy is great. Some ferret-free zones don't think twice about removing your furry family member out of his safe, secure home for good. If the ferret's lucky, he may get shipped to a shelter in a ferret-friendly zone where his life can begin again. If he's unlucky, his life will be abruptly ended because of your carelessness. While confiscation of the fuzzy is almost always inevitable, you may also be slapped with fines. I hear that some are pretty hefty, like $2,000 per ferret offense.

If you live in a city that doesn't enforce its policy on ferrets, proceed with extreme caution. Often, all it takes is a couple of complaints or a nip or scratch for the ferret to be confiscated and/or euthanized. This outcome apparently happens even where ferrets are legal due to the fear of rabies, unfounded though it may be. Be smart and cover your own and your fert's behind.

Part II

Finding Your Ferret and Hanging Up the Welcome Hammock

The 5th Wave

By Rich Tennant

"Hey—that's a record! Honey, I just clocked the ferret at 28 mph coming through the living room!"

In this part . . .

Now you're getting more serious about living happily with fuzzballs, but you don't know where to start. Where do you shop for ferrets? How do you know whether you're getting a healthy one? What about cages and ferret accessories? And what exactly are ferret accessories, anyway? What are the do's and don'ts when making out your shopping list? I help you with that — sharing everything you need to know to both find your ferret and set up his home. This part also lets you know what else you need to do to prepare for his arrival and what you need to do to get *your* house ready: things like ferret-proofing, finding a vet, and, finally, introducing your new baby to his new family. In a nutshell, this part deals with finding your ferret and preparing for his arrival.

Chapter 4

Your Ideal Furball

Most people who want a ferret have an image of what a perfect ferret is. Friendly, sweet, loving, playful, adventuresome — those are just a few of the characteristics ferret lovers dream about their ferret having. But, when it actually comes down to choosing a ferret, friendly, sweet, loving, and all the other nice adjectives only get you so far. You also need to think in terms of health, gender, and even age. And when you've got that all figured out, you probably want to consider whether you should get more than one.

This chapter deals with choosing the perfect ferret for you (Chapter 5 tells you where to go once you decide what perfect is). Here you can find out what the normal and ideal traits are, as well as some characteristics to avoid. Some sections talk about the differences in genders and ages. You may be surprised what you discover in this chapter. Color should be the last deciding factor, especially because many coat colors and patterns have a tendency to change and lighten over time.

Ferrets are very adaptable to new people and new environments. All it usually requires is a little time and patience, a lot of love, and a box of raisins.

The Basics

Until you become more experienced in ferret care, it's important to choose a healthy ferret that has a pleasant personality. And here are some other things to keep in mind:

✔ The fur should be soft and shiny. He should have no patches of missing fur.

✔ The eyes should be clear and bright. No discharge should be coming from the eyes, ears, or nose.

✔ The underside of the ferret should be clean and healthy looking. Look for signs of diarrhea or bloating, which can be evidence of parasites or illness.

✔ Do *not* buy a ferret out of sympathy. You may run into the occasional sickly kit (baby ferret) at a pet shop that you feel you can't pass up. Pass him up anyway. Help the fuzzy by calling your local shelter or ferret club and informing someone of the situation so they can intervene. But leave the rescuing and more difficult cases to the experienced ferret humans who know what they're getting into.

✔ The ideal ferret should be inquisitive when you approach, not cower or run to a hiding place. He may be jumpy and playful.

✔ Don't look at nipping in a younger ferret as an obvious warning sign. That's normal for a youngster. However, do avoid a ferret that bites aggressively out of fear. You'll recognize the difference. Problem ferrets hang on and draw blood.

Many wonderful shelter ferrets need good homes, too. Some of these ferts require special attention. Most do not. For information on where you can find your ferret, see Chapter 5 or the shelter listing in the appendix at the back of the book.

But I felt so sorry for him . . .

I can't tell you how many people bring animals to our shelter, ferrets included, because they hadn't really thought long enough about their decision to take on such a responsibility. I always ask why they acquired the pet in the first place (I'm the curious type), and many people say they felt sorry for the animal. Getting a pet out of sympathy rarely leads to a win-win situation. Caring for an animal you know inside and out and have prepared for is difficult enough. But taking on an animal that you know little about or that has underlying problems you're unable to deal with can lead to frustration, anger, and a sense of hopelessness on the parts of all involved.

New or Used?

Some people automatically think that they should start off with a baby ferret for many reasons, some of which just don't make sense with ferrets. The thought that you must begin with a baby so that he'll bond with you properly doesn't hold true in the ferret world. Most adult ferrets adapt well to change and will love you no matter how long you've had them. But what about the "I want little Johnny and the ferret to grow up together" reasoning? The fact is, both adult and baby ferrets make good pets. The decision should be made based on your experience and lifestyle.

Kits (baby ferrets)

Baby ferrets, or *kits,* are absolutely adorable and hard to resist. Youngsters are delightfully bouncy and mischievous, with seemingly perpetual energy. They're just a tad more energetic than their adult counterparts. Here are some things to know about kits:

- ✔ Kits are more active and playful and can be more demanding of your time. They are also notoriously nippy because they are still in the learning and testing stage.

  Biting is not cute and should not be encouraged through play. It can get out of hand and become a behavior issue instead of a learning issue if not dealt with immediately. To find out how to deal with biting, see Chapter 19.

- ✔ You need to train and socialize the kit. You'll be the one who teaches this ferret kit what is and isn't acceptable.

- ✔ You need to make sure that he has all of his baby shots. Medically speaking, a baby fuzzy should have already received his first distemper shot by the time he goes home with you. He may need up to a total of four shots, depending on how old he is and what he's already received (see Chapter 13 for details).

If you have small children, I recommend that a kit not be your first choice. If just you and maybe one or two other adults are in the household and there's lots of extra attention to give, a kit may be just what you're looking for.

Older ferrets

Adult ferrets make wonderful first-time pets. You don't have to get these guys as babies to get them to bond to you. Unfortunately, thousands of wonderful adult ferrets wait patiently in shelters for that just-right home simply because people believe the older kids are damaged in some way. Some people even dare to think adults aren't as cute as kits. I beg to differ. Ninety-five percent of all my ferts have been hand-me-down adults. And each one, with his unique personality, melted my heart right away. If you're thinking about adopting an older ferret, keep the following points in mind:

- Because the life span of a ferret is relatively short (average 6–8 years), getting an older or adult fert means possibly having less time with him down the road.

  This isn't always the case, though. I've lost younger ferrets to disease and had some of my older adoptees live years beyond what's expected. The life span is just something you may want to think about.

- Generally speaking, older ferrets seem to be a bit more relaxed with themselves and wiser to their surroundings (see Figure 4-1). They're still inquisitive and mischief makers, though. Unless they are ill, most adults are wildly amusing and playful. Some can even get into as much, if not more, trouble than their young counterparts. They just seem to have had the edge taken off.

Figure 4-1: Older ferrets — like Ginger — can bring a smile to anyone's face.

✔ Adult ferrets can be more set in their ways. Behavior difficulties, if they exist at all, can be more of a challenge to correct. Some have surely been neglected or abused. They may need a little more understanding and patience. On the other hand, adults that have been treated well (and even many of the neglected and abused ferrets) adapt well to new environments and have little or no difficulty bonding to their new human.

✔ The majority of these older guys have had at least one other caretaker. Most are already trained to use the litter box and have been taught that nipping is unacceptable. However, adult ferrets that haven't been properly socialized may bite out of fear. If you decide on an older ferret, take the time to play and socialize with him awhile. It won't take long to determine if any special needs exist.

Boy or Girl?

Another decision you have to make is whether you want a male or female.

✔ Females, called *jills* (unspayed) and *sprites* (spayed), are typically smaller and daintier than males, called *hobs* (unneutered) and *gibs* (neutered).

✔ As ferrets mature, the boys seem to become more cuddly and couch-potato-ish. Females tend to remain more squirmish, as though they'd rather be anywhere else than in your loving grasp. I hate to say that this is a rule, however, because I've had some that were quite the opposite of this stereotype. Sometimes, all it takes to get a ferret, particularly the girls, to settle down is a bit of human intervention, such as rubbing the ferret's ear or other "grooming" gestures.

Unless they are very sick or old, ferrets are amusing bundles of energy with a propensity to please and make trouble, regardless of gender.

Altered Versus Whole Ferts

Because most ferrets entering the pet trade come from mass ferret producers, more than likely your ferret, regardless of gender, will already be neutered or spayed. Spaying or neutering is done at a very early age (as young as 4 weeks), and sometimes the only way to know for sure is by a tattoo in the ear. But not all breeders tattoo their ferrets.

If you happen on a whole, or *unaltered,* ferret, the altering procedure should be done by the time the ferret is 6 months old, unless you're planning to breed. Some people suggest that males be neutered as late as 12 months and females be spayed as late as 9 months so that they'll reach full growth. However, if you choose to wait, watch your ferret closely and alter him or her just before he reaches sexual maturity.

In the male, neutering is more of a behavioral necessity. Neutering also dramatically decreases the odor of boys. In the female, spaying is a medical necessity. Unlike other mammals that go into heat for short periods of time, the female ferret stays in heat until she is bred. This unending heat cycle more often than not leads to a life-threatening condition called *aplastic anemia.* Spaying your fert can save her life.

Very few differences exist between altered male and altered female ferrets. In fact, every altered ferret I've ever encountered had his or her own very unique personality that was unrelated to gender or age. Ferrets are all amusing and hyper to various degrees and are easy to please as long as you meet their needs.

Boys will be boys

You'll know your male is whole if his testicles begin to drop (appear) and his odor becomes stronger as the *rut* approaches: Like many animals, from the little prairie dog to the large moose elk, unneutered male ferrets enter a period of rut when all they can think about is passing on their superior genetic makeup. For ferrets, rut can start in the spring and last six months, all the way until fall. In most individuals, though, it typically lasts only a few months.

At this time, males on the prowl can become quite aggressive toward other male ferrets, neutered or unneutered. In fact, even the females are not safe from the male in rut. For their own safety and the safety of cage mates, unaltered males should be house separately during mating season if not used for breeding. During this period, the boys' weight can also fluctuate a great deal; they usually lose weight while preoccupied with the girls. Some males even become depressed or anxious if they fail to find the girl of their dreams and have a night of unbridled romance.

Do them all and yourself a favor and neuter.

Girls will be girls

Females, while less intent on finding the hob of their dreams, enter a period of heat if unspayed. Telling whether your ferret is in heat is very easy because her vulva (genitals) swells a great deal from the increase in hormones.

Unlike many other mammals whose heat cycles last for a given period of time, a ferret stays in heat until she is bred. If the heat cycle lasts long enough (she remains unbred), your little girl will most likely develop a life-threatening condition called aplastic anemia. If you're faced with a female in heat, your vet may choose to administer a hormone shot to bring her out of heat before spaying her. Or she may be bred to a vasectomized male, to fake her out of heat, and then spayed. Spaying your female while she's in heat can be done, but it's considered dangerous due to the risk of hemorrhaging.

Swelling of the vulva can also be a sign of an incomplete or partial spay. While it's uncommon, altering ferrets at very young ages can result in this surgical error. Unfortunately, a swollen vulva is also a common symptom of a female ferret with adrenal problems. Do not overlook this symptom. If you have a ferret with a swollen vulva, a visit to an experienced ferret veterinarian will yield the answers you need in order to proceed with the proper course of action.

You Want How Many?

One ferret can be happy and content in a cage as long as he also gets a lot of playtime out of the cage every day. If you have a busy schedule and your ferret isn't going to get out as often as he should, you may want to consider having two or three ferrets. In fact, I advise that all ferret homes have at least two fuzzies. (If you're already caring for one fert, two ferts aren't that much different. And neither are three. In fact, three is probably a perfect ferret number.)

Almost all altered ferrets get along with other altered ferrets with little or no problem (see Figure 4-2). Although ferrets have a deep rooted solitary instinct, most ferrets view other ferrets as littermates and play and bop around accordingly. As usual, there are exceptions.

One reason three is a good number

I've heard of many stories where a fert became severely depressed when his long-term cage mate died. The best thing to do for the grieving fert, in my opinion, is to get another ferret as soon as possible. Here's where always having three ferts comes in handy. Having three means the loss of one fert will never leave another fert completely alone, and you'll have more time to bring another fert into your life and the life of the surviving ferts. But that's just my opinion, and some people think I'm nuts.

Figure 4-2:
If one is
good, then
two must be
better, right?
Right.

Ferrets aren't territorial to the extent dogs are, but they are territorial critters by nature. In the wild, polecats mark out territories and chase off other polecats of the same gender. In a cage, ferrets have little, itty-bitty microterritories and squabble over seemingly insignificant things. While they usually share just about everything from the water bottle to the litter box to the sock stolen right off your foot, they do make claims to certain things and even stuff like a section on their bed. So if you already have one ferret and are considering adding another, do so with some caution:

✔ Introduce new furballs in neutral territories with neutral toys, just to be sure there's no bad chemistry.

✔ Keep in mind that an older ferret may not find the antics and energy of a kit or an adolescent as amusing as you do. On the other hand, a younger ferret may be just what the doctor ordered for the sometimes lazy and depressed carpet shark, assuming no serious illness is going on.

✔ It's not unusual for the more dominant ferret to act a little bullyish and make the first tackle. They may screech at each other with humped backs and roll each other for a moment or two. Tails may get puffed like pipe cleaners or bottle brushes. One may take all the toys and stockpile them in a guarded corner or hidey-hole. These aren't unusual acts associated with introductions.

✔ Watch for the warning signs of true aggression, like ongoing screeching and puffed tails. There should be little to no screeching, and tails should return to normal size within 10 minutes of the initial meeting. If one or both ferts is doing more biting and screaming than playing after 5 or 10 minutes, then call it a day and try later.

It's unusual to have one ferret kill another, but occasionally you'll come across an oddball that just simply hates other ferrets and makes an honest effort to injure the other. These guys should remain single. One ferret drawing blood or literally scaring the poop out of another ferret indicates a serious problem, and a mismatch has likely occurred.

One ferret is amusing; two or more ferrets are a stitch. Whether in or out of the cage, multiple ferrets wrestle and tumble together. They chatter and screech and fuss about. They steal each other's treasures and then collapse together in a cuddly pile until one decides to start the routine over again. My thought is you can never have enough ferrets. But that's just me, and poop doesn't bother me very much. I have the lifestyle and dedication that allows me to live this philosophy. However, if you're even questioning how many to bring home, get at least two.

Two lessons in one

I had a situation where I tried to introduce a single female into a group of 10 ferrets. Mischief was very docile and passive, but none of the other ferrets liked her or allowed her to join in ferret games. I could introduce any other ferret to that group, and the newcomer would be fine. Mischief was just an oddball.

I might also add that this was the first time I'd ever been bitten by a ferret. I was consoling Mischief right after another ferret attacked her. Stupid me. I went to give her a kiss on the nose,

and she latched onto my chin. Bit all the way through to the other side.

Had I read her warning signs (puffed tail and agitation), I could've saved myself the pain. Of course, it was definitely my fault, not hers, and I felt foolish rather than angry. Moral: Never kiss an agitated ferret (or take more caution when a ferret has just been in a fight and is upset). Mischief never bit again and was so happy playing by herself or with me.

Chapter 5

On the Trail of a New Fuzzy

*W*hen you have an idea about what type of fert you're looking for (see Chapter 4 if you don't), you're ready to seek your dream fuzzball out. You have several options to consider, all having pros and cons.

You can adopt or purchase a ferret from many places. It all depends on what you're looking for and how far you're willing to go to get your ferret. No matter where you go and what you choose, there are certain things to look for in a ferret.

Pet Shops

Perhaps the most often thought-of source for a baby ferret is the local pet shop. Here are some things to think about if you get your ferret from a pet shop:

✔ Pet shops are convenient, and often ferret kits are readily available, but your choice can be limited.

✔ The majority of the kits come from ferret farms or mass producers. Occasionally, a pet shop buys kits from a local breeder. Sometimes, you'll even find an older fuzzy that wasn't bought as a kit or one that was returned by his previous owner.

✔ Ferrets originating from mass ferret producers (farms) tend to be on average a little smaller. Many private breeders put out larger and bulkier fuzzbutts. For this reason, if size is important to you, know where your youngster came from.

✔ You may or may not get a health guarantee with your new purchase. I suggest you request one in writing or look elsewhere for your ferret. Reputable pet shops usually sell healthy animals and therefore should be more than willing to offer a health guarantee.

✔ Pet shops are sometimes more expensive than many private breeders and shelters, although the expense may be worth it if the ferret is in top health and has a great personality to match.

✔ In good pet shops, the kits are played with frequently to ensure socializing, and the staff has been trained extensively in the care of the animals they sell.

In some pet shops, the kits are left in their cages until a potential buyer asks to see one. This practice can lead to poor socialization at a critical point in the ferret's life. Pet shop employees are sometimes unknowledgeable in the care of specific animals and recite words of miswisdom to unknowing customers. Other pet shops don't offer solid after-sale support. To find out whether the pet shop you're considering is one of the good ones, keep these things in mind:

✔ Pet shops should be clean, as should the animal cages, and the animals should look and act healthy and have clean food and water.

✔ Employees should be knowledgeable about the animals you're inquiring about or be willing to seek out the correct answers to your questions. They should also be sensitive to your concerns regarding buying a particular pet and shouldn't have the "sell sell sell" attitude.

✔ If you have enough time to do actual research, try to find people who have purchased animals from that shop and get their opinions. Also check with the Better Business Bureau for prior complaints. You can also call your local Humane Society or the government agency monitors pet shops and ask them. If complaints were made, they would know.

✔ Don't purchase on your first visit. Make several visits to see how the animals are truly cared for.

Remember that the goal of a pet shop is to ultimately sell you something. Do your homework on the ferret and research the pet shop before buying your new carpet shark.

Private Breeders

Another logical place to find a ferret is a private breeder. Like pet shops, there are good breeders and there are bad breeders. Locating a reputable one can be difficult since few private breeders are out there. Good sources of ferret breeders are small-pet magazines, particularly ferret-specific magazines, such as *Modern Ferret*. This wonderful magazine not only offers readers up-to-date ferret information on a bimonthly basis, but also advertises breeders and other ferret-related resources. Also, word of mouth in the ferret community can point you toward respected breeders.

People breed carpet sharks for several reasons, and you must keep these in mind when finding a breeder. Some breed for money or profit; others breed because they love fuzzies. Yet for others, it's a combination of both things.

A good breeder will be very honest and up front with you about the responsibility of having a ferret as a pet. While a breeder should be pleasant and easy to talk with, you may end up feeling like you're the one being quizzed. This can be a good thing. A breeder too eager to part with babies may be in it only for the profit and not the well being of the ferret or the buyer.

Here are some suggestions for finding a reputable breeder:

- ✔ Be sure to get references from people who've recently bought kits from the breeder and check them out.

- ✔ If geographically feasible, ask to come out and see the breeding facility to get a sense of how the ferts are kept.

- ✔ Ask about vaccination schedules and any illnesses encountered. (Make sure, if you purchase a kit, that a health guarantee is given.)

- ✔ Another important service a good breeder will offer is after-sales support. Ask how willing this person will be to chat when you call with an emergency question regarding your newly purchased baby.

- ✔ A good breeder may only have one or two pairs of breeding ferts, or the breeder may have many more. While you certainly don't want inbred ferts, the amount of breeding pairs doesn't tell you if it is or isn't good breeding.

A good look at the animals in stock will tell you more about the breeding practices of a private breeder than anything else. A good breeder, regardless of the number of ferrets, will have humane conditions, active, alert ferrets, with intensely curious kits.

When you find a good, honest, reputable breeder, you may have to wait for the next litter to arrive. Some breeders even allow you to special-order certain colors or patterns.

My, what big ferrets you have!

Private breeders often put out bigger ferrets than the ferret farms. The reason is often because private breeders don't neuter/spay their babies early. Hormones, after all, play a role in growth. Most ferret farm babies are altered at 4–6 weeks. Ferrets from private ferret breeders are usually neutered/spayed at the new owners' expense and discretion. Preferrably the procedure should be done before sexual maturity is reached. A reputable breeder will discuss your options with you. It's also possible that private breeders produce bigger ferrets because they may be more particular about their breeding ferrets' diets.

Ferret Shelters

Perhaps the most overlooked source of a wonderful pet ferret is the ferret shelter. At a shelter, you can find ferrets that come in all colors, patterns, and personalities. Some are youngsters that proved too energetic for their uneducated owners. Some are well past their own life expectancy when given up and need a gentle and loving home for their final months. Some have been abused and/or neglected. Many have been well cared for until their surrender. Some shelter fuzzies have special needs, such as daily medications or special feedings. Some may bite out of fear and require experienced, patient ferret homes. If you're considering getting your ferret from a shelter, keep these things in mind:

- Shelters rely on ferret adoptions for financial assistance as well as making room for more incoming fuzzies. Many shelters frequently have no less than 60 ferts at any given time.

- People in the business of ferret rescuing and sheltering are usually only in it because of their undying devotion to ferrets. Even though I run an animal shelter and get in ferrets, some of my fuzzies have come from our local ferret shelter. With every visit to the Greater Chicago Ferret Association (GCFA), I make them promise they won't let me bring another home. I usually run a 50–50 chance of taking one home despite my own lectures to myself.

- Expect shelter operators to conduct a friendly yet thorough interview and ask a lot of questions of potential adopters. That's okay. The job of the shelter folks is to be sure the poor fert that was dumped on them will be put into a lifelong, loving home. Their goal is to find the best families for these homeless fuzzies.

✔ Many shelters may have certain restrictions or requirements that some breeders and pet shops may not have. Almost all shelters require that the ferret be returned to the shelter if the relationship doesn't work out.

✔ Most ferret shelters also have veterinarians working closely with them to monitor the health of each and every ferret in their care. The ferrets should already be vaccinated before adoption, and a general physical will have ruled out most illnesses. Some shelters have blood work performed on their older fuzzies just for peace of mind.

✔ Adoption fees are usually lower, but they vary depending on the age and health of the ferret you adopt.

✔ Most ferret shelter people are eager to extend after-adoption support — when they aren't up to their elbows in poop. You're bound to make friends with ferret shelter people, which also means a lifetime of support and continuing knowledge.

The number of ferrets that wind up in shelters is overwhelming. No matter what type of fert you're looking for, a shelter is bound to have him. Adopting a ferret from a shelter is a great way to support the ferret cause. An extra perk may mean a membership in the shelter's ferret club if it has one. Membership may include newsletters, ferret shows, holiday parties, and fundraisers. So in addition to adding a wonderful new family member, you get to meet other furball fanatics and have a connection to a lifelong support group.

The Classifieds

If none of the options discussed in this chapter seems workable for you, then you can always try the newspaper classified ads or bulletin boards at veterinary clinics or pet supply shops. If you live in a larger city (one where owning a ferret is legal), it's not uncommon to come across posted signs or ads for ferrets needing homes. Sometimes the seller is willing to part with the cage and supplies as part of the fee. Most often, the ferts being sold are older, but the previous owner can provide a wealth of background information on that particular fert that you may not otherwise get.

Buyer beware: Like a pet shop, the seller's ultimate goal may be getting the cash in hand. Others are kind animal lovers who just want their fuzzies to go to a good home and wish to recuperate some of the investment they initially made. Be wary of the husbandry information you receive from a private seller. Stick with the advice of real experts.

The Wayward Weasel: Stray Ferrets

Sometimes people find ferrets that have been lost or abandoned by their previous caretakers. Always be cautious with a found ferret since you don't know what the poor little guy's been through. He's likely scared and hungry and probably very confused. He doesn't know if your intentions are good or bad and may bite out of fear or defense.

Also, some people mistakenly identify mink and long-tailed weasels as ferrets. To date, I've gone out on seven separate stray ferret calls where I've come home with minks. While they're awfully cute, these wild animals can pack a powerful bite and should not be approached. Be sure what you're "rescuing" is indeed a ferret!

If you find a ferret, you should make every attempt to find his home because someone may truly be grieving the loss of this little furball. Place an ad in the paper and post notes on boards at pet shops and veterinary clinics. If a home isn't found and you want to keep him, be sure to quarantine him before introducing him to the other fuzzies. He may be sick or have fleas. A trip to the vet with your newly found friend is a must.

If you can't keep him, do not abandon him. Many excellent ferret shelters are out there that would be more than happy to find him a proper home. Many ferret fanatics are also out there who will reply quickly to an ad.

The majority of dog/cat shelters accept ferrets, but most also kill them instead of going to the trouble of finding them good homes. Don't take a found ferret to your local shelter, no matter what they tell you their intentions are. Find a good ferret shelter to take him in or find a good home for him yourself.

Chapter 6

Home Sweet Home: Setting Up Your Ferret's House

In This Chapter

▶ Getting your ferret's house ready

▶ Picking a food dish and water bowl

▶ All sorts of accessories that you and your ferret will love

*B*efore you bring your ferret home, it's only fair that you're completely prepared for his arrival. If you're all set for your new bundle of joy before he arrives, you'll spend less time ferreting for forgotten items and more time bonding with your baby.

This chapter contains the must-haves for any ferret to live comfortably and safely in your home. This chapter covers both the needed basics and accessories. With the info in this chapter, you can find out everything you need to know about ferret accommodations: from the house and furniture to the wardrobe and wall coverings. If you already have a ferret, please read this chapter anyway to make sure you haven't forgotten something. With so many things to think about, overlooking an item or two is easy.

Set Up the Cage

This is where true fuzzball lovers often show their fanatical yet creative sides. Cages can be simple, single-level ranches to multilevel mansions with guesthouses. It all depends on your taste and what you can afford, both financially and spatially. The effort is worth it. After all, your ferret will have to stay in his house when he's not out playing, so work on creating as stimulating an environment as possible.

Ferrets are carnivores. You should house ferrets only with other ferrets or by themselves. While most pet ferrets don't recognize a small animal as food, ferrets often play a small animal to death. Many ferrets have a strong predatory urge. I've known people who've lost rats, mice, sugar gliders, and guinea pigs to pet ferrets. If you insist on interaction between ferrets and other animals, supervise them closely and cautiously.

Size

Cages should be at least 3 feet wide by 2 feet deep by 2 feet high, and this is a *minimum* for one fert. As a rule with most pets, the bigger, the better. Whatever size you choose, be sure he has enough space for a playroom, kitchen, bedroom, and bathroom. You wouldn't want to eat, sleep, and play in your toilet, and neither would your ferret (see Figure 6-1). You can find a suitable habitat at a good pet shop, pet supply store, ferret specialty catalog, and even ferret shelters.

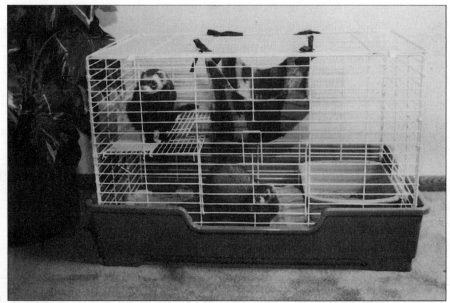

Figure 6-1:
This cage is much too small — especially for two ferrets.

Design

Many, many types of cages are out there that are more than adequate for your ferret. Pick up a ferret magazine and see how creative fert humans can be. The keys to a good cage follow:

✔ **Ample size.** The floor space should be large to allow for ample playing and comfortable snoozing.

✔ **Good ventilation.** Poor ventilation combined with stinky, damp patches of urine can lead to illness and disease.

Ferrets are not fish. Avoid aquariums and similar enclosures for housing your ferret. They lack proper ventilation and can in turn cause serious illness in your ferret. Besides being too small and cramped for an active carpet shark, they were made with fish, not ferrets, in mind.

✔ **Small openings between wire and secure doors.** Ferrets are master escape artists. They are tempted to stick their heads into or through any opening they can get their snouts into. They can and will push open doors with their heads.

Severe injury or even strangulation can occur in an unsuitable cage. So make sure that no large openings are anywhere in the cage design and that, if necessary, the doors on the cage are reinforced with snap bolts (the snaps at the end of a dog leash).

✔ **Sturdiness and easy access for cleaning.** Certain ferret cages also come with pull-out trays to catch the litter and food crumbs that fall to the bottom. If you're lucky, you'll find one that also has a built-in metal litter box that also pulls out.

Cages made of wood are impossible to completely sanitize because the urine and poop are absorbed into the wood. The wood may also be chewed and ingested. Certain treated woods can also contain harmful chemicals. Likewise, certain metal surfaces can contain lead, which, when ingested, can be harmful to your fert. Do your cage research before putting out the money. Doing so will save you a pile of trouble in the end.

I found a company called Corner Creek Acres located in Ottumwa, Iowa. These folks build beautiful, spacious cages for incredibly reasonable prices. They ship, too. They have many designs but will custom-build any cage to your specifications. Their cages are by far the best cages I've come across for small critters such as ferrets. I have about 20 of this company's cages — all different sizes in attractive black vinyl-coated wire. You can contact them by calling 515-684-7122. Or visit their new Web site, at www.cornercreek.com.

Materials

Perhaps the best types of ferret cages out there are those made of sturdy galvanized wire. I prefer the black vinyl-coated wire because it's not only decorative but also easier on the ferret's feet. If the floor is made of wire, be sure the little squares are no bigger than ¼ inch by ¼ inch. Ferrets have little feet, and the wire can be hard on their sensitive pads. You certainly don't want anything wide enough for their feet to fall through.

One or multilevels?

While a single-level cage will do, it just doesn't seem appropriate for the lifestyle of a ferret. Ferrets are active and inquisitive. As ground dwellers, they love to burrow under piles of stuff, but they also enjoy racing up and down the ramps in a multilevel cage (see Figure 6-2). Obviously, the ramps should be made of wire because solid ramps act more like slides than ladders.

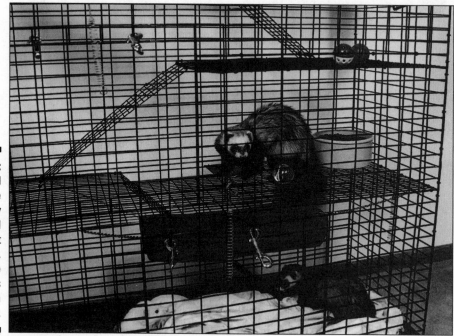

Figure 6-2: Multilevel cages are greatly appreciated by most ferrets. Notice the snap bolts for extra security.

Multilevels also add more opportunity for you to attach cage accessories that are almost as important as the cage itself (see the section "Cage Accessories and Other Stuff"). Multilevel cages should have multiple doors to access the different levels. Consider adding a litter box to the upper level also. At some point during the routine cleaning process, you'll be reaching into the far corners of all levels of the cage, so be sure you can access them.

A room with a view: Finding a place for the cage

Placement of the cage is vital in the health and happiness of your ferret. If you can, place the cage where he can see you several times a day. It should be a quiet, comfortable place, conducive to snoozing when necessary, and

Cage stress

Cage stress is often associated with the ferret's inability to escape to a safe place. You can identify a ferret suffering from cage stress by watching his behavior. Some signs may include constant pacing back and forth and gnawing on the cage bars or scratching incessantly at a corner of the cage. He may even have sores on his head and face from trying to push his way out of his confines. Cage stressed ferrets are overly destructive in their cages, tipping bowls and litter boxes more so than "normal." It's imperative that the fuzzy have somewhere dark and warm to hide and get away from all that's going on around him. You can use piles of fluffy bedding or a snooze sack, for example. Providing safety and security helps prevent cage stress. If you have a particularly nervous fert, covering part of the cage with a sheet or large towel may be helpful.

Wooden parrot nest boxes can make great hidey-holes and sleeping spots for ferts. In addition, a nest box can make for a fun climbing experience. Insert a few cuddly pieces of bedding into the box and place the box into the cage or in the play area. Watch for wood chewing. If you notice a lot of wear and tear, either replace the box or scrap the idea altogether.

yet not so far out of the way that the fuzzy's forgotten in your daily routine. Some ferret lovers actually dedicate an entire room to ferrets and their cages. I have cages that are connected by colorful tubes. I never know which ferret will be sleeping in which cage. Sometimes as many as eight of them are piled snuggly onto one hammock, although there are four to five hammocks throughout the maze of cages.

Here are some other pointers:

✔ He should be indoors. Ferrets are not outdoor pets, and keeping them outdoors can lead to escape, disease, illness, and/or possible death. Short, supervised outdoor excursions are okay, but ferrets should not be kept out for long when the weather dips below 40 degrees Fahrenheit.

✔ Just as dangerous as cold is the heat of the sun. While ferrets enjoy the warmth that sunlight provides, direct sunlight with no relief can be deadly. Ferrets can get heat stroke or heat exhaustion if kept in hot places even for just a short time. If sunlight comes in contact with your fert's cage, be sure a large part of the cage is shaded at all times so the fuzzy can escape the sun's hot rays.

✔ Drafts and moisture can also cause your ferret to get sick. Do not keep the cage below a drafty window, next to a door leading outside, or near the airflow of an air conditioner. Basements and small, poorly ventilated rooms are often damp and great breeding grounds for bacteria. Consider your fuzzy a part of the family and keep him comfortable and close by.

✔ Do yourself a huge favor and place the cage on tile if at all possible. And pull the cage at least 6 inches from the wall. Toilet habits can get sloppy, and you'll most definitely be cleaning both the floor and wall surrounding the cage routinely. You may want to consider putting up a large piece of Plexiglas to cover the wall closest to the cage. And if you absolutely must put the cage on carpeting, invest in more Plexiglas or a large piece of linoleum to place under the cage. Ferrets love to scoot up into the corners of their cage and poop out the side.

Make the Bed

Ferrets absolutely love to tunnel and nestle in their bedding, so knowing what and what not to use is important. Wire-bottom cages should always be covered with as much soft stuff as possible to prevent sore or injured feet.

✔ Some people cut a piece of carpeting and fit it into the bottom of the cage. If you use carpeting, you must take it out and wash it thoroughly or replace it, as necessary. Because dirty bedding usually accounts for most ferret odor, your nose will tell you when the time has come! Also, you need to supervise ferrets with carpeting. They love to dig at the fibers, and some ferts find the fibers simply delicious, which can be dangerous. Also, be aware that claws can also become snagged on carpet fibers and other fabrics, which may cause the ferret to become trapped or injured. Keeping nails trim will help, but not necessarily prevent this problem.

✔ Other people may use a fitted piece of linoleum flooring or Plexiglas to cover wire floors. I like the linoleum because it's flexible and easiest to clean.

Whether or not you cover the cage bottom is up to you, but be sure to fill the major areas and bedroom area with plenty of old T-shirts, sweatshirts, pillowcases, or towels. Do so no matter what, just to provide good snoozing sites and hiding places. Another neat piece of bedding is simple to make: Simply snip off the legs of an old pair of pants or blue jeans. You can also buy custom ferret snooze sacks and fabric tunnels. They're attractive and cozy. But if you're handy with a sewing machine, they're also easy to make. Remember that all bedding should be washed regularly to aid in reducing odors. Keep a clean, fresh supply of bedding on hand to use when the dirty stuff is being washed.

Inspect bedding routinely. Some carpet sharks find cloth an irresistible delicacy and chew holes in the fabric. The danger comes from the fert actually swallowing chunks of cloth. You'll find that certain ferts need stronger types of fabric, such as denim, to prevent "cloth grazing" or ingesting pieces of bedding. Small holes also pose a danger when your fert is playing or digging around to get comfortable. He is apt to poke his head through a hole. If he twists and turns just right, he may find himself trapped and strangulation may occur. So toss the holey stuff. Also, raggedy fibers and stuff like terry cloth are easy to catch on long claws, so toss the raggedy stuff and avoid fabrics like terry cloth.

Set the Table

Picking out your ferret's food dish and water bottle doesn't have to be as tedious as picking out the good china for the newlyweds. However, not all dishes will live up to your ferret's high standards, and he may put them through a battery of destruction tests before you can finally settle on the best one. Ferrets are extremely cunning little buggers, and the average ferret can master even the most ferret-proof dish — meaning, almost all the dishes out there can be flung about the cage, tipped over, chewed up, pooped in, dug out, or slept in. It's likely that you'll need to find the best possible dish and attempt to outsmart your ferret by adding a few of your own clever additions to aid your attempt in keeping the food clean and in the dish where it belongs. Remember, it's all in the presentation.

The food dish

Dishes come in just about every size, shape, color, and texture. They guarantee amazing things, such as nontippable, indestructible, and easy to clean. And for the average pet, these claims are true. But a ferret sees a challenge in all that surrounds him, and a simple dish is no exception. It's important for you to choose one that best suits your ferret's needs. Remembering a few things may make your purchase easier and more successful.

Your ferret is bound to find the one weakness of the bowl you purchase for him. He may even appreciate you throwing in a decoy bowl used only for playing with. Provide him with plenty of toys and soft bedding to play with, to keep his mind off the dish he finds so irresistible. Almost any bowl, attached or detached, will be subjected to his sleeping in or on it. Unless you have an itty-bitty bowl or a ferret the size of a housecat, you'll just have to be amused with this enchanting trait.

Less amusing is how many ferrets love to dig their food out of the bowl. This is another trait you must learn to live with. If your ferret cage has multiple levels, either place the food dish anywhere on the top level or away from the corners on the lower levels (ferrets like to poop in corners). Food that has been contaminated should be discarded immediately. Likewise, a poopy food dish is an unsanitary food dish. Wash it right away.

Here's a solution to curbing some cage destruction that's easier and cheaper than cementing down the bowls and litter boxes, and it's more fun for both you and your ferret: Challenge your ferret in other ways. Although ferrets can be quite devilish, a lot of destructive behavior can be modified simply by providing more environmental and intellectual stimulation. Provide more toys and a variety of them. Give your ferret more play time outside of the cage. Remember: Boredom = destructive behavior. (See Chapter 10 for more ideas on enrichment.)

Attachable bowls

I have found that attachable bowls are the best choice. However, even these bowls have flaws. Not all are ferret-proof as far as becoming detached. The round stainless steel bowls that fit snugly into an attached round wire hanger are great until the fit becomes just a tad loose. Being the predator he is, the ferret senses the minute weakness of the dish. With a push and a shove of his back feet, a ferret lying on his back can easily flip the dish right out of its holder and into a soiled litter box.

Small metal C-clamps from the hardware store can be fastened around the bowl, hanger, and side of the cage to prevent this dish tragedy (see Figure 6-3). While they don't prevent digging, they do prevent tipping and catapulting. You can also drill a couple of holes in a sturdy plastic dish and fasten it to the sides with cable ties or even thin wire. If you choose one of these types of bowls, though, you must be willing to detach it for its cleanings so that the freshest food is available. It's always a good idea to have an extra bowl — one for using while the other's being cleaned.

If you choose the wire dish hanger that simply hangs over the wire of the cage, grab your pliers and bend the holder until it can't be lifted off the wire. Often times, this same type of holder falls prey to the "flip and tip" method of kill. With only the top fastened to the cage, the bottom can be lifted and the food flung up and out of the cage. A simple garbage tie or piece of wire can secure the bottom of the hanger to the cage, making it more secure. Good-quality ferret food is certainly not cheap, so choose carefully the manner in which you present it to your ferret.

Weighted bowls

Unless your ferret is Hercules (and he may very well be), a heavily weighted dish or one made of a heavy material such as thick ceramic helps minimize the distance the dish is catapulted across a cage. If you can't fasten your ferret's bowl to the side of the cage, you'll want to get the heaviest bowl possible — preferably one that's wider at the base, making it more difficult to tip over.

Figure 6-3:
Use a C-clamp to secure your ferret's bowl, and you'll come to believe that they were made with frenzied ferret owners in mind.

Heavy ceramic bowls should always be placed on the lowest level of the cage. On higher levels, these bowls can become quite dangerous if they are pushed off and tumble onto a fuzzy below.

Plastic bowls

If you're determined to buy plastic, make sure that it's the heavy-duty type. The less porous the composition of the bowl, the more sanitary and easier to clean it is. Also, avoid lightweight plastic. It's easily damaged. As a result of constant scratching and gnawing, small grooves and holes, which can be difficult to see, accumulate and may harbor harmful bacteria. To fully sanitize a plastic dish, you need to dip it briefly into boiling water.

Stay away from materials such as flimsy plastic and unglazed pottery or ceramic. Stick with a stainless steel, thick plastic, or heavily glazed ceramic dish.

The water bottle

Up until now, little has been said about water dishes. There's a simple explanation as to why. Most ferret owners don't put their ferret's drinking water in bowls. Ferrets love to play in water and view a water dish as a minipool.

The water bottle is perhaps one of the greatest and least appreciated inventions made available to pet owners. It is easily cleaned, doesn't tip over, and provides uncontaminated water throughout the day. Providing a constant supply of clean, fresh water is essential in your ferret's well being.

Unlike with food dishes, there are only a few things for you to consider before purchasing a water bottle.

- **Size:** Sizes vary from those suitable for a mouse to those large enough for dogs and cats. Fortunately, the makers have taken some of the thought out of the process and made several specifically for ferrets. If you can't find one, the guinea pig or rabbit water bottle is appropriate. A bottle too small yields little water and empties quickly. One too large, such as those designed for dogs, can be difficult for the ferret to operate because it requires a much harder push on the heavier ball.

- **Narrow or wide mouth:** Both work well, but the wide-mouth is easier to clean because its cap opening is wider, which makes getting a brush or cloth inside for cleaning easier.

- **Type of plastics:** Some plastics are made specifically for indoor/outside use (polyethylene bottles), while others are strictly indoor functional. Because you'll be cleaning your bottle on a regular basis and your ferret lives inside, either material is suitable.

Attaching it to the cage

Ferret water bottles are designed to mount on the outside of the cage. Go with the ones mounted on the outside. A bottle hung on the inside is fair game and quickly seized and dismantled by most ferrets. Also, outside mounting is convenient for you (the water should be changed daily and you

Training your ferrets to use the water bottle

Most animals quickly discover that water flows from the tube when the stainless steel ball is gently pushed in. I have even witnessed my ingenious ferrets holding the ball in with a toenail to allow for more water to flow out. Water bottles work best when they're filled at least halfway, so keep this in mind when feeding and watering.

While training a newcomer to the water bottle, place a shallow dish of water just beneath the water bottle until the water bottle level indicates that it's being used. Separate a ferret that's still learning to use a water bottle until you know he's drinking from it. It's not going to do him any good if the other ferts are drinking from the bottle and you assume he is too. Taking away his water bowl prematurely could lead to dehydration. Keeping the water dish filled and the cage clean can be temporarily tedious, but it's well worth the effort in the end. Just through curiosity, most ferrets will figure out the workings of the water bottle and will have done so without risking dangerous dehydration, illness, and possible death.

have easy access to the bottle). As with anything your ferret sees, if the bottle is not firmly attached, you'll find it on the floor the next time you check it. And you'll have at least one ferret staring pitifully out at you with his "What took you so long to get here?" look.

A water bottle doesn't work too well if your fuzzy can't reach it. I've seen many people place their pet's water bottle way too high or way too low without even thinking about it. It should be positioned at a comfortable height so that the ferret doesn't have to strain himself by reaching too high or too low to snatch a drink. Also keep in mind the number of ferrets residing in the cage. If you have three or more in one cage, consider adding another bottle. For multilevel cages, providing water bottles on the top and bottom levels of the cage is a good idea.

Prepare the Bathroom

Ferrets are naturally clean animals that can and should be trained to use a litter box. Therefore, your ferret's deluxe townhouse needs to be equipped with a suitable bathroom. Believe it or not, there are even some things to consider here before running out and buying the first plastic cat box you see. The first thing is the size of the cage door through which you plan on shoving the cat box. This is where custom cages with built-in pull-out litter pans can be convenient (see Chapter 30 or the previous section, "Set up the Cage," for info on how to contact Corner Creek Acres, a company that builds custom cages). In most instances, you won't have a problem, but double-check the size of your doors. I've had many brilliant ideas foiled due to the width of the doors. There are some very big housecats out there and some very big litter boxes.

Your fert's cage should have at least one litter box. Large cages and cages with several ferts should contain a minimum of two boxes. You'll find that corners are coveted spots for pooping, and a corner is the best place for a litter box. Keep that in mind when shopping for cages, as well.

The litter pan

The type of pooper(s) you have determines the most suitable litter box for your ferts. Age and health status make a difference, too. Here are some things to think about:

- Ferrets who aim high (those, for example, who scoot their butts up to the corner and aim for the peak of the poop hill) need boxes with high sides. Those who don't much care where they go (the ones who enter the box and, once all four feet are in, squat down to do their business) are probably okay with a low-sided litter box.

✔ As ferrets age, some lose mobility in their hind legs, which can make getting into a litter box more difficult. The same holds true for the little sick or injured guys. Invest in a low-sided box for the debilitated fuzzball, even if it's a temporary condition.

Baby ferts are full of energy and can and will get into almost anything. If the ferret is too small to get into a litter box, then it's probably too soon to be training the fert to use it. (Check out Chapter 20 for more info on litter-training.)

✔ Never, ever use plastic litter box liners in any ferret litter box. They'll be torn to shreds, and ingesting this material can cause serious blockage.

✔ If you have a super-duper big cage, maybe a covered litter box is feasible. Perhaps you need a combination of both: A low-sided box may do well on the bottom level and a high-sided one on a top level, if it fits, or vice versa. Also available are smaller triangular boxes that are designed to fit only in the corner of the cage. They are low in the front and very high in the back. However, most ferrets prefer to use a litter box that they can get all four feet in.

Finding the right litter box for your fert may be a crapshoot at first. If you're a good observer, you'll figure out what your fert's litter box needs are. On the other hand, I am a good observer, and I have ferrets that make me move the boxes all around. I think they do it just to keep me on my toes.

Plastic litter boxes

Your fert's litter box will most likely be made of a durable plastic and come from a pet shop or pet supply store. What about those plastic boxes with rims around the top to help keep the litter in the box? Some people like this feature. I find the rim to be an ineffective weapon against the talented litter pitchers, which most ferrets pride themselves in being. Additionally, most are not fitted well enough to the litter box itself and become just another object tossed about the cage.

Attached metal litter boxes

Some cages have metal pull-out litter boxes built right in. Just open the little door and pull out the box for easy cleaning. It fits snugly into its own space, which eliminates the need to secure it. This kind of litter box can be nice, but it has its own problems. My ferrets drag their bedding into it, so I inserted a short Plexiglas barrier to prevent this. But, perhaps the worst thing about this type is that after a year or so, and depending on the amount of urine, the bottom of the pan slowly corrodes, which leads to eventual holes in the bottom of the metal pan. Here are a few things you can do to prevent this problem or at least delay it:

✔ Some people line the bottom and ½ inch up the sides with contact paper. The contact paper is okay, but it doesn't last very long and eventually peels or crack when you clean it.

✔ Others cut a fitted piece of linoleum and place it on the bottom. This fix works fairly well, but the linoleum must be removed regularly for you to clean beneath when urine leaks under it.

✔ Another solution I've heard of is regularly spraying the bottom of the metal pan with a safe coating, such as Pam cooking spray, in between cleanings or painting the bottom with a nontoxic paint or coating, such as Teflon.

Most metal pans are longer than a typical litter box. However, I put a plastic litter box on my ferts' favorite side of the metal box and fill the space that's left over with litter also. So the large metal box is now divided into two, and the unprotected side gets little use except for when I fail to clean the box as often as I should. This solution may seem to defeat the purpose of the built-in metal box, but it still fits in snugly, pulls out with the metal box, and isn't tossed about the cage.

The perfect litter

Don't think that the cheap, generic litter you force your housecat to use will do for your ferret. In most cases, cats are cleaner about their toilet habits. They go in, do their duty, may or may not politely cover it up, and exit quickly to be sure no one saw who issued that smell. Ferrets are different. They dig and burrow in their litter. They toss it about as they roughhouse with each other or a favorite toy. Some may drag their bedding into the litter box and go to sleep. A litter box is to most ferrets what a sandbox is to a creative child. That's why picking litter for your ferret requires more than simply picking up the cheapest litter in the kitty aisle of your grocery store.

The litter you choose for your litter-snorkeling fuzzball should be absorbent and as free of dust as possible. Also, the bigger the pieces the better because litter gets stuck in the strangest of places and can cause illness.

✔ **Clay litter:** Clay litter is very popular among both cat and ferret fanciers. It's cheap. It's abundant. It's fairly absorbent. And you can find it anywhere, even the grocery store. Most clay litters, however, even the ones that claim to be 99 percent dust-free, produce a ton of dust. Just because you can't see it once the dust settles after the initial pour doesn't mean the dust's not there. And regular playing, digging, and walking on the litter upsets the dust. Your ferret constantly breathes in this dust.

Respiratory problems can develop over a period of time if too much dust is inhaled. Also, bits of clay litter and scoopable litter easily find ways into the fert's ears, eyes, nose, and mouth. Clay and scoopable litters stick between little fert toes, not to mention cling to his little butt when the fert scoots his behind across the litter after going.

✔ **Scoopable litter:** Scoopable litter is another popular choice. The absorbency with the higher quality scoopable litters is excellent, making it convenient and easy to clean. It may have a pretty smell (before use of course) or may be odorless. Many, not all, can be flushed right down the toilet along with the poop and urine. However, scoopable litter is also incredibly dusty. The consistency is as fine as sand, making it easier to inhale and ingest.

Extra caution must be taken for newly bathed or wet ferrets. Like dogs, ferrets go bonkers after baths. They roll around and wipe themselves across every surface available, including the litter box, and water + scoopable litter = cement. It dries quickly and can be very tedious to clean. Eyes, ears, noses, mouths, toes, and behinds can be subject to scoopable-litter impaction.

✔ **Corncob litter:** While it's decorative to some degree, my experience with it says you're just asking for trouble here. First off, it's so light and airy that most of it is out of the litter box in no time. It's not very absorbent, and it molds quickly. And many ferrets just can't resist nibbling on it a little here, which can lead to a bowel impaction. Perhaps the only good thing I've found with corncob litter is that it's not dusty.

✔ **Wood shavings:** Avoid wood shavings such as pine or cedar as litter or bedding. Although many cedar shaving packages have cute pictures of small animals on the front, be aware that it's been documented that these vapors have caused asthma in rabbits as well as humans. Additionally, long-term exposure has caused liver damage in rodents. While the tests have not been specifically designed with ferrets as subjects, I have seen ferrets come into the shelter with respiratory problems after being housed for long periods of time on cedar shavings. Although it may just be a coincidence, I'd rather not take the chance.

✔ **Pelleted litters:** I prefer pelleted litters to the other types of litters available. Pelleted litters, which are perhaps the best litter for ferrets, exist in many forms on the pet market. Most are made from plant fibers or recycled newspaper. For the most part, they rate high on the absorbency scale. Some of these litters are even considered digestible in case of accidental or intentional ingestion. Most are fairly dust-free and free of perfumes, and they are difficult for the ferret to shove up his tiny nose. While no litter is completely safe from the throws of ferret paws, pelleted litter is also heavier and bigger, making it a little harder to toss overboard. My favorite is Yesterday's News. It is highly absorbent and holds its form when wet.

✔ **Newspaper:** You may find that a plain sheet of newspaper of shredded newspaper works well for your ferret. While it's not pretty, it's cheap and does the job. It's the only reason we subscribe to our local newspaper.

Cage Accessories and Other Stuff

Ferrets are curious and intelligent creatures. Picking out a suitable cage and throwing in the basic necessities are not enough. A fert needs stimulation. Add some extras for his amusement and yours. Have a little fun and regularly rearrange his townhouse. Doing so also makes the cage look neater in your home.

Extra snooze sites and stuff

No ferret home is complete without at least one hanging hammock. Hammocks come in all shapes and sizes. You can either purchase one from a pet store or make one yourself. It should be made from soft yet durable fabric and have hooks or clasps on all four corners to hang from the top of the cage. Make sure that your fuzzy's hammock is located near a shelf or ramp so he has safe, easy access to it.

Some hammocks look more like hanging sleeping bags. The fert can choose to sleep right on top or snuggle between the two layers of fabric. I've had some squished inside with another pile of ferts heaped on top of them. It reminds me of circus clowns crammed in a VW Bug. Just when you think it can't possibly hold anymore . . . .

It's very important to provide warm, dark places for the fert to hide out and sleep in. Ferrets need to burrow and feel safe in a secure hideout. Even though your fuzzy's cage may be out in the open, give him a place to escape to. His sanity may depend on it. If he doesn't get it, he'll likely suffer cage stress (see this chapter's sidebar about cage stress for more info).

Because tunneling is a ferret's favorite extracurricular activity, you may also want to hang some plastic tubes. Ferrets enjoy running through them and even curling up for a nap in there. The tubes are easy to clean and colorful, and they brighten up the cage area.

'Round and 'round we go: Exercise wheels

Most ferret owners are surprised to hear that ferrets will even use a wheel, but it doesn't take long for many ferrets to figure it out. Our large ferret cage also has a custom ferret exercise wheel in it, and after staring curiously at it for months, most of my ferrets took to it. Now they gallop on it for quite a while before collapsing for a nap.

Unfortunately, I've never seen an appropriately sized wheel made for ferrets in any store. Size is important because a small wheel is dangerous and can cause stress to the ferret's back (most wheels you see in pet stores are designed with hamsters and other small rodents in mind). Also, traditional wheels have bars on the running surface which are impractical for fuzzies.

Fortunately, you can special-order ferret wheels. I ordered mine (a huge wheel that's about 15 inches in diameter with a flat running surface) from Ain't No Creek Ranch (see Chapter 30 for contact information). If you special-order a wheel, remember that you have to get it in the door to your ferret's cage. I had a heck of a time squishing mine through the cage door and even had to bend it a little and then reshape it once it was in. It easily hangs to the side of the cage. Here's another little tip: Cover the running surface with those rubbery no-slip things that you put in the bottom of a bathtub. Doing so helps the ferret keep his grip when running. You can also put a fitted piece of fine sandpaper on the bottom to help keep their nails trim.

As with any open wheel, risks can be involved. I've heard of other pets, such as rats and sugar gliders, getting their long tails or heads caught in their own wheel as it passes the supporting spoke. I don't know many people who use ferret wheels but haven't heard of any incidences. Ferret wheels don't pick up the speed that rodent wheels do. Use your best judgment and supervise closely, if necessary, while your ferret figures out the trick of the wheel. You may even want to try having them use it on the floor. However, my fuzzies are too busy exploring and getting into trouble during playtime to stop to run on a wheel. When they're bored in the cage, however, they take to it like a duck to water.

Toys galore

Ferts are materialistic critters with an eye for valuables. While you probably won't be able to prevent the thieving of some of your own prized possessions by a roving fert, you must provide him with his own valued toys. Toys also help to satisfy your ferret's natural instinct to hoard food.

Good toys

Your ferret should be able to enjoy an assortment of toys both in the cage and out. Try to keep up with his level of intelligence and curiosity. Provide him with as much excitement as possible. Here are some toys you can use:

- Hard rubber balls, maybe even one with a bell safely inside
- Cat toys that are made of hard plastic
- Tennis balls and racquetballs
- Paper bags and cardboard boxes
- Human infant toys such as plastic keys and rattles and terry-cloth-covered squeaky things

- ✔ Large ferret balls — the kind that have holes in them for entering and exiting
- ✔ Fun tunneling stuff like PVC piping, clothes dryer hoses, and ferret tubes

Ferrets love noisy and squeaky toys, so find some safe toys that have bells inside or squeak. Hang some toys in the cage for extra fun — large, dangling parrot toys work well.

Inspect toys routinely. Throw away any that have stuffing pulled out and pay close attention to squeaky toys. Ferrets have been known to pull out the squeakers and ingest them.

Toys to avoid

Caution must be exercised when purchasing playthings for your fuzzball. Most of the toys out there have been designed for dogs and cats. Ferrets love to chew and gnaw and destroy the stuff they covet so fiercely. But their bodies don't process the junk in quite the same manner as dogs and cats' bodies do. You'll find occasional bits of foreign gunk, such as rubber or plastic, in the poop. However, more often, what doesn't choke them usually finds a nice place to settle in the stomach or intestine and cause just enough damage to warrant immediate medical attention — not to mention extreme panic for you. A best-case scenario: a major dose of Laxatone to help push it on through. A worse-case scenario: surgery to remove the blockage. And the most awful scenario of all is death that could've been prevented.

Here are some things you don't want to use as ferret toys:

- ✔ Any toy made of latex of soft rubber/plastic, including squeaky toys unless they're used only to call or get your ferret's attention
- ✔ Anything with small pieces that can be chewed off and swallowed
- ✔ Plastic bags
- ✔ Objects small enough that your fert can get his head stuck in them
- ✔ Toys that show signs of ferret wear and tear

Your fert will pilfer through your belongings and come up with a few toys you've obviously forgotten about. These toys may include socks, shoes, car keys, lipstick, and various other sundries. If you're a smoker, watch your cigarettes, too. Ferrets find them wonderfully fascinating, but they're not only toxic to ferrets, the filters can cause obstructions.

Ferrets love to chew up stuff and ingest small things. An obstruction can be deadly and, at the very least, expensive to fix. Avoid all soft or rubbery toys, such as latex squeaky toys, and stick with hard plastics and other nonchewable items. Avoid bedding that contains foam rubber or stuffing.

Leashes and harnesses

Ferrets can learn to be walked on leashes provided that they have a comfortably fitting harness. Leashes and harnesses are especially important if you plan on taking your ferret outside for romps or if you have guests over who'd like to get to know your fuzzbutt. Many types of harnesses are on the market, but the long, slender body of the ferret makes him a difficult fit. Choose one made specifically for ferrets. They are H-shaped across the back and fasten around the neck and belly of the ferret (see Figure 6-4).

Figure 6-4:
Leashes and
harnesses
keep your
ferret safe
outside.

Just like a new puppy, your ferret will resist this sudden restraint on his freedom. He'll twist and turn and play tug of war as though he's truly claustrophobic. He'll do the typical alligator roll and fake a horrible torture. Believe me — he'll get over it. As long as you can squeeze your finger under the harness, be assured that it's not too tight. Ferrets are master escape artists. Any looser and your ferret will back right out of it in no time. Be patient and persistent and reward him for good behavior. Unless you only use the harness when taking him to the vet, he'll eventually associate it with playtime. For tips on getting him used to the harness, see Chapter 20.

The travel taxi

This is probably one of the first things you'll want to purchase after you have your cage set up. After all, your baby needs to arrive home safely. Ferrets are

What about collars?

Some people put collars on their ferts with little success; others do so with good success. I suppose how successful it is depends on the fert's personality and his ability to tolerate having a collar around his neck. A ferret's head isn't much wider than the neck it's attached to. It's next to impossible to keep collars on for long, including those "designed specifically for ferrets." A collar is a collar. They're all round and none are a match for a ferret who wishes to eliminate them. Collars become coveted objects for the hidey-hole, though.

neat, and it's fun to show them off, but a car isn't a safe place to do that. He can get stuck under the seat and under your pedals. He can obstruct your view by cruising on the dashboard. This stuff can cause an accident, and an unrestrained fuzzy is too vulnerable to come out of a serious car accident in one piece.

- A simple, small, plastic cat carrier comfortably accommodates a couple of ferrets for short trips to the vet or to grandmother's house. All carriers should contain a soft towel or other type of bedding for comfort and snoozing. Most carriers are designed for adequate ventilation, so that shouldn't be much of a worry for you.

- Avoid those folding cardboard carriers that shelters or pet shops send you home with. It doesn't take long for a fert to figure his way out of one either by scratching or chewing. Those carriers also can't be properly sanitized. It's no fun to have ferret pee leak through the bottom of a cardboard carrier onto your car seat.

- Some carriers open like suitcases. These carriers are okay for short, short trips. For longer trips, a carrier with a wire-grated, front-opening door is more appropriate. Larger carriers of the same type (made for small or medium-sized dogs) are appropriate for temporarily housing ferrets on trips because they can hold a small litter box in addition to the ferts and their bedding.

As much as I hate to admit this, not everyone enjoys ferrets as much as I do. When traveling to the vet or other places, it's important to keep your ferret contained in case you run across one of these oddball people. My vet doesn't like it when I come waltzing in with a 10-foot snake draped around my neck. It scares the poodle owners. So I bring snakes in reptile carriers. The pet carrier (minus the snake) is the safest place for your furball anyway. Strangers poking at him may be too much stimulation for your little guy, and he may nip out of fear or excitement. Unless you're in a comfortable and ferret-friendly environment, keep your fuzzy safe in his carrier.

Chapter 7

Other Things to Do Before Your Ferret Comes Home

• •

• •

*Y*our home can be a scary yet stimulating jungle to the tiny ferret just waiting to find or cause trouble. And believe me, if trouble is to be found or caused, it will be. Carpet sharks are notorious explorers and excavators. They like to push and pull and carry and toss every little thing they can. They can fit into the tiniest of tiny places. They can manage their way to the highest of places. And all of them put their leaping skills to the greatest challenge. Whoever came up with the phrase "Curiosity killed the cat" obviously hadn't been exposed to ferrets. Curiosity, one of the ferret's most amusing qualities, can be his worst enemy.

In this chapter, you find out how to get your house ready for your new arrival, what habits you can change to keep your ferret safe, and how to find a good vet.

Ferret-Proof Your House

Some people leave their ferrets out of their cages unsupervised all day. I believe this practice can be dangerous to the fuzzy. With the possible exception of a single closed-off room (a rubber padded cell?) with no furniture, holes, or floor vents, most areas in the home can't ever be completely ferret-proofed. You can only do your absolute best to minimize the possibilities of ferret tragedies. Like the parent of a toddler, *you* must keep your pet out of trouble and out of harm's way. However, unlike a human toddler, the ferret will rarely scream for Mom when he hurts himself or gets wedged somewhere. Your fuzzbutt depends on you to remain alert at all times when he's out of his cage. The following sections explain the various danger zones and what you can do to keep your ferret safe. Here, though, are some general guidelines:

- ✔ Put up security gates to keep ferrets from danger zones. And I don't mean those easily climbed children's gates, either. Those are just neat obstacles to be scaled and mastered as easily as a ladder. You'll probably have to build something at least 3 feet high out of wood or Plexiglas or another material that can't be climbed.

- ✔ Be careful what you leave lying around the house. Anything is fair game to a ferret. Remember that intestinal blockage is one of the leading causes of death in ferrets. Some things to think about include pen caps, rubber bands, cotton balls and cotton swabs, coins, latex/vinyl/rubbery things, sponges, plastic bags, jewelry, and Band-Aids.

- ✔ Watch where you store chemicals, such as cleaners or antifreeze. Ferrets can knock the containers over, causing a spill, and ingest these poisonous chemicals. They'll at least lick the containers just for a taste and ingest possible chemical residue.

- ✔ Put your medications out of reach. While prescription meds can be extremely dangerous and toxic to your ferrets, keep in mind that many over the counter medications, such as Tylenol, can be as deadly as rat poison to your ferret.

You get the idea. Think and prepare as though you have a toddler exploring your environment. Everything a toddler touches ends up in his or her mouth. A ferret isn't that different. Don't forget also that ferrets can jump. Anything less than 30 inches off the ground or that can be reached by climbing should be ferret-proofed.

The following sections point out dangers that you may not have thought about. The knowledge and wisdom in these sections are made possible by all the close calls, injuries, and fatalities experienced by thousands of ferret lovers all over, including myself. Learn from our mistakes.

Laundry room

Usually, utility/laundry rooms are loaded with danger and practically impossible to ferret-proof, so keep these rooms off-limits altogether. Dryer vent hoses are easily chewed, and ferrets tunnel right out through them, sometimes to the scary outside. They quickly crawl up into the clothes dryer for a nap beneath all those soft clothes, especially when they're warm. You don't see them go in, and it's too late when you do find them.

Kitchen

Block off the kitchen if you can. With all those dangerous appliances in the kitchen, keep your fuzzies far away. Refrigerators and other appliances have fans that can abruptly turn on and injure or kill your ferret. Ingested fiberglass insulation causes blockages or severe illness. Stoves have pilot lights that can cause severe burns. All appliances have electrical cords that can cause electrocution if chewed on. I've known ferrets to climb into dishwashers, refrigerators, and freezers when no one's looking. You can imagine the worst case scenarios!

Inside appliances are places where your fert can get severely wedged or suffocate before you get the chance to rescue him. And if you're like I am, you keep your bottom kitchen cabinets filled with cleaners that are both poisonous and fatal if swallowed by your fert. Ferrets are adventure seekers. Remember, they'll try anything once. Sometimes once is all the chance they'll ever get.

If you can't block off you kitchen, keep a close, supervised eye on your ferret at all times. If you find that the obvious dangers, such as open flames and fans in appliances, cannot be rectified, find another room to allow your ferret to play in.

Moldings, baseboards, and under cabinets

Get on your belly and make sure that the moldings and baseboards are intact and complete all around the room. Double-check with your hands beneath cabinets to make sure that the ferts can't get up into the cabinets from under the ledge. Home builders seem to skimp in this area.

Check for holes that lead into walls or to the outside. Any hole wider than one inch is a potential hidey-hole or danger zone. Board them up. If the hole is less than one inch wide, can your fert widen it with his teeth or claws? After all, drywall and similar materials are no match for a fuzzy's weapons.

Windows and doors

To prevent escapes and falls from high places, double-check windows, doors, and screens. Make sure that screens are securely fastened and doors are shut tight. It's probably best not to open any window that a ferret can get to when he's out. A screen, likewise, is not very hard to tear open or pull out with teeth or claws.

How big is the gap between the bottom of the door and the floor? More than one inch? Better lower it to prevent the fert from scooting under or getting stuck (see Figure 7-1). Don't underestimate the average furball. Some ferrets are seemingly smarter than we are.

Figure 7-1:
Ferrets can get through the smallest openings — even under some doors.

Also, it doesn't take a ferret long to realize he has the strength and smarts to open some doors and windows. So use snap bolts to keep him safely inside (see Figure 7-2).

Fuzzies are extremely good with their paws. Don't underestimate your fert's ability to open doors and windows just far enough to escape. And screens are hardly a match for those teeth and claws. Many ferrets have fallen from great heights from pushing through screens. Most ferrets don't land on their feet, and they certainly don't have nine lives.

Floor vents and air returns

Floor vents and air returns can be easy to pull off. I know my floor vent grates just lay loosely on top of the hole (for decoration, I guess). Once a ferret gets in, he can tunnel through the house, get stuck somewhere, or fall to a place

Figure 7-2:
Snap bolts
can keep
your ferret
safely
confined
when you
can't
supervise
him.

where he can't get out. You can try to fasten the loose grates securely with small pieces of Velcro. It's effective and the strips are hidden from view.

Floor fans can also be dangerous. A moving fan blade can easily remove a toe, paw, or tail tip (or worse). If the blade protector (the cage covering the fan) is broken, you may end up with a decapitated fuzzy. Don't use fans near your free-roaming ferts.

Plants

Some plants are poisonous, and your ferret *will* taste all plants, as well as promptly remove every trace of dirt from the pot. Ferrets are excellent diggers. Some dirt contains harmful bacteria or chemicals from fertilizers or pesticides.

Either remove the plants or try to outsmart your fuzzy. Wire mesh across the top of the planter works okay for some ferts. I prefer to cover the soil with large, decorative garden rock that is both attractive and functional. It keeps the ferret from digging, and it weighs the planter down to prevent tipping. Friends may think you have an artistic eye for gardening. Ferret and cat owners know the truth. Picking up a rock here and there beats the heck out of replanting your plants every day or treating a very sick ferret.

Heights

Look around you. Everything in your house is a potential stepstool, ladder, or launching pad, including the fuzzy townhouse. It may be necessary to move certain items to prevent the ferret from getting too high. Pay close attention to stairwells, curtain rods, and countertops. A significant fall is almost always injuring, and sometimes it's fatal.

Electrical cords

Ooooh, these are yummy chew toys to the grazing ferret. In the eyes of gnawing-pet owners, electrical cords are electrocutioners and fire starters. Try applying Bitter Apple or Bitter Lime spray (available at pet stores) on the cords to help deter the fert's gnawing urge. Another simple solution is to wrap the cords in aluminum foil. Ferrets don't normally enjoy chewing on foil. However, it's best to keep electrical cords completely out of the ferret's reach or enclose them in special cable/cord moldings.

Reclining chairs/rockers and foldout couches

These furniture items can be death traps. It's easy to quickly plop down into a rocker or recliner and forget the danger of crushing your romping fert in between the moving parts. Don't use them when your ferrets are out playing or keep them out of your ferret's play-designated space. I make everyone sit on the floor when my fuzzies are out and about.

Fireplaces

There's nothing quite like a little walk on the wild side for your fuzzy. And fireplaces have it all: wood, dirt, and sometimes even rocks. If you want to keep your ferret and house free of soot, make your fireplace off-limits to snorkeling ferts. If you need to, invest in a heavy-duty fireplace grill that can't be climbed and that can be pushed flush against the fireplace. We scrapped ours all together and installed glass doors on our fireplace.

Mattresses, couches, and chairs

It's easy and tempting for a ferret to crawl beneath most couches and chairs or the cushions. Mattresses are just as luring. Those places make good hidey-holes, plus the fabric beneath the furniture is awfully enticing. Ferrets can be squished between the cushions if you unknowingly sit on them. Also, many ferrets are tempted to dig and chew and tear at the underside fabric, often creating holes. Besides being detrimental to your furniture, furballs find the stuffing that's revealed behind the protective fabric cloth to be a ferret delicacy. The same goes for mattresses. Ferrets love to chew on soft, foamy, rubbery things. If the foam or other stuffing is ingested, intestinal blockage can occur.

Some ferret people use futons instead of traditional couches and chairs. Or, when it's time to replace the furniture, other ferret people choose to buy only couches and chairs that are flush against the floor so the ferrets can't get under them. If this isn't an option for you, turn your chairs and couches over and see if you can staple some heavy-duty cloth to the bottom of it to keep the ferrets out. Remember to staple close together so they can't get in between the staples. Most ferret owners don't need to go to such extremes if they keep a close eye on their fuzzy during play time and inspect furniture routinely for signs of destruction.

Toilets, bathtubs, and buckets

Supervised recreational swimming can be fun for some fuzzies, but even the most athletic ferret risks drowning after a while (see Figure 7-3). Keep lids down on toilets and keep doors closed to bathrooms that may have a bathtub full of water. Buckets of water or other liquid can also pose a drowning threat. Even if your ferret doesn't drown, he may become violently ill if the liquid is a chemical of some sort.

Lots of bathmats and area rugs have rubber backings to prevent slippage. These backings are delicious and sometimes deadly to fuzzies. Even the little rubber tips on door stops are just the right size to block up your fert's intestinal tract. Watch for signs of interest in these items. You can easily pick up bathmats and rugs during playtime. If necessary, remove the baseboard doorstops and replace them with the ones that fasten to the top of the door.

Cabinets

A ferret is quick to discover that he can easily pry open a cabinet door. I don't recommend most child latches as a solution. Most are designed so that you have to slip your hand in and release the latch to open the cabinet. If you can slip your hand in, that means the cabinet opens just enough for a ferret to completely get in or get his head caught. On the other hand, there are a few child latches designed that will work fine. One even uses a magnet to release the latch on the inside of the cabinet door.

Figure 7-3:
A tub filled
with water
can be
deadly to an
unsupervised
ferret.

Supervise your ferret around cabinets and be sure that none contain dangerous chemicals or small ingestible objects. Also make sure that there are no holes in the cabinets that can lead to other awaiting danger. I have one cabinet that has a poorly fitted pipe coming through the bottom of it. I can see right down to the basement. . . .

Trash cans

Garbage cans are simply irresistible to roving ferts. Think of all the disgusting and dangerous things you throw away on a daily basis. Would you want a fuzzy kiss from a fert that just had his nose in all that?

Keep all garbage cans up high and out of reach when your fuzzies are out. They *will* tip them over or find a way into them. Depending on what's in the trash, your ferret's curiosity could kill him or make him terribly ill. And who's to say you won't accidentally throw your fuzzy out with the trash if he climbs in and curls up for a snooze with a stinky banana peel? Keep sturdy lids on your trash cans or keep them completely out of reach from your ferrets.

Change Your Habits

Those of you with children may remember those selfish days when you could do just about anything your own way without needing to take into consideration another life. Ferret owners: You too can kiss your selfish days goodbye. Well, maybe it's not as drastic as all that, but be prepared to adjust your habits and daily routine. You furball is depending on you.

✔ Watch where you step and don't carry stuff that blocks your vision. A ferret's favorite place is under things: carpets and rugs (carpet sharks), clothing, pet beds, you name it. They're all viable snooze spots or hiding places.

Shuffle your feet if you have to. Ferrets are quick, and they're quiet. They're underfoot in a flash. Tread lightly, for a ferret is bound to be close at foot.

✔ Check the clothes dryer and washer thoroughly before operating either of them. Also check carefully before tossing that load of clothes into the washer. Ferrets aren't bulky and heavy like bricks. You'd hardly notice if one had burrowed into your dirty underwear (assuming you're not wearing them at the time).

✔ Don't just plop lazily down onto the couch or chair. If the fuzzy's not under the furniture, he may be under the cushions. Also, the moving parts in a reclining chair or sofa can injure or kill your ferret!

✔ Don't leave small objects around. Stealing is an endearing but sometimes deadly ferret trait. If your fuzzy doesn't eat it or chew it up, he may hide it — and hide it well. You may not find your stolen objects for a very long time. This is particularly annoying if the item is valuable.

✔ Don't open or close doors quickly. The same goes for cabinets, drawers, and even refrigerators, freezers, washers, dryers, and dishwashers.

Get a Vet

Ferrets have different medical needs, and not all veterinarians are equal when it comes to the health and well being of your ferret. Although they're the third most popular carnivorous pet in America, topped only by dogs and cats, they are far less common in the vet's office. Some vets don't like ferrets, while others get hung up on the common misconceptions. Therefore, it's a good idea to seek out a veterinarian who is comfortable and experienced with ferret medicine before bringing a fuzzy into your home. Doing so helps ensure that your ferret will have the best routine care available. More importantly, you won't be forced to jeopardize your pet's life while doing the panic shuffle if an emergency arises. You'll have already done your research, and you'll know who to call.

To find out what to look for and what questions to ask, head to Chapter 13.

Chapter 8

Introducing Your Ferret to His New Family

. . . .

In This Chapter

▶ Helping your new pet adjust to you and his new environment

▶ Making introductions: Hello to other ferrets, the cat, the dog, and other pets

▶ Teaching your kids how to safely interact with the ferret

▶ Introducing your ferret to strangers

. . . .

*B*ringing home a new ferret often means that you must also face the delicate issue of introducing the new family member to existing family members. It may not be as easy as you think. Take, for example, your domestic kitty who, up until now, was king or queen of the roost. An arrogant ruler, no doubt. Your cat will be dethroned, as will your spouse or any other member of the household, human or otherwise, when the ferret enters the act.

Knowing how to interact safely with your fuzzy on a one-to-one basis is imperative, and this chapter tells you how. This chapter also offers insight into the social aspect of ferrets. Ferrets are not all they appear to be; they're even more wonderful than I can put on paper. That said, I also talk about sticky subjects (not raisins) such as how to teach kids to be safe and appropriate around the fuzzbutts. I include how to deal with Fido and Fluffy, as well as those neighbors who just have to stick their noses in your business.

It's a good idea to quarantine any new ferret for at least a week until you know for sure he isn't sick. While he may look healthy when you bring him home, he may be harboring parasites (rent-free) or transmittable illnesses. Some of these illnesses will only flare their ugly heads during stressful times, like a sudden change of environment.

Ferrets as Social Animals

Ferret-owning humans swear up and down that ferrets are incredibly social critters. Yet polecats, ferrets included, are solitary animals with territorial tendencies. They aren't dogs, which seek out other dogs, form packs, and travel around in groups. If you were to release three ferrets of the same gender in your backyard, they would more than likely go three separate directions. In the wild, polecats defend their territories fervently against polecats of the same gender. (Naturally, if a member of the opposite sex enters their territory, they are more than welcome to stay for awhile.)

The need to be solitary and territorial is, for the most part, kept pretty well under control by our beloved domestic ferrets under normal circumstances. But make no mistake about it: While they play with and tolerate each other to the delight of all onlookers, ferts maintain little unspoken territories and at times squabble with trespassers or thieves. So why is it that thousands of ferret owners out there coo to themselves as they watch their babies pile in one big sleepy heap at the end of the day? Ferrets view other ferrets as litter-mates and play about accordingly. They wrestle and dance about as though they were the best of buddies, and in most cases they are the best of buddies. But ferrets do establish a sort of hierarchy among themselves and stake out microterritories in their tiny domains.

You and Your New Ferret: Making the Most Out of Your Friendship

Most ferrets enjoy the companionship of humans. It usually won't take long before your new fuzzy sees you as the perfect playmate, assuming you're willing to play nicely with him. Sometimes it takes a little bit of patience and extra understanding before you begin to feel that your ferret has bonded with you.

Your body movements and tone of voice can influence his reactions to you. The age of your ferret and his history (some come with emotional baggage) may also determine how quickly he'll blend into your family. Before introducing him to other family members, get to know him better and learn how to properly interact with him. Once you know your ferret, you'll be able to properly introduce him to others.

Hold me gently, please

Scruffing, if done correctly, is a safe and painless way to hold a ferret when you need him to remain still for things like trimming nails and cleaning ears. Simply grab the large, thick patch of skin behind the ferret's neck with your entire hand and lift him. His hanging body should naturally remain still. His bottom should be supported, especially if he's a heavy furball. However, the more support his bottom receives, the more he can move around. Scruffing should only be used when more control is necessary for his safety or yours.

Many healthy ferrets maintain the "I'd rather be anywhere than in your arms" position. In most cases, it has nothing to do with how you're actually holding the little guy (see Figure 8-1). There are always exceptions to the rule, though. I've run across many furkids that love to be held and cuddled. Usually, they're older, more mature ferrets who have come to appreciate us humans over the years.

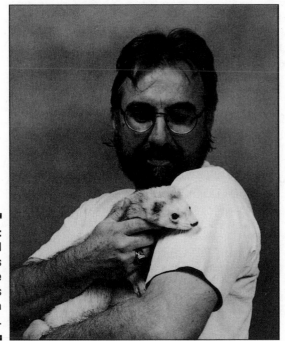

Figure 8-1:
David demonstrates one of the proper ways to hold a ferret.

When holding your ferret, supporting his entire body is important. Support both his front and back legs in your arms. I can assure you that he'll be moving around quite a bit and probably trying to crawl up your chest and onto your shoulder — maybe even your head. You can adjust his position but remember not to squeeze his little body too tightly. You may find that sitting down and holding him on your lap works better for you. Use a treat such as Linatone or Ferretone to entice him into sticking around for a while.

If your ferret decides to nip you in protest of being held, do not reward the behavior by putting him down to play. You'll have given in to his bad behavior, and he'll know what to do in the future if he wants down. Instead, if he nips, immediately tell him "No!" and place him in his cage. This way, he'll begin to associate biting with jail time.

Getting him settled in

I always advise people to allow their ferret to get used to his new cage before introducing him to the wonders of his new surroundings. Doing so gives him the chance to soak in all the new smells, both good and bad (people can give off funny scents). Each fert has a different personality that you need to also become familiar with. Only time will allow this to happen. Ease him into your routine slowly. Better yet, let him slowly ease you into *his* routine.

Keep his cage in a convenient location but don't allow your 100-pound Bullmastiff to rattle the cage every time he runs by. Likewise, the cage shouldn't be a resting shelf for your curious cat until your fert has become comfortable with having that particular cat around. Children and other family members should be instructed to keep fingers out of the cage until the ferret has become comfortable with all human family members. Partially covering the cage may also be a good idea until you all get to know each other.

After a day or two of letting your ferret settle into his new home, take him to a safe place, such as a bathroom. Sit down with some toys and let him explore you at his own pace. Move slowly and quietly, talking softly as you encourage him to play. By watching his body language, you can see how comfortable he is with you. Some fuzzies are more laid back and eager to accept the change. Others may maintain a pipe cleaner tail for hours until they become more relaxed.

Once you're comfortable with the ferret's temperament, give him more freedom when the kids are at school and the other pets are confined to another area of the house.

Most ferrets get right into the swing of things and want to graduate to bigger and better things. The goal of the slow introduction is for you to become comfortable with having a fuzzy around and handling him properly. After all, how can you teach other people or introduce pets if you aren't feeling okay about your own relationship with him?

Fuzzy Meets Fuzzy

Introducing a ferret to another ferret can be tricky business. Like many other species of mammals, littermates vie for the top position. They do so through play wrestling and biting. Some ferts are natural leaders, while others are natural followers. And there are those who'd rather venture through life without ever encountering another ferret. You never know which type you're bringing home until you see him spring into action. Here are some suggestions:

- Kits are perfect squeaky toys for older ferts. However, the kit rarely sees it this way. Adult ferrets can be quite possessive of youngsters. Adult fuzzies may drag them around, often trying to stuff them in hidey holes and guarding aggressively against curious visitors. A kit should be allowed to play and socialize with the older kids, but house the kit separately until he can kick some butt, too.

- Newly introduced ferrets often display their frizzed tail for the first 10 minutes or so. This is normal. Pay particular attention when one ferret aggressively tackles the other and performs an immediate alligator roll. Sometimes a frightened ferret screams and hisses as the more aggressive ferret tries to engage in play. Keep in mind that ferrets play rough, but if one fuzzy seems overly bullied or frightened, separate them and try again later.

- Unaltered males are particularly aggressive toward other ferrets, particularly males. Older ferrets may look at kits as possessions and drag them around like rag dolls for a while. Ferrets that have been isolated for a long period of time may feel particularly frightened at the sight of another fuzzy.

- While ferrets are capable of severely injuring — and even killing — another ferret, it rarely happens. Of course, always end the meeting if blood is drawn. And always have a spare cage for the newcomer in case the introduction turns sour.

Most ferrets eventually learn to get along with another ferret. There are some signs that will almost immediately tell you that the new relationship probably won't work out: Drawing blood, one ferret literally having the poop scared out of him, and persistent screaming. If they only display bottle brush tails and keep coming back for more sniffs, things should be okay. All that said, you can do certain things to encourage a successful introduction.

Meeting on neutral ground

You can choose a ferret-proof room that hasn't been explored yet by your established ferrets. Another neutral place can be in your yard with all ferrets harnessed and leashed. Place them together and watch cautiously to see how they all react. If the introduction is a rough one, place them in their own cages and try again later.

Even if this type of introduction is successful, I suggest that you clean all toys and bedding in the main fuzzy cage before lumping them in together. Don't forget to also clean the cage and change the litter boxes. Doing so gives the new ferret ample opportunity to get his scent in there at the same time as the others.

Messing with their sniffers

Ferrets have a tremendous sense of smell. They identify each other and objects through the unique scents they give off. The scent of a new ferret can be intimidating and provoke aggression or fear. So, in addition to completely cleaning the cage and all its contents before adding the new furkid (see the preceding section), you can do other things to get them used to each other:

✔ Your ferrets are probably due for a bath anyway, so break out the most fragrant shampoo you can find and give them all baths. The boys will be busy feeling embarrassed at how girly they smell, and the girls will be walking with their heads held high. The newcomer will be noticed, but everyone will smell pretty much the same at this point. If you want to try for a more exotic smell, add a little vanilla extract to the rinsing bath. Since a lot of disagreements arise from one fert not liking another fert's special smell, having them all smell alike can help to curtail fuzzy tension.

✔ Another good tactic is to switch the cage bedding of the new ferret with the cage bedding of the established fuzzies and vice versa. This way, they have no choice but to live with the stink. They'll either get used to it or resent the newcomer even more. Usually, they get used to it. I use this tactic when introducing most animals to each other, from rabbits to foxes. While it doesn't always work, it's got a high success rate.

✔ The other thing I often do when introducing animals to others of the same species, ferrets included, is place the cages side by side. I start off with the cages about a foot apart and gradually move them closer together in a day or two so that they're touching each other. The ferrets can touch noses and exchange sniffs but not attack each other. It's a safe way for them to become acquainted with each other.

It may take only a few minutes for a newcomer to be welcomed into an existing fert home. Or it may take hours, days, or even months before the introduction is safely completed. Still, some ferrets just won't, under any circumstances, have anything to do with another ferret. These ferrets should remain single.

Fuzzy Meets Fido and Fluffy

If you love ferrets, the chance is good that you also have other pets in your home. Ferrets can usually be introduced successfully to dogs and cats, provided that you take the necessary steps to minimize tension between all of them. Not all ferrets are the same. Likewise, every cat and dog has a unique personality that will influence the relationship. In addition, some breeds of dogs (generally speaking) aren't as good with ferrets as other breeds.

Sometimes the relationship can be stronger when a ferret kit grows up with a kitten or a puppy. As a rule, ferrets get along better with cats. Ferrets and dogs together present different conflicts that should be monitored closely.

Heeeere kitty, kitty

Ferrets and cats can make great companions for each other, depending on the temperaments of both (see Figure 8-2). I have three fat cats, and each responds differently to my ferrets. Butch is usually neutral around ferrets, sometimes feeling too crabby to fert around. Other times, he gets a wild hair up his heinie and waits patiently around the corner for a ferret to amble by before making the tackle. Old man Smokey has zero tolerance for fert behavior. He either stays up high or throws haphazard swats toward any fuzzy that's curious enough to cop a sniff. Then he runs away and hides. Snickers, the youngest of the clan, is always up for a good wrestle. He tolerates ferret antics and gets down and dirty with all the furballs. They bite each other and take turns chasing. They play hide and seek. Snickers, however, usually wears down the ferrets. They run and seek solitude in a hidey-hole after an hour or two. Similarly, some of my ferrets show little interest in the cats, while others do what they can to provoke a good wrestle.

Figure 8-2: Ferrets and your other pets can become the best of friends, but always supervise interactions.

To smooth the feline-ferret introductions in your house:

1. **Once your ferret's comfortable in his new surroundings, allow Kitty to move freely about the outside of the ferret's cage.**

   Let them sniff each other and watch how they react. You may see no reaction at all.

2. **Take the ferret out and hold him securely while both he and the cat explore each other.**

   New smells are intriguing to ferrets. Both he and the cat may have puffed tails.

3. **If all seems calm, put your ferret down and watch cautiously as they interact.**

   It may take a few meetings before everyone's completely comfortable. If conflict arises, end the meeting and try again later.

Many people think that the ferret is the one in the most danger during cat-fert encounters. My experience has been that most healthy adult ferts can hold their own against a cat and can even be more aggressive ("little fert complex") toward the cat than is healthy for the poor cat. Until you're sure that the ferret and cat can play nicely together, always supervise their games. And even after you're comfortable, supervision is a good idea.

Adult ferrets have been known to kill kittens, so never leave a ferret and kitten unsupervised. Better yet, let the kitten develop into an arrogant adolescent before subjecting him to ferret torture. It's only fair.

Nice puppy

The relationship between a dog and ferret can be a little more complicated than that between a cat and ferret. While cats come in different breeds, they all maintain pretty similar characteristics and are similar in size. Dogs, on the other hand, can be itty-bitty or massive in size. Purebred dogs are bred for certain personality traits and job functions. You must take all of these things into consideration when introducing your ferret to any dog.

I've heard of many ferrets being killed by dogs, and the owners blame the dogs. The fault usually lies with the human who wasn't supervising or who didn't take into consideration the personality of the dog. Remember, it's your responsibility to keep your fuzzy safe and healthy. It's a dog's responsibility to be a dog.

While good dog-fert relationships are out there, I tend to mistrust most dogs around ferrets for several different reasons:

- Some breeds of dogs (like Terriers) are bred to hunt ferret-size game and may find a ferret awfully tempting. Supervise with extreme caution.

- Some dogs are very territorial. An otherwise laid-back, ferret-friendly pup may snap at or kill a ferret that ventures too close to the dog's food, toys, or den. Keep dog stuff out of the ferret's territory and watch for signs that your dog is getting possessive with other objects.

- A nursing dog can get extremely aggressive toward all other animals when she's protecting her litter.

- Large or hyper dogs may inadvertently paw a ferret to death or injure the ferret's spine in an attempt to engage in play.

- Some dogs just aren't good with other animals, including ferrets.

- Some dogs don't like little animals or young animals and are very freaky around them. My dog Ara was great with cats but was unpredictable around kittens.

- Some dogs do well with ferrets until the ferret nips or chases the dog. A ferret is bound to nip and chase in play. If your dog can dish it out but can't take it, don't allow him to play with a fuzzy at all.

Those are rules that I live by, but, of course, many exceptions exist. Some nursing dogs allow a ferret to snuggle in with the rest of the litter. Some big dogs tiptoe gently around ferrets. Because every animal is an individual, it's be up to you to decide how to allow you fuzzy to interact with your dog. Use common sense. If it feels or looks unsafe for your ferret or other pet, it probably is.

No matter how well a dog and ferret seem to get along, never leave them unsupervised. Dogs can be funny critters, and I don't mean funny ha-ha. Some people know their dogs' personalities way too well to even think about introducing a ferret. Others know their dogs and trust them completely. Use your head. If you're in doubt, go with your gut. Dogs should only be given one supervised chance with a ferret. If the dog blows it and shows any sign of aggression toward the ferret, assume it won't be the last. Likewise, if your dog has been fine around ferrets for some time and suddenly displays aggression towards them, it's time to end all interactions between dog and ferrets for good.

Introducing a fuzzy and a dog is almost the same as introducing a fuzzy and a cat. It's a slower process, however:

1. **Once your fuzzy is feeling settled in his new home, allow the dog to roam freely and investigate the ferret's cage with you present.**

   Allow this type of interaction for several days. If you have a large dog, do not allow him alone with the cage. I have a friend who lost eight fuzzies to a large dog that tore apart the cage in a matter of 15 unsupervised minutes.

2. **When cage sniffing seems to be going well, take the ferret out and hold him securely; then let the dog and ferret sniff each other.**

3. **If the mutual smelling goes well, put the ferret down on the ground with the dog in the room.**

   You should harness and leash your fuzzy before letting him on the ground with your dog.

Be extra vigilant. Dogs are quick, and you may not be able to rescue your ferret if he needs help. Dogs are also curious and are usually overly interested in fuzzies. Your ferret may also be scared of the dog's size and back away. Some ferrets nip at the dog's toes or tail. If, after several attempts to introduce the dog and ferret, you still seem uncertain, it's probably a clue that you should keep them separated altogether.

Other small animals

Ferrets are carnivores and predatory by nature. Allowing them to play with other small animals (such as rabbits, hamsters, birds, hedgehogs, guinea pigs, and lizards) is, in essence, messing with the laws of nature. As I mention in Chapter 9 (the food chapter), most kibble-raised ferrets won't even recognize these animals as food. But the quick movements made by such small pets may trigger the predatory reaction in your beloved fuzzbutt. Even if the small pet stays perfectly still, the ferret's curiosity could take over, and, like a dog pawing during play, the ferret may very well kill the small animal accidentally.

Yes, exceptions to this rule exist. But I wouldn't want to risk the life of my other pet just to see if we fell into the exception category. As a general guideline, keep ferrets separated from any animal the ferret's cousins might prey on in the wild.

Enter the Kids

Some adults think kids automatically know what to do and what not to do around animals. Not so. They need to be taught about interacting safely with animals. While some youngsters have more common sense than their adult counterparts, the adult is still responsible for keeping both the child and the pet safe. Children often get bitten or scratched by an animal because the adult wasn't closely supervising the interaction.

Never allow any pet, ferret or otherwise, to interact unsupervised with a baby, toddler, or incapacitated person. Doing so is incredibly stupid and irresponsible. Not only can the human get severely injured, but so can the pet, particularly if it's a small animal such as a ferret.

Not all kids are the same around animals. I was a real pain-in-the-butt kid but had great common sense around animals. Know your kids. If you think they're too young or immature, a ferret may not be a good pet for your household. Typically, ferrets make wonderful pets for older or more mature children.

Preparing your child for the ferret

Children can activate the insanity button in even the calmest person. Fuzzies are already strung out on excess energy, and kids easily manage to activate the overload switch in them. That's a given. Behavior aside, kids are smaller than adults. They are clumsier, and they have much higher pitched voices. These things alone can make an already nervous ferret more excited. When you factor in the added hyperactivity a kid brings in, you've got double trouble.

Your job as a responsible adult and ferret-owning human is to teach the child what you know about ferrets in terms the child will understand. When you're done explaining this stuff to your kids, explain it again to any young friends who may also want to interact with the fuzzbutt:

 ✔ Many kids get frightened easily, particularly when they get nipped or scratched by a pet. Explain to kids that ferrets are very active and playful.

 ✔ Stress the importance of not running or rough-housing where ferrets are loose. Give them reasons so they'll understand.

 ✔ Teach your kids how to properly hold a fuzzy. Insisting that they always hold the ferret while sitting down is a good idea. That way, even if fuzzbutt squirms away, he won't end up plopping to the floor.

For safety reasons, always supervise children until you feel confident that they know how to properly interact with the fuzzy.

Making the introductions

Children have a tendency to squeeze things in order not to drop them. And they also insist on holding things and then rapidly and without warning change their minds and let the object or animal drop to the floor. Kids can be quite unpredictable in this sense. That's why it's important to go slowly and explain things as you go along. The first step is to go over the rules mentioned earlier. Once that's done, the following can help ease the ferret safely and comfortably into the child's life:

 ✔ Because most children automatically shy away from being bitten or scratched, make sure the child has on long pants and long sleeves to prevent the ferrets claws from making direct contact with the child's skin. This way the child will find handling the ferret easier.

✔ Have the child start off slowly by sitting on the floor in the same room with the ferret. Allow the ferret to approach the child on his own. This is a good time to practice patience.

✔ If the ferret seems relaxed and the child hasn't gone into hyper mode, pick up the ferret and demonstrate the proper way to hold a ferret. Point out his sharp claws and teeth and explain why it's important to properly hold the ferret.

✔ With the child still sitting on the ground, place the ferret in the child's lap and allow the ferret to get used to being with a new person. Encourage the child to gently pet the ferret.

✔ If the meeting is going well and everyone is still calm and under control, place the ferret into the child's arms, again showing him the proper way to hold the ferret. Make sure your hands are just below the ferret in case the child decides he no longer wants to hold him.

✔ If the you and the ferret both seem comfortable with how the child is holding the ferret, demonstrate how to put the ferret back down. At this time, you'll also want to show the child how to properly pick up the ferret. Picking up the ferret and putting him back down are as important as learning to hold the fuzzy.

With the rules listed previously and these simple guidelines to get you started, you should be able to determine how responsible your child will be with a ferret and how your ferret will do with a child. Some kids and some ferrets take a little longer to get the hang of it. If this is the case, then go slow! Never force a child or pet to interact with each other until both feel and act comfortable. Moving to the next step before the prior step is completed may lead to an injured child and an injured pet. Remember, it's your responsibility to keep both the child and pet safe.

Stranger Danger

You ferret may have several opportunities to encounter strangers. It may be at the vet's office or in the park during playtime (with you attached at the end of the leash, of course). It may be in your child's classroom during a visit or in your own home. Not everyone shares our fuzzy enthusiasm, and some will be taken aback at the quick display of curiosity shown by your ferret. Others may be annoyed at how bold the ferret can be as he tries to steal their personal possessions and mow through their new hairdos. You'll also be sure to find more who are just like you and me. These people will be tickled pink at the fert's charming personality.

Some ferrets are natural social butterflies. Others quiver with nervousness when encountering new people or places. Use common sense and don't risk the stranger's health or your fuzzy's life if you already know that the ferret reacts badly to change or strangers. That said, here are some suggestions for dealing with strangers around your ferret:

- When allowing a stranger to touch your ferret for the first time, keep the ferret's head under control. Offer the stranger the ferret's heinie and back to pet in order to minimize any chance of biting.

- If you're entertaining guests at your home or the kids have friends over, once the fuzzy curiosity has passed, it's best to keep the ferret caged. With so much else going on, supervising a roaming ferret would be difficult. He could be mishandled or injured with all the feet moving about.

- For frequent visitors, give them a brief education on the common behavior of ferrets and the proper way to handle them. I can't stress the education factor enough. That, along with common sense, has allowed me to show off my fuzzies hundreds and hundreds of times with no incidences.

I was once told by a friend to never allow a stranger or an acquaintance to touch or hold any ferret I wasn't willing to immediately part with should it bite. The reason has to do with the overblown fear of rabies exposure. Many states used to immediately confiscate any ferret that bit or scratched. The ferret was then killed, decapitated, and sent off for rabies testing. Many states are now beginning to impose the lighter, more appropriate sentence of quarantine. Nonetheless, always keep your ferret updated on shots and keep proof on hand.

General guidelines for kids and animals

Here's a basic checklist that goes for teaching young kids about any pet. I use it during educational lectures:

- Never approach a wild, unfamiliar, or stray animal.

- Ask an adult for permission before petting an animal or removing it from its cage.

- Always keep the animal away from your face.

- While handling animals, keep fingers and hands off your face and out of your eyes and mouth until after your hands are washed.

- Do not pick your nose and then pet the critters.

- Do not "feed fingers to animals." In other words, no poking fingers in cages.

- Do not physically abuse any animal. Abuse includes pulling on fur, tails, and ears. It includes using legs, tails, and ears as handles. It also includes poking fingers in eyes, ears, and noses, as well as hitting, biting, or kicking the poor little critter.

- Remember that anything with a mouth can bite.

- Also remember that anything that eats must poop. (Telling kids this fact never lessens the "Gross!" reaction when an animal poops anyway, but at least you can't say you didn't warn them.)

- Never go near an angry, injured, frightened, or fighting animal.

- Never sneak up on an animal or wake it suddenly.

- Never tease or chase a pet.

- Don't forget to wash your hands after handling an animal (it's always necessary to repeat this piece of advice).

- Pets do not teach kids responsibility. Pets are only for responsible people (this advice is for the adults).

Part III
Basic Care and Feeding

The 5th Wave   By Rich Tennant

"We keep her diet high in protein, high
in nutrients and high off the floor
behind a locked door."

In this part . . .

Ferrets are complicated critters with complicated needs. This part deals with the basic necessities: how to keep your ferret and his cage clean, what his nutritional requirements are, what activities he needs to stay healthy and active, and what to do when you go a-traveling — with or without him. Most of us can keep a ferret alive, but keeping him healthy, happy, *and* sane is another matter. This part also takes caring for your ferret a couple of steps further and delves into issues such as an alternative diet and environmental enrichment for your fuzzy.

Chapter 9

Filling Their Bellies

- -

In This Chapter

▶ Dietary requirements for ferrets

▶ Types of food: Which are good for your ferret?

▶ How to change your ferret's diet

▶ Supplements: What they're good for

- -

A suitable and complete diet is essential for your ferret's good health. The keys to a good diet are fat, animal protein, and proper amounts of vitamins, minerals, and amino acids. Yet finding this perfect diet can be difficult and challenging to even the experienced fuzzy human.

That's why this chapter is extra-important. It covers the basic stuff like water (how much and how often), traditional diets, supplements, and treats. I even explain how to switch a ferret's diet if you find it necessary to do so.

The wrong foods can lead to obesity, food-related illnesses, and a shortened life span. Just how big a part diet plays in terms of ferret diseases is still being researched. We may all be surprised at what is discovered.

Water, Water, Everywhere

Obviously, no living thing can live without it, and your ferret is no different. But not all water is equal. Some people prefer to use bottled or distilled water. However, it is strongly argued that distilled water lacks many important nutrients that our pets need, so you should probably avoid it all together. Unless your tap water has tested positive for high levels of harmful chemicals, tap water should be sufficient.

Some ferrets' systems have difficulty adjusting to a change in water, whether it be from city water to well water or vice versa. Even tap water varies from place to place. This simple change in water can possibly cause diarrhea for a day or two. If the diarrhea is severe or doesn't subside after a couple of days, seek veterinary advice.

Make sure that your ferret's water bottle is full at all times. Common sense mandates that the more ferrets you have, the faster the water level in the bottle will drop. Warm or hot weather causes the water level to drop more quickly, too. So always be sure that your ferret has a fresh supply of water at all times. If you have many ferrets or a particularly large cage, provide two to three bottles. Keeping spare bottles around for when the others are being washed is also a good idea.

The Traditional Diet

It's easy to tell that your ferret is a carnivore just by looking at his sharp canine teeth. They were designed for tearing flesh and meat and cutting bone. Because ferrets are carnivores and get most of their nutritional needs met from animal-based products, the food should contain taurine (which helps keep their eyes and heart healthy) and be composed of no less than 20 percent fat and no less than 34 percent animal protein. Table 9-1 gives you a quick rundown of the pros and cons of various types of food.

- ✔ The pet industry has come out with several foods formulated just for ferrets. The majority of them meet the protein/fat level and are considered the best food choices for your ferret.

- ✔ Some high-quality dry kitten foods have the necessary taurine and higher fat and protein content. But many don't. Before you make dry kitten food a staple of your ferret's diet, make sure that it has the nutritional content your ferret needs.

- ✔ Dog food is not a source of proper nutrition for your ferret. It doesn't contain the taurine additive that your ferret needs to help keep his eyes and heart healthy. As an infrequent treat, dog food is fine.

- ✔ Raw meat is a great food, assuming that the meat is free of dangerous germs or parasites and as long as it isn't the ferret's only food. By itself, raw meat lacks many of the necessary nutrients, particularly calcium. If you opt for the more natural diet, you may choose raw meat as a part of the whole diet. See the section "An Alternative Diet" for information on feeding your ferret a more natural diet.

- ✔ Avoid fishy stuff. While fish in moderation is a good food, most ferrets just aren't crazy about fish.

If you have a young ferret, do your best to offer a variety of different quality foods from the get go. Ferrets imprint on food smells at an early age. The older they get, the less likely they'll be able to recognize the smell of a new food as being yummy. Ferrets that have been exposed to a wide variety of good foods have less difficulty switching diets or taking to a new food item.

Table 9-1	Types of Food for Your Ferret
Type of Food	*Comments*
Moist ferret foods	Difficult to find high quality, but it can be the best man-made substitute.
Dry ferret foods	Equal or slightly better than the best dry kitten foods.
Dry dog foods	Too low in protein and fat and lack taurine. Okay as an occasional treat.
Moist dog foods	Higher in protein and fat but still not balanced enough for a ferret. Okay for an occasional treat or change of pace.
Dry kitten foods	Have the necessary taurine and higher fat and protein content.
Moist kitten foods	Have less grains and some brands are better than dry, but they make ferret poop even stinkier.

Don't expect a pet shop clerk to know what's best. I've overheard one or two telling unaware ferret owners to feed canned dog food or only hamburger meat. I even heard one tell a customer that ferrets are herbivores (plant eaters).

Fuzzies aren't built to digest fiber. If you were to take a peak at the inside of a ferret (not advised), you'd see that his large intestine is short and tubular and that the ferret lacks a cecum. The *cecum* is the gut cavity — the place where fiber is digested. Too much fiber in your ferret's belly leads to extra-squishy or mucousy poops.

Improper food can shorten your ferret's life span, so make sure that you check the food package labels. The main ingredient should be meat or poultry; avoid products that list corn meal or another plant material as a first ingredient.

The fuzzy is constantly eating and converting the food into energy. Therefore, the quality of food you choose is also extremely important. Of course, you'll pay more for a good food, but it'll be well worth the investment.

Wet or dry?

Some people like to stick with a dry food, while others prefer to feed their fuzzies moist. Some alternate or mix the dry and moist. I personally try to give as much variety as possible. Here are some things to think about when deciding what's right for your furball:

✔ Dry kibble helps wear down the tartar buildup on the fuzzy's teeth. But hard kibble fed as the sole diet can cause tooth wear. Sprinkling a few drops of water over the hard food and microwaving it briefly can help soften it up a little but not make it the consistency of canned food.

✔ High-quality moist kitten or ferret food is easier on the teeth and, depending on the brand, may be more nutritional than dry. It's also more expensive and can cause stinkier poops. This shouldn't be the only food in the ferret's diet. Some harder foods should be added to help with tartar buildup on the teeth.

Feeding schedule

Your ferret's metabolism is very high, and food passes right through and out the other end in only 3 to 5 hours. Therefore, your ferret replenishes his belly with many meals — 10 plus — throughout the day. Because of his high animation level and quick metabolism, food should be available at all times (see Figure 9-1).

Figure 9-1:
Ferrets eat many meals throughout the day, so always have fresh food available.

Some people think that leaving food out all the time leads to obesity. They must be thinking of us humans. Normally, ferrets aren't gluttons and consume only the amount of fat needed to make the energy to terrorize the household in their normal capacity. This is called *eating to caloric need*. If the diet is poor quality, your fuzzy will start to develop a nutritional deficit and begin eating more to make up for it. With the added extra calories comes the added weight. However, if you think your ferret is getting chunky, take him to the vet to rule out an enlarged spleen or fluid in the abdominal cavity. Enlarged spleens are common causes of rapid weight gain.

Some ferrets do get slightly wider with age, and some get wider in the winter. In general, obesity is rarely a serious problem in ferrets, especially if the diet is balanced.

Knowing you've got it right

If your ferret is eating a well-balanced and nutritious diet, his fur will be soft and shiny. He will have bright, clear eyes, supple skin, and well-formed poopies that don't smell too bad. He'll also have a high activity level and look happy overall.

If your ferret has itchy, flaky skin, a brittle coat, large, overly stinky poops, and lethargy, you may need to change his diet. Before you do, however, first visit the vet to rule out any underlying medical conditions.

Changing diets

Sometimes it's difficult to convince your ferret that he needs the correct type of food, especially if the fuzzy's been fed a different or improper diet before coming into your care. You need to switch the ferret over to the good stuff, despite any protest he may display. Doing so can be tricky in some cases. I've had some ferrets eat any type of cat, kitten, or ferret food, no matter what. They weren't very picky at all. On the other hand, I've had some that refused all food until I could figure out exactly what they had been eating before coming into my care.

The best way to switch your ferret's food is to mix the previous food with the new food. If your ferret eats around the new food and devours everything else, give it time and don't give up. The health of your baby could depend on it.

Start off by adding just a small amount of the new food to the food the ferret is accustomed to. (It's important not to switch completely to a new food immediately. Such a drastic change can lead to upset tummies, diarrhea, and a generally crabby fert.) Gradually increase the amount of new food and decrease the amount of old food over the course of 10–14 days. This process usually works well and gives you fuzzy's system a chance to get used to the change.

If multiple ferrets are in the cage, telling whether the new ferret has taken to his new food can be difficult. As the food level is quickly depleted, you're unaware that your new ferret is slowly starving, which can be extremely dangerous. Watch for any significant weight changes in all your fuzzies, particularly newcomers. In fact, I recommend that you house a new ferret separately until you know for sure that he's eating what the rest of the gang is eating. This practice gives you the opportunity to monitor his food intake closely and prevent a possible slow starvation.

An Alternative Diet

Up until now, people have fed their ferrets manmade foods, mostly out of convenience, tradition, or lack of anything else good to feed. But there's been a growing movement to switch to more natural diets for all pets, including the ferret. Some people believe the only way to true health is to feed a diet that the animal evolved eating, and kibble certainly wasn't around 2,500 years ago. Here's what proponents of a natural diet believe its benefits are:

✔ A natural diet is a way to ensure that your ferret is getting the essential nutrients. In terms of essential amino acids, for example, those that the ferret can't produce himself can be found in the food his wild cousins eat: rabbits, mice, rats, birds, frogs, lizards, squirrels, and even berries. Calcium is another example: Many manmade cat or ferret foods lack quality bone meal, so your ferrets are losing out on calcium.

✔ A healthy ferret on a varied and natural diet doesn't need to have food available at all times. This makes sense when you look at the ferret's cousins, who eat only once or twice a day, sometimes even skipping a day when food is scarce.

✔ Many people who feed their fuzzies a more natural diet believe that the variation of food consistency (bone, skin, meat, etc.) helps to flush out the intestinal tract regularly, causing the ferret to be less prone to hairballs and other obstructions. (Even if this is true, all experts agree that a good hairball preventive such as Laxatone should be kept on hand for emergencies, especially for ferrets that eat or chew foreign objects.)

✔ The design of the ferret's jaw leaves him with little chewing capability. His teeth were designed for cutting meat and bone but not all the time. Kibble can be as hard or harder than bone. People who favor the natural diet believe that kibble leads to too much wear and tear on the teeth and gums.

The following sections explain the staples of a natural diet: bone and meat.

Naturally dissecting pet food labels

You'd be surprised at where the 30 percent protein listed on that kitten food label may really come from. Labels, even those from reputable manufacturers, can be and are often misleading. Unless the label says all the protein is from meat, you can be sure it isn't. The protein can come from other sources thrown into the recipe. The hair in a hairball is 100 percent protein. Fecal matter (trace amounts are allowed in by-products) is also made up of protein. Ick. So even if your ferret's food is 30 percent protein, how much of it actually comes from meat? Even if meat is listed as the #1 ingredient, it doesn't mean that's where all the protein comes from.

Most pet foods have meat or chicken by-products listed as a first ingredient. What the heck are meat and chicken by-products, anyway? Hold onto your lunch. By-products are leftover gunky animal bits that aren't fit for human consumption. They don't even qualify to be stuffed into a hotdog casing (that's really bad). By-products include such yummies as heads (chicken), skin, feet, blood, guts, beaks, tendons, stomach contents, discarded organs, and fecal matter

(trace amounts). Once in a while, by-products may include bits of less-than-fresh meat. The protein from by-products may not be easily digested by your pet ferret. The key is meat, not by-products.

And even if by-products are listed first in the ingredients, that doesn't mean there's a lot of them. They may be only 10 percent of the meal. They may be listed first only because they're the highest percentage in terms of total ingredients. There may be 20 other ingredients listed afterward, making up the other 90 percent of the food. Hmmmmm.

Of course, we all see other things on the labels, too, such as colors and additives. Some we recognize; most we can't pronounce. We don't even know why they're thrown in there. Some say "to preserve freshness." Sure. Can you imagine? And did they remember to add all those essential vitamins, amino acids, and minerals that our ferrets evolved eating? Some manufacturers may try their best to make up for it in some way, but how do we really know the job was accomplished?

Bones

Bones contain an incredible amount of good stuff, calcium being the most obvious. The bone marrow itself is made up of tissues rich in protein and fat. Bone and marrow contain high amounts of fatty acids, fats, iron, and other vitamins essential to the health of carnivores. Most of this good stuff comes from the ends of the bones, which are softer and easily bitten and swallowed. The ends of the bone are the best part of the bone. This is the part ferrets are most interested in. They usually leave the rest if they can find something else to eat.

No bones about it?

Most people have been ingrained with the idea that bones are bad, bad, bad. You may have heard horror stories about bones splintering and getting caught in the throat of the poor diner. Or maybe it was a choking story. Those stories scared the crud out of me and made me paranoid about even thinking of feeding them to my pets.

Many of these fears have arisen from experiences with dogs. Dogs gulp down huge pieces of food and bone without a second thought. They don't cut the pieces into manageable sizes, so choking on bones can be a problem. I know that my dogs are constantly urping up rawhide or other things that they prematurely swallow.

A ferret, unlike a dog, can't swallow anything bigger than what fits down his throat because of the way his jaw is designed. The teeth of a ferret are designed to cut bone into tiny, manageable pieces. These tiny pieces can then be swallowed safely. If a piece of bone is too big, the ferret usually coughs it up from the back of the throat and bites it into smaller pieces before trying to swallow it again. Once the piece makes it past the throat, it's as good as gone out the other end.

Think about it. What were ferrets eating before man forced them to feed on kibble? What do their cousins eat today? Why aren't carnivores all over the place dropping dead left and right from eating bones?

Fact is, bones are a wonderful source of natural nutrition. But if you're not comfortable giving bones to your ferrets, then don't. If you think your ferrets would benefit from the calcium and other nutrients in bones, then try it.

When comparing the skeleton of a domestic ferret to a wild polecat, the polecat's bones are usually thicker. Experts think the reason is partially due to the natural diet of the polecat — who consumes more bones (thus, more calcium) than the domestic ferret. Another reason is that neutering/spaying ferrets also reduces the thickness of bones to a slight degree.

Can feeding bones to your ferret cause harm? Certainly. On rare occasions, a splinter may cut the esophagus, causing bleeding. A bone fragment can even puncture the intestinal tract or stomach. But in my experience, these scenarios happen less frequently than choking on commercial food. Plus, the middle piece of the bone is the part that would most likely cause the damage, and most ferrets only eat off the ends of the bones, leaving the middle for the garbage can. The middle piece is too big to be swallowed anyway.

If you're nervously thinking of giving bones to your ferret, try these suggestions:

✔ Start off with something you know is too big to swallow and too hard to splinter, like a cooked ham bone or soup bone. The more marrow, the better. You can see for yourself that this type of bone is too hard to bite in pieces and too big to be swallowed. The fuzzy still gets the benefit of the marrow and a bonus toy for later.

✔ Some people feed raw bones, but I suggest briefly boiling the bones first. Besides softening the bone a little, boiling eliminates any bacteria and, hopefully, your paranoia.

✔ Try feeding only the softer ends of long bones or backbones. People who've become more comfortable with feeding bones to their fuzzies offer cooked chicken or turkey bones. I've chatted with many of them who say they've never had a problem with feeding these types of bones over the years; their ferrets are happy and healthy, and many are quite up there in years.

When trying anything new, stick around for a while to see how it all plays out. The odds are in the favor of your ferret being just fine. Ferrets did well before being domesticated, and they should still do so now.

Meat

Most people agree that cooked meat is the ideal choice. Others fight diligently to prove that raw meat is the best. Still others say, "If you must feed meat, feed it in the form of human baby food." And, of course, when discussing meat, there's always the issue of live or dead and the pros and cons of doing either (as explained in the section "Is it live or. . .?").

Well done or rare?

It's common knowledge that cooking meat kills off any harmful bacteria that may cause illness to the unfortunate human diner. Some people suggest that you rinse raw meat in a food-grade hydrogen peroxide to make it safe for pets. If you're comfortable with those answers, then stick with them. However, I don't see little barbecue pits scattered throughout the forests, nor do I see dead coyotes, foxes, hawks, or other predators on the sides of the roads (unless they're car casualties). Carnivores eat raw meat. That's a fact of life.

What affects humans is different from what affects other animals. Humans have very different digestive tracts than carnivores, who evolved eating other animals. The Europeans continue to feed their ferrets mostly rabbit, and they're the biggest, healthiest, and most muscular fuzzbutts around.

If you're still unsure about raw meat, cut off the outside layer of the meat. The inside meat is generally sterile and safe. Make sure that the meat is fresh. I have fed live, fresh-killed, and thawed frozen meat to a number of animals over the years and have never had an incident of illness resulting from raw meat.

While clean raw meat (okay, cooked meat, too) is a wonderful food for ferrets, it can't be the sole food. Wild polecats eat the whole animal — bones, guts, and all. Domestic ferrets need all the good nutrients that come from the rest of the prey animal, not just the meat. They also need some hardness to help clean their teeth. The same goes for fish as a food source. It's good, but it shouldn't be the only food source.

Is it live or . . .?

For those who agree to feed a whole animal to a carnivore, the question is always, "Should a carnivore be fed a live or dead animal?" This is a topic that people argue aggressively both ways. Whenever possible, I always try to feed prekilled animals to the carnivores. My decision to feed prekilled vs. alive rests on what type of carnivore I'm feeding and the experience of the predator.

An aggressive myth

Many people believe that feeding live animals (and some even believe raw meat) makes your ferret more aggressive. This is simply not true. And, by the way, *domestic* doesn't mean unnatural. It only means tame, made fit for domestic life, adapted or bred to live with and be of use to man. Humans are domestic. Does that mean we can't cater to our primal urges once in a while?

Take a good look at the average housecat. Some of these sweet, purring kitties can be killing machines, responsible for millions of wildlife deaths each year. While they could be quick killers, they more often than not kill slowly, often playing and toying with the victim before death. And yet, our housecats remain dear to our hearts, sharing our pillows at night and claiming us as their possessions in the morning by rubbing up against our legs. Why would a ferret be any different?

All ferrets have a natural predatory instinct. It shows in the way they play with their toys as well as in how they interact with each other. Feeding your ferret what he would naturally eat in the wild won't unleash some fantasy wild beast inside. It only gives him an opportunity to experience and benefit from something more natural than what he's used to. In the end, he'll be the same lovable character, except maybe a little happier, healthier, and more energetic.

Polecats, ferrets included, are by nature efficient and quick predators that normally kill with a lightning-fast bite to the back of the neck. But most pet ferrets don't recognize small animals as food. Some are quick to kill. Others play with the food until it happens to die. And still others could care less and lazily watch a potential snack waltz on by. For a ferret eating a more natural diet that includes mice or chicks or whatever, I see no reason to offer live food unless he's a quick predator. That's my opinion. I don't like to see the prey animal suffer anymore than it has to.

Converting the ferret naturally

Polecats hunt by sense of smell. This sense is so powerful that the critter can sniff out a frog under a foot of mud. Thus, the frog becomes dinner rather quickly. Ferrets, like their cousins, are also olfactory hunters, meaning they follow their nose to the dinner table. Whatever the ferret has consistently eaten during the first six months of his life, he'll see as food in the future — called *olfactory imprinting*.

Getting a ferret to initially betray his own nose after chowing on kibble for so long can be challenging. Over time it's well worth the effort if you're a true believer in the natural diet. Of course, the conversion should occur when your fuzzy is as young as possible, but you can teach old ferts new tricks. The idea is to broaden the ferret's culinary horizons. However, not all ferrets can be brought around, particularly the older kids. Make sure that you've given it your all before giving up. Here's how you do it:

- If you haven't already been feeding any canned food, start introducing high-quality wet cat or kitten food. You can add it in a separate bowl, but mixing it with dry will force the ferret to taste it. Occasionally, switch to a high-quality canned dog food just for variety. The poopie smell gets worse with canned, but the end result (oh crap, a pun) causes less stinky poops.

- Invest in baby food. Yep, you heard right. Often you can use meat baby food, from infant to toddler, as an enticement for your ferret to try a new food. Chicken works well. Rub some on the ferret's nose if he won't readily accept it. He'll surely lick it off.

- Put aside some freezer space for some frozen mice. Some people feed prekilled chicks instead of mice. I know, gross. You can usually purchase prekilled mice or chicks at a pet store, particularly one that sells reptiles. Store them in the freezer and thaw them as needed. Don't feed your ferret mousicles or chicksicles. Remember, these are dead animals, so they aren't feeling the ferret tossing them about and testing their chompers on them. Once a ferret discovers the mouse or chick is tasty, he'll be hooked.

✔ **Experiment with poultry.** You can try chopping up small pieces of chicken, turkey, or other poultry (bones and all) and allowing the ferret to taste it. You can use either cooked or raw poultry, depending on your comfort level. If you don't want to make a special ferret meal, save a couple of cut-up pieces after your next poultry dinner.

✔ **Organ donors needed.** Chicken, pork, and beef livers, as well as chicken and beef hearts, are great treats and full of nutrition. Slice them up and offer the cuts to your fuzzy. Liver, by itself, is a great meal.

✔ **Be creative with hamburger.** We've all had those days when we mix anything we can find in the cupboards or freezer with hamburger. My mother called it junk, but we ate it, and it actually tasted good most of the time. Cook some up. Add some raisins or ground bones or kibble. Form it in shapes like the kibble if you must. Just be creative.

✔ **Use natural juices.** Many people forget how tasty the juices from cooked meat can be. I always use the juices as gravy over the dogs' dry food. Natural juices can be a great introduction to a new taste, either in a separate bowl or over a small amount of kibble.

✔ **Throw in some fishies.** Canned tuna in spring water is yummy to many ferrets. Try it. You can also try other prepared fish, such as trout or salmon, cooked shellfish, shrimp, and crawdads.

✔ **Don't forget the bugs.** Even my dogs and cats eat bugs. Your fuzzies, once they get used to the idea, will only eat the squishy, juicy parts and leave the rest for you.

Don't expect a change overnight. Persistence and experimenting are the keys to converting your ferret over to a more natural diet. All ferrets are different. Some take several days to convert. Others take a week or so. And some, maybe never at all. The younger ones will probably convert more easily. You may find that one of your ferrets loves liver, while another prefers hamburger. It may take a little patience on your part. And don't forget that these foods spoil quickly. Don't let any linger around for too long. If it's still there in 12 hours, get rid of it! If you have to, try something different later.

Once your ferret is switched to the natural diet, he'll be likely to try just about anything. That's important since you don't want to stick to just one food item. He still needs a combination of soft and hard foods. Besides, some of the foods mentioned in this section aren't complete diets. It's the combination of them that makes them so good. So don't rule kibble out for good. If you do keep your ferret on a more natural and varied diet, his poop will most likely stink a little less, too. That's good news.

Supplements

A *supplement* is something added to make up for what's lacking in the diet. If your healthy ferret is on a truly balanced and suitable diet, he doesn't really need supplements. Although supplements may have been a necessary part of a ferret diet years ago, today most kitten and ferret foods are better formulated, thus more balanced for a fuzzy than years ago. Often, giving supplements is more a matter of choice because your ferret enjoys the taste and sees them as a treat.

Even if your ferret doesn't need a supplement, you can use them as treats and rewards, as well as emergency first aid. Keep supplements on hand just in case.

You can buy supplements at many pet stores and certainly the larger pet supply stores. Some ferret shelters and veterinarians also carry these products.

The two ferret supplements commonly used can be beneficial at times if given as directed by your veterinarian. Overdosing a ferret on a supplement can be detrimental to his health, so always consult with a knowledgeable ferret vet.

Fatty-acid supplement

The most common supplement is a fatty-acid oil-based solution, which ferrets find pleasant to the taste buds. Sometimes in the colder months, the ferret's coat and skin get a little dry. Linatone (for cats), Ferretone (for ferrets), or other fat soluble vitamins can add just the right amount of fat to the otherwise complete diet to help during these dry times. Also, I give my little guys a few drops once or twice a week during the dry, cold season. They lick it right off the spoon. Pouring a small amount over the food can also work, but keep in mind that the supplement will spoil on the food over time. This spoilage can be harmful to the ferret.

Supplements that contain Vitamin A should not be used in excess. Vitamin A can be toxic in larger amounts.

A calorie boost

The other supplement ferrets often enjoy as a reward during training or after being groomed is a gooey vitamin supplement that tastes very much like molasses (yes, I've tasted it). The two products commonly used are Nutri-Cal and Ferretvite. The supplement is a high-calorie paste that can give an extra boost to a debilitated ferret or one suffering from low blood sugar. Using such a supplement as a medical aid should be done only with the guidance of a good ferret vet; too much can be very harmful and even deadly.

More often than not, though, it's just a treat given in small quantities just for fun. I give no more than ⅛ teaspoon (about an inch of goo) daily. Some ferrets lick it right off the end of the tube. I prefer using a spoon so that I can monitor the dosage better. Remember, however, that this is a sugary item that should not be given excessively, especially in ferrets with certain medical conditions such as insulinoma.

Treat Time!

There is such a thing as loving your pet to death. Many dog and cat owners do so unknowingly with large amounts of treats and table scraps. Treats can be a vital part of your relationship with your ferret, as long as they are the right types and are given in moderation.

Some fuzzies come to expect a favorite treat at a certain time of day or after performing a neat trick. All beg for them no matter what. Of course, *all* ferrets deserve treats. But, before starting your ferret on treats, discuss doing so with your veterinarian. Some treats can actually aggravate medical conditions such as insulinoma or chronic bowel disease. Better safe than sorry.

Keep the pieces of food small so that they can easily be chewed and digested. Remove any stashed treats that may get spoiled before consumption. Ferrets hoard everything they can.

The good stuff

Even the good stuff can be harmful to your ferret if overfed! Here are some treats that you can offer you ferret in moderation (remember to feed these in very small pieces):

- **Nonacidic fruits:** Raisins (a must-have), melon, banana, apple, and papaya. No more than 1–2 two small pieces of any of these per day. Also, most fruits are high-sugar treats, so watch the insulinoma patients!

- **Cooked veggies:** *Only* cooked. Uncooked vegetables may get lodged in the intestinal tract. Chopped green pepper, broccoli, and cucumber (no skin) are good. Veggies have little nutritional value for ferts and come out the other end basically undigested.

- **Cereals:** The key to a good cereal treat is low salt and low sugar. Two good ones are Cheerios and Kix. Other good ones are out there, too. No more than 1–2 pieces a day.

- **Eggs:** Hard-boiled or scrambled. Egg yolks (cooked or raw) can be very good. However, some people won't risk feeding raw eggs due to the possibility of germs or harmful bacteria. Raw egg whites also contain a substance that binds to the biotin in the diet, so avoid uncooked eggs.

- **Peanut butter:** Smooth only. It can cause diarrhea if you give too much.

- **Meat:** Cooked meats are great treats. Special favorites are chicken livers and hearts. Beef and turkey are good, also. Avoid processed meats such as lunchmeat or salami. They're full of salt and additives.

Ferrets can become "addicted" to treats if they're fed too much and too often. Here's a little trick for people who don't want to feed a lot of treats. Most ferrets view a piece of their regular kibble as a treat if you feed it to them from your hand. If this works for them, they not only get a treat, but aren't straying too far from their diet! This is also a good way to introduce a new food item.

The not-so-good stuff

While we know there are some acceptable treats that will be fine for your ferret if given in moderation, there are some not-so-healthy treats you should avoid altogether no matter how much your ferret begs:

- **Alcohol and other high-sugar drinks:** Too much sugar is a bad thing. And a drunk ferret can quickly become a dead ferret. (Besides, you must be 21 to legally drink.)

- **Coffee and tea products:** No caffeine either, please. Like they don't speed around enough.

- **Dairy products:** Even though ferrets love milk and cream and have a history of being fed milk, dairy products can cause diarrhea in ferts. No milk mustaches here, please.

Many experts argue about lactose intolerance in ferrets. Some vets say it's prevalent, while others say it's not. A single lick of vanilla ice cream probably won't harm most healthy ferrets. In fact, heavy cream (the real stuff) is frequently used by ferret owners and vets as a high fat supplement to add weight on and boost energy in the debilitated ferret. And cheese contains very little lactose, so very small amounts of cheese are probably safe. Use your best judgment. If it comes out the other end of your ferret in smelly liquid form, he's probably sensitive to lactose.

- **Seeds and nuts:** These things are indigestible and hard to pass out the other end, not to mention painful. They can cause blockages.

- **Chocolate:** Contains theobromide, which, in high doses, can be fatal in some pets (such as dogs). No one knows for sure if chocolate is as dangerous to ferrets. Don't panic if your guy accidentally happens on a tiny piece, but don't make a habit of using chocolate as treats. Carob makes a good occasional treat as a substitute for chocolate.

- **Sugary foods:** For obvious reasons. A small lick here or there won't do any harm, but try to resist the urge.

- **Salty foods:** Save the beer nuts for the bar. Again, a small taste here or there won't kill a ferret.

- **Raw egg whites:** Raw egg whites contain an element that binds with biotin. Ingestion of this substance can cause anemia. Cooking egg whites destroys this biotin-binding substance and makes egg whites safe for consumption.

- **Fingers:** Just seeing if you're paying attention.

Treats are not a part of the main diet and can alter the fert's intestinal tract if given in excess. Many treats contain sugar, and large amounts of sugar are bad, bad, bad. Other treats lack nutritional value, so don't skimp on the regular meal just because you overindulged and treats were plentiful one day. Treats listed as good can be bad in large quantities. Likewise, a tiny taste of the bad treats won't make your ferret keel over and die. Moderation and common sense should keep you and your furkid out of trouble.

Chapter 10

Playtime and Exercise

In This Chapter

▶ Teaching an old fert new tricks

▶ Being creative with toys

▶ Developing a ferret enrichment program

F errets are as intelligent as some small primates, which is just more proof that ferrets need a lot of action-packed play and quality time for exploring a ferret-safe environment. Without a constant supply of this type of stimulation, ferts can become cage-crazy or depressed. They may begin chewing on cage bars, digging out litter and food more frequently, and spending most of their awake time trying to find a way out of jail. Physically, they can become unfit, develop love handles, and frequently fall asleep on the hammock while watching reruns of old sitcoms.

This chapter is designed to give you a little more insight into the play behaviors and needs of fuzzballs. I tell you how you can get right down on the ground and play with your ferret as though you, too, were a weasel. I discuss wonderful toys that you can buy at the store, as well as some cool things you can easily make on your own to keep your fuzzy amused. Also, you'll find a section on ferret enrichment to give you an idea about how to keep up with your fert's need to experience new things. In case you were wondering, you can even teach ferrets a trick or two. And finally, for those of you who are convinced you have the perfect furkid, I give you an inside peek into ferret shows and fun matches.

Getting Down and Ferty

At least half of your ferret's playtime should be spent with you (see Figure 10-1). Now your mother may have propped you up on a pillow, stuck a bottle in your mouth, and placed you in front of the television as her idea of playtime, but it wasn't exactly what you craved for attention. A ferret likes to play, and his human should be willing to join in the fun. It's good for the soul, as well as funny for the bone.

Figure 10-1:
Ferrets need
to interact
with you.
What better
time than
playtime?

✔ Stimulate chasing by rolling balls past your fert and squeaking toys to get him to come running.

✔ Let him grab the end of a toy and play tug of war with you.

✔ Let him exercise his acrobatic talents by encouraging him to jump for toys. Dangling a toy at the end of a stick or pole is great for this activity. Cat toys are often great for ferts.

✔ Use a stuffed animal for him to wrestle with and roll your ferret around.

✔ Play hide and seek with your ferret. Use a squeaky toy when he starts to "get cold."

✔ Lie on the floor and let your ferret explore you.

When it's time to put your ferrets away for the day, many people often use a squeaky toy to call them out from hiding. I call this direction Last Call.

You can and should come up with as many safe ways as possible to interact with your fuzzy. Your main goal, besides having fun, should be to stimulate the ferret's natural curiosity, as well as his many play techniques. People do the silliest things when they're playing with their fuzzies. And fuzzies do the silliest things because, well, they're fuzzies.

Teaching an Old Fert New Tricks

With such a short, wandering attention span (I'm speaking of ferrets), believing that you can teach a fuzzy some basic tricks is difficult. Attention span aside, these guys are extremely intelligent and can learn some cool things as long as you're willing to make it worth their effort. Of course, I'm talking treats and praise and extra time out of jail. When using food treats as rewards, use small or cut up pieces of the ferret's favorite food. A lick of Linatone also works wonders.

Your fuzzy will be more receptive to the idea of learning tricks, no matter how humiliating, when he's semi-pooped out from playing. Those with human kids can relate. Ferts have short attention spans. Use short, 5- to 10-minute sessions with lots of positive reinforcement. Negative reinforcement never works. Don't forget patience, consistency, and repetition. Here's another tip: Train one ferret at a time to avoid constant distraction; some ferrets will learn just by watching the other ferret perform!

I beg your pardon?

The easiest trick to teach a ferret is to sit up and beg. It comes naturally since they often have to stand up high and peek for the things they're about to pilfer. Once your furball learns this trick, he may even run in front of you every chance he gets to beg for a treat doggie style. Teaching this trick requires a favorite treat and a human hand — preferably attached to the rest of a human body (see Figure 10-2).

1. **Sit on the floor with a treat in your hand or Linatone on your finger.**

2. **Reach away from your body and let your ferret sniff the treat/Linatone to know it's there.**

   You can even give him a tiny taste.

3. **Slowly raise your hand until he has to raise himself to reach the treat.**

4. **While he's reaching to get it, use the command you want to stick with, such as "Up," "Beg," or "Sit up."**

   Choose a simple word and be consistent with it.

Don't let him rest his front paws on your lap or grab your hand. If he does so, gently nudge him away or move further from him and start over. The idea is to get him to do the trick without cheating.

Once the ferret begins to associate the verbal command with a treat, start using only the hand motion. Deaf ferrets can't read lips, but they can read body language and beg for treats just as frequently.

Figure 10-2:
Bouka in the leap-and-catch position.

Scooter, I think your human's calling

Many people have taught their ferrets to come a-runnin' when their names are called. Teaching this trick is almost the same as conditioning them to respond to a squeaky toy or another noise with a treat in mind. However, many people proclaim that each of their ferrets knows his name separately from the others and that some even recognize the names of their cage mates.

There are a few ways to go about teaching your fuzzy his name and having him respond to it. Repetition and reward play the biggest role. How you go about it may vary, but here's one method that works well:

1. **During playtime, call your ferret's name.**

   If he doesn't even notice a noise came out of your mouth, make visual contact with him and call his name again.

2. **Crouch down and let him know you've got something good to show him, all the while calling his name.**

3. **If he appears interested and comes toward you, reward the action with a small taste.**

4. **Move farther away and call him again, repeating the process several times as he figures out that his name really means a treat.**

Treats are great motivators and help in training your fert. However, an unfit fuzzy won't come running when his name is called because he'll have turned into a slug from all the yummy treats. Use verbal praise and lavish petting as alternate rewards for desired behavior. Doing so will keep your ferret healthier, and he may enjoy the surprise of the reward.

You can also call your ferret's name and squeak his favorite toy at the same time. This combination usually gets a furball's attention, and he'll come to investigate. Keep verbally calling his name as well as using the toy as added motivation. Once he masters this trick, use the squeaky toy less and less until you cut it out all together.

Make the trick tougher by hiding from your ferret and calling him. Ferrets are extremely intelligent. Once they know a positive reward is at the end of the voice, they'll listen for their name and come bouncing eagerly to greet you.

Jumping through hoops

This is a relatively easy trick to teach. All you need is a small plastic hoop (or something similar) about 1 foot in diameter. Hold the hoop up on the floor between you and the fuzzy. Show him a treat to entice him through the hoop; when he walks through to get the treat, say "Jump" and then reward him when he passes through. Note that at this point, he has no clue what the heck you're talking about. He thinks you're nuts and just wants the treat. In time, though, he'll make the connection between the hoop, the command, and the treat.

The goal is to continually raise the hoop and have the ferret jump through on command. You can do accomplish this feat in several ways. Some ferrets just jump through as you raise the hoop. Others go under or around the hoop. If you have a difficult fert, use a corner or narrow passageway to make it necessary for him to pass through the hoop. Always keep the treat up high so the fuzzy has to look up and over the hoop rim to get to it. Don't forget to say "Jump" any time the ferret passes through.

Once the ferret masters walking through the hoop and learning the Jump command, you can also try to place him on a slightly raised platform like a pet carrier and place the hoop in front of it. Raise the treat up high and say "Jump" as he hops through.

Several creative ways are available to teach this trick to your ferret. You may come up with something that works even better for you. Tossing the fert through the hoop and hollering "Jump" isn't a good way. Remember to be gentle and creative and pour on the positive for a job well done.

Some fuzzies are cautious and anxious; don't traumatize your ferret by insisting that he learn a certain trick if that trick obviously bothers him. Other ferts, on the other hand, will learn trick after trick. They may teach you a few and still have room to invent new tricks of their own. Remember that fuzzies are individual characters with different personalities. All are extremely intelligent, but some have less interest in learning stupid pet tricks for the delight of the human. Having your ferret act like a ferret is always delightful enough.

Roll over, Beethoven

A Cheerio or piece of raisin can work wonders with teaching your ferret to roll over on command. Some fuzzies don't like to be placed on their backs and manually rolled over, so your ferret may give you a hard time at first. As usual, I know several ways that have been successful. Following is one method that works well, but you may come up with a variation that works better for your fuzzbutt.

1. **Hold the treat in your hand and allow your fuzzy to lick it.**

   The treat will distract him while you gently roll him over.

2. **While still holding the treat, move the treat in a circular motion over the ferret's head while you roll him over.**

   Many times, the ferret's head will roll and his body will naturally follow as he tries to keep up with the treat.

3. **As the ferret is rolling over, either on his own or with your gentle help, say "Over" or "Roll over."**

   Be consistent with the term you use.

In the beginning, you may have to roll the fuzzy over 100 percent of the way. Eventually, you can taper off to a three-quarter push to a half push to a slight nudge. Your fuzzy should need only the motivation of a treat by the time he's learned what you want him to do.

Using the circular hand motion is great for deaf carpet sharks that can't hear the command. They simply roll as you give them the hand signal. Once a fuzzy associates rolling over with treats and affection, you may find your fert running in front of you and rolling over to get attention, be picked up, or get a treat. It's quite amusing.

Mom, I think fuzzy's dead

Playing dead is a difficult trick to teach, and it's different from the dead bug thing where your fert randomly collapses during play and rolls over onto his back with all four feet in the air. That's a normal fuzzy quirk. Like the temporary speed bump oddity in which he drops to the ground and lays motionless for a moment, he jumps up and is back to his normal mode of hyperactivity within seconds. Still, I hear that many talented ferrets are out there that can play dead on command. I think it takes a human with a lot of time and patience on his or her hands to teach this trick.

To teach a ferret to play dead, you need a fuzzy that is comfortable lying on his back — preferably one that has already mastered the Roll Over trick. You also need the most irresistible treat to mesmerize him with. That treat will vary from ferret to ferret. I know one person who uses a small piece of watermelon. Whatever you choose, it must be the most treasured treat for the learning fuzzy.

1. **Place your fuzzy on his back and hold the treat just above him and to the side.**

2. **Choose the word or phrase you'll be using, such as "Dead" or "Play dead" or "Dead fuzzy," and say it repeatedly while teaching your ferret this trick.**

3. **If he begins to move, slowly move the treat over to the other side of his head so that he focuses on the movement of the treat instead of wanting to get up.**

4. **Repeat the verbal command.**

    You can use your hand to reinforce the desired behavior but be gentle. This is a tough trick to teach a critter who'd rather be hopping about.

5. **If he stays still, lower the treat so he can get a taste but keep repeating the phrase.**

You can have several training sessions a day but spread them out. Or you can have one session a day. Some ferrets are quick learners. Others seemingly refuse to learn a certain trick but quickly learn another. Have I mentioned the thing about patience, consistency, repetition, and positive reward?

Diving for treasures

This trick is pretty cool and fun to watch, but you need a ferret that's comfortable with water and likes to snorkel around otter style. Find a treat that sinks and is easy to spot underwater. Raisins are perfect for this trick.

1. Get a large litter box or something similar and fill it with water.

2. Place a piece of raisin in your open palm and rest your hand on the water's surface. Allow your ferret to grab the treat.

3. Repeat Step 2, but this time lower your hand just enough to soak the raisin. Again, let your ferret grab it.

4. As your fuzzy gets used to this trick, lower your hand more and more until he's (voluntarily) submerging his head in the water to get the treat.

5. When your fuzzy snorkeler is a pro at bobbing for goodies, toss the raisin into the tub and watch him dive in.

   If he doesn't, bring the raisin up from the deep and show it to him in the palm of your hand. As he sticks his head in to get it, drop the raisin to the bottom. He should go directly to it and snarf it up.

Sometimes during playtime, I fill my bathtub with water, place several ferts on the edge (it's big enough for them to walk around on), and toss in a few pieces of raisins. Usually, all the ferrets dive in after them. Once they get the treats, I usually lift them back onto the ledge so they can eat them. It's hard to eat and swim at the same time. Besides, you're supposed to wait at least 15 minutes after eating before going back into the pool.

Enriching Their Lives

Since our sanctuary is a USDA-licensed facility that is also a caretaker of lemurs (members of the primate family), I am legally required to develop an enrichment program to improve the lives of these captive animals through various means of stimulation. The reason is to prevent these critters from going crazy — literally — from lack of stimulation. I use environmental, sensory, and dietary changes.

So what does this have to do with ferrets? Ferrets are as intelligent as some small primates and, I might add, obviously more intelligent than our lemurs. Is it possible to bore fuzzies to death? I think so. Have you ever had to listen to Uncle Ned tell the same tediously long war story for the 100th time? At least you can usually get up and walk away. A ferret, on the other hand, only gets to experience what you have to offer (see Figure 10-3).

To keep up with a carpet shark's constant need for stimulation, you must be creative. Fortunately, hundreds of ways are available for you to impress your ferret with your inventiveness, and most often, a great financial investment is not involved. Think safety, fun, fresh, exciting, and artistic.

Figure 10-3:
Ferrets need
a lot of
stimulation
and play-
time, as
Panda and
Buster
demonstrate.

The goal is to give your ferret something new to experience every day. Think about it this way: A fuzzy uses his nose to experience the world. Stick him in a cage, and he'll explore every inch of it until he knows it well. Then what? Boredom. Sleep. Sleep. Boredom. That's why playtime and how he spends it are so important. Here are some ideas to help liven up his ferthood:

- **Diet:** Give him some variety. Take a look at Chapter 9's alternative diet section and see if something works for you. If you had to eat hot dogs every day, you'd go nuts. The traditional ferret diet is boring, not to mention unbalanced in the eyes of many.

- **Toys:** Rotate toys you give him to make old toys seem new. Get him new toys frequently. Make some of your own. Make a ferret castle: Cut holes in boxes and tape the boxes together. You can do wondrous things with tubes and empty oatmeal canisters. Buy plastic Easter eggs and glue a tiny bell in them. (They don't quite roll like regular balls.) Hide toys in safe places and make him search for them. Drill a small hole in a ping pong ball and push a dozen BB's in there. Then seal up the hole really well with epoxy or crazy glue. The noise drives them wild!

- **Food:** Hide food in various places (remember where) and let him find the treats. Put food in hard-to-get-at places, like a box or Tupperware with a tiny hole cut in it. Make him work for the treat. Put a piece of treat in an Easter egg or a milk carton or a 2-liter pop bottle.

✔ **Cage:** Rearrange his cage regularly, if you can. Change bedding. Add new accessories, such as a ramp or different type of hammock. Maybe add some hanging parrot toys (no small parts). Play musical cages: If you have another cage, routinely switch the furkids from one cage to the other.

✔ **Scent:** Rub a small amount of cooking oil on a toy. Some people use non-toxic perfumey scents. If you have several cages of ferrets, switch the bedding occasionally. Visit the hunting section at the local department store and invest in a bottle of deer scent. Rub a drop of it on a toy and watch your furkids go crazy. (Varying the diet also falls into the scent enrichment category.)

✔ **Games you invent:** Fill a box with dirt, sand, or hay, and let him go bonkers digging for gold. You can also use plastic whiffle balls, balls of paper, or cellophane instead of the messy stuff. Float some Linatone-laced ping pong balls in a shallow tub of water. Give your ferret a ride across the floor on the edge of a towel. Create plastic tube slides (using PVC pipes) and prop them up on the couch. Watch your fuzzy's inner kit come out.

In addition to the things listed, you can enrich your fert's life by altering the ways you physically interact with him. Let him explore outside more frequently and go to different places with him. Encourage his digging instincts by putting him into the your kid's sandbox. Hide some toys in there and let him find the treasures. You've never experienced true ferreting until you've hidden fuzzy valuables in the sand.

Never let anyone tell you ferrets are low-maintenance pets. That's simply not true. Sure, you can keep a ferret alive for many years in a small cage and feed him the basic diet. But to keep a fuzzy healthy and happy requires a great deal of care and attention. In this respect, they're a lot like human children. Without constant stimulation and positive interaction, ferrets become sluggish and depressed and fail to thrive. They may become cage-crazy and develop behavioral problems. It's your responsibility to see to it that more than just the basic needs are met.

Bringing Home the Blue Ribbon

People love to show off their fuzzies, whether they're *au naturel* or dressed up in silly little costumes. Ferret shows and fun matches do exist. They're a lot of fun, and everyone comes out a winner. Many ferret clubs sponsor holiday parties with contests and games. Many larger organizations hold fancy ferret shows — just like the dog shows, only with much more style and taste.

Do you think you have the greatest, most talented character in the world? Do you think your fuzzbutt is the epitome of beautiful? Then why not enter him in a local ferret show or ferret fun match? It's a great way to meet other fuzzy devotees and compare fuzzy notes. You can swap stupid and silly stories, most of which are related to the bodily functions of ferrets. You can also learn about new medical treatments, tips on overcoming behavioral problems, and ferret-proofing. Also, many vendors set up booths and sell ferret-related items, from food and ferret costumes to jewelry and other novelty items.

One good way to keep informed of any upcoming shows is to subscribe to a top-notch ferret magazine. In addition to giving you show listings, a magazine dedicated to ferrets and their humans is the best way for you to get fresh information on problem-solving techniques and the latest medical discoveries and procedures, and it keeps you in touch with people who are as devoted to fuzzies as you are. Two wonderful ferret magazines you may want to consider subscribing to are *Modern Ferret,* (Crunchy Concepts) and *Ferrets Magazine,* (Fancy Publications). More information on these publications can be found in Chapter 30.

Fun matches

Fun matches are a great way to have fun with ferrets and their nutty humans. A little competition is good for the soul. The contests have nothing to do with how beautiful and well behaved your ferret is. They have everything to do with creativity, personality, and skill. Sometimes it's just fuzzy luck.

The first ferret competition I ever entered was a yawning contest, and my Cookie took the prize. She yawned seven times in 60 seconds. I was so proud. Back then, you were able to scruff your ferret, which helped the yawns come on. Most contests now rely more on natural yawns. I might win that contest, but none of my current ferrets would. Other fun contests include tube racing — the first ferret out the other side wins. Sometimes you're allowed to use squeaky toys or stick your face through the exit hole to encourage your ferret through. I think my Nikki curled up and went to sleep in the tube. We had to lift the tube and slide her out. Can't win 'em all.

Other contests usually include the great paper bag escape, silly pet tricks, and, of course, the costume contest. I don't know — I could never subject my ferret to the costume humiliation. Maybe that's my own ego getting in the way. While some costumes are often adorable and very creative, many are downright embarrassing.

Can you be too careful?

In my opinion, ferret humans *do* tend to baby their ferrets a little too much. Ferrets are prone to many ailments in their short life span, but they really aren't fragile creatures when they're properly cared for. You'll hear a lot of "don't do this" and "be sure to do this" in the ferret community. Much of it is sound advice from the experiences of long-time ferret humans. Some of it is just fear-based jabber with no sound backing. Take, for example, my advocating an occasional romp in a sandbox. Many ferret owners will be appalled that I even suggest this activity since the sand can get in the eyes and nose and ears or be ingested. I'm not suggesting using sand as a bedding and subjecting his little body to it all the time, but the ferret's wild cousins frolic in sand and dirt and rocks all the time with few problems. Go figure.

Ferret shows

Some of the larger ferret societies and shelters also hold ferret shows. Rules, regulations, and standards vary from organization to organization. They can be quite competitive. If you decide to show your ferret, he or she may be competing with generations of champions bred for show by private breeders.

Depending on the type of show and who's sponsoring it, you may have many entry classes to choose from. They can be color or pattern classes, breeder classes, kit classes, and geriatric or disabled classes. The list goes on. Some shows have a class specifically for rescued or shelter fuzzies. Also, depending on the type of show you enter, points are awarded to winners just like with dog shows. To reach a certain level or tier in the show circuit, your fert must obtain a certain number of points.

Naturally, looks aren't all that matter. Personality is a plus. While points are awarded for clean ears, clean teeth, and a nice manicure, the most gorgeous, well-groomed ferret won't take home a ribbon if he bites the judge on the nose.

Chapter 11

Cleaning Time: It's Not All Ferret Fun and Games

• •

In This Chapter

▶ Cleaning up the mess

▶ Cleaning up the furball

▶ Checking the cracks and crevices

▶ Giving fuzzy a manicure

• •

*I*t would be nice to have the butler deliver our clean, happy ferrets to us on the couch and have nothing more to do with them other than the romping, playing, and cuddling part. However, most of us don't have butlers, so we must face the routine chores of keeping ferrets. I'm talking about odor control, grooming, and general sanitation stuff here.

If you're anything like I am, you'll find little more satisfying than watching your gorgeous, clean, and healthy ferrets dashing about with ferret enthusiasm and then collapsing in their unsoiled condo for a long nap. Besides giving you an opportunity to bond with your furkid and discover possible health problems, cleaning and grooming are necessary for both your and your ferret's continued happiness, as well as everyone's health.

In this chapter, I discuss things like cleaning the cage, bedding, and dishes. I provide the much-needed information on cleaning your fuzzy, too. Cheer up. Into every life a little poop must fall.

Cleaning House

When I say *house*, I mean the entire house. What good is a sparkling cage if the bedding still has poop stuck in it or the toys are crusty from heaven knows what? Sometimes people forget to do the whole overhaul. I admit it. I'm guilty at times. You and your fuzzy will be happiest when the cleaning tornado hits the entire ferret condo.

So you think you're allergic to ferrets

Human allergies are one of the most common reasons that ferrets are dumped in shelters, even though true allergies associated directly to ferrets aren't really common at all. Ferrets have even been called hypoallergenic pets. Maybe it's not your ferret you're allergic to at all. Maybe you're allergic to the ferret's kitty litter or the bedding you've chosen. Maybe you're getting sick because of another allergen that's present at the same time the ferret coincidentally arrives. The human baby's cold may have worsened since the fuzzy arrived, but chances are, it's not the ferret. It's everything else.

If you insist that you're allergic to carpet sharks, you can do some things to help ease the symptoms of the allergy or asthma. My husband and I always have an inhaler on hand because of our asthma. You can also try the following:

✔ Vacuum more frequently and use filtered vacuum bags. Don't forget to vacuum the tile, too. Sweeping just spreads the junk around. If you're really serious about attacking the problem, get rid of the carpeting altogether.

✔ Purchase a heavy-duty HEPA filter air cleaner. If necessary, purchase a couple.

✔ Treat carpets with anti-allergen sprays and shampoo them more often.

✔ Bathe your ferret more frequently.

✔ Keep your ferret out of the rooms you spend the most time in, such as bedrooms.

✔ Wash the ferret's bedding more frequently to get rid of loose fur.

✔ Wash your hands after handling your furball and don't put him or your furried hands to your face or mouth.

✔ Get those nasty allergy shots a couple times a week or take medication to stifle the allergy symptoms. This one's for the serious pet human.

Allergies don't have to shatter your relationship with your fuzzballs. They may not be the source at all. As a true fuzzy lover, you should aim for a solution before dumping the suspected culprit.

Doing dishes

I tackle food dishes and water bottles first since I think one of the most important aspects of good husbandry is providing clean, fresh food and water at all times. You should probably have extra food dishes on hand to swap with the dirty dishes that you'll be cleaning.

Since pooping and peeing are frequent activities with ferrets, you're likely to find an occasional poop in the food dish or poop smeared on the side of it. If you notice this, or an unusually dirty bowl, take it out immediately and clean it thoroughly. If you ignore it, the poop/dirt doesn't go away. Trust me. I've tried. Otherwise, regular cleanings with soap and warm water every couple days are usually sufficient.

A more effective cleaning solution is a mixture of warm water and a touch of bleach. At least once a week, clean all dishes with the bleach water solution.

Unless you have bionic eyes, you'll be unable to see all the bacteria condos going up on your ferret's dish. Come to terms with the fact that they are there and wash frequently. Your ferret will thank you.

Properly rinsing the food dish is just as important as cleaning the food dish. While a trace amount of soap won't kill your ferret, it tastes pretty bad and can cause diarrhea. In addition, the residue attracts more dirt and bacteria. Bleach, on the other hand, can cause your ferret to become very ill. Take care when washing the dishes and be sure to rinse well. As a safeguard, I wash with soap and water after using bleach. After all, can anyone be too careful when dealing with these precious furballs?

Maintenance on the bottles is simple. Soap and water are usually adequate when coupled with a gentle scrubbing with a bottlebrush. A mixture of vinegar and water or baking soda and water can also be used. The key to good husbandry, however, is to scrub the inside thoroughly to remove any particle or algae buildup. Do not neglect the tube and stainless steel balls. Keeping these things free of mineral deposits helps eliminate any leakage from the tube. Always remember to completely rinse the bottle before refilling it.

Stripping the bed

Your ferret's bedding can get pretty raunchy after a while. Because ferrets spend so much time running in and out of the litter box, chances are good that traces of poop and urine are on the towels or other bedding. Also, particles of litter and food crumbs get mixed in there as well. Your fuzzy spends much time snuggling and sleeping in this bedding, so thoroughly washing it at least once a week is important.

If you have multiple furballs, you may find it necessary to wash more frequently. I'm lazy, so I have a lot of spare bedding put aside to switch with the dirty stuff. When I get a full load of ferret laundry, I wash it all.

Doing ferret laundry is no different from doing your regular laundry. I use laundry soap and hot water. Sometimes I add a half-cup of bleach to the load. Make sure that the finished laundry doesn't have a strong bleach odor. If it does, another regular wash should fix the problem.

Another thing to consider is the health of your washing machine. I always take the bedding outside and thoroughly shake it out before throwing it in. That way, most of the loose litter and debris is discarded before the bedding is washed. Look for little poopies that might be stuck to the bedding and pick them off (real ferret people use their bare hands). You don't want that stuff being thrown into your washing machine, and bits of it will remain mixed in the load. There's nothing like wearing a "clean" shirt with a poop stain on it. Worse yet is having someone point it out to you.

Scrubbing the toilet

Litter boxes should be scooped as often as needed (see Figure 11-1). Doing so also helps reduce the number of accidents outside of the litter box because most ferrets hate to get their feet dirty — unless they're playing outside in dirt and sand. Obviously, if you have many ferrets, it doesn't take long before the poop starts to pile up. Scoop it as often as you can, refilling with litter as needed. You'll notice that the insides of the litter box start to get pretty dirty after a short while because most ferrets poop in the corners or at an edge. Some hang their butts over the side, and the poop lands on the litter box edge.

Figure 11-1:
Your ferret spends a lot of time in the bathroom, so cleaning litter boxes frequently is important.

You'll soon find out that the litter box can be a nasty undertaking. Use common sense when cleaning it. I take out all litter boxes and empty them completely at least once a week. I use a rag or dish sponge (not the one from my kitchen) and scrub the bottom and sides of the litter box. Usually, soap and water are sufficient. At least twice a month, I use bleach water. Don't forget to clean the C-clamps that hold the litter box to the cage. They can get quite nasty also.

Tearing down the house

Cleaning the entire cage itself can be the most time-consuming and tedious chore. If it's nice outside, I drag the entire cage outside and hose that sucker down with high-pressure water at least every couple of weeks. Since I can only do that seven months out of the year, the rest of the time I'm on my hands and knees reaching into the cage to get it clean.

You need to pull out any catch pans and change the newspaper or catch litter. In addition, sweep up the displaced litter and food particles from the flooring. A little hand held vacuum is perfect for this task. Spray the flooring with a safe cleaner and wipe it thoroughly, remembering to leave no residue behind. That's all the easy part.

The hard part is getting any solidified poop off the corners of the wire shelves. I actually use rubber gloves and pull it off. What doesn't come off with the initial tug is pushed off with a long metal stick (mine is actually a shish-ka-bob skewer). You can also use a scouring pad, but it can be too abrasive and wear down the paint on the wire. Once most of the poop is off, use a wet rag and thoroughly clean the areas.

If you have short arms like I do or a cage that's difficult to reach into, you may find that one or two far corners always have a small bit of poop residue. That's when hosing can be effective.

Getting the gunk off the toys

Don't neglect the fuzzy's toys; they get dragged about the litter box and buried in dirty bedding. Most cloth toys can be safely thrown in the wash with the rest of the bedding. If they're super disgusting, just toss them in the garbage and pitch in the few bucks for a brand-new toy. After all, fuzzbutts deserve new toys as often as possible.

As far as plastic toys are concerned, I simply soak them in bleach water or plain warm water until all the grime can be easily scrubbed off. The important part is always remembering to thoroughly rinse them and leave no residue. I have friends who put dirty fert toys and fert dishes in the dishwasher. Some even use the dishwasher for dirty litter boxes. Okay, this works, but I don't ever eat at their house.

People often overlook toys when cleaning the fuzzy's environment. Toys get pretty disgusting and crusty after a while. Include them in your cleaning routine. If you happen upon a toy buried beneath a pile of pooh, it's okay to pitch it and buy your ferret a new toy. Some things are just too gross to clean.

Bathing Fuzzy

You've got lots to think about when bathing a smelly little fert — from choosing the right shampoo to knowing when and where to bathe him. Not all ferrets like baths, however, so knowing what to do and what not to do can help ease the anxiety both of you may be feeling.

When it comes to official bath time, not all ferrets enjoy water like their otter cousins. Some act more like the stereotypical housecat when they get the slightest bit of water on their paws. Others take to it with Olympic-like style. Yet other ferrets merely tolerate the wet stuff. Oftentimes, a ferret's first few encounters with water determine his attitude. Whether the disdain for baths is simply personality or post-traumatic stress disorder, your job as a ferret human is to make the bathing process as pleasurable as possible for both of you. If the fuzzy looks at bath time as treat and reward time, your battle may not be as big next time.

Water anxiety, of course, magically disappears after bath time. I frequently find myself spending lots of time racing to keep the ferrets out of full coffee cups, toilets, and the dogs' water bowls. It may just be a control thing on the carpet shark's part. Who knows for sure?

One bath too many?

It's hard to believe that bathing a ferret may defeat your purpose of wanting to make the fuzzy smell fresh. But bathing strips the skin and fur of their natural oils. Then the skin works overtime producing these oils to replace what was originally washed down the drain. You may even notice initially that your ferret has a stronger smell than before the bath. Don't worry. It improves within a day or two.

While bathing is important, equally important is not washing too frequently. Excessive bathing can also lead to dry, flaky skin and coarse fur. In addition, you'll want to give the scratches on your arms ample time to heal up before bathing the furball again.

Unless your ferret gets into something really nasty, do not bathe him more than once a month. I suggest bathing only a few times a year. You need some good supplies before you begin: an appropriate shampoo, plenty of clean dry towels for both you and the ferret, and hip boots and goggles (for you).

 No matter what, only attempt to bathe one ferret at a time. I once tried six ferrets in a bathtub, and it was a personal disaster. The ferrets had a blast. I was miserable and exhausted by the time I dried off and treated my own battle wounds.

Do they make acne cream for ferrets?

Ferrets are prone to blackheads just like humans are, but they usually show up on the ferret's tail. Usually, hair loss and a reddish-brown waxy film come with blackheads. The cause is dirt and oil that are clogging their fuzzy pores. While blackheads aren't too attractive, they're nothing to worry about. Simply wash the tail every couple of days (the tail only) with a shampoo containing benzoyl peroxide or salicylic acid (you can get this from your vet). Gently scrub the tail with a washcloth and let the suds sit for a minute or two before rinsing.

Picking a shampoo

The shampoo you use on your ferret should be very gentle, like baby shampoo. Your vet may also carry some good shampoos that are great for sensitive skin. Don't use strong shampoos and regular dish soaps; they can lead to dry, itchy skin and brittle fur. Some over-the-counter pet shampoos work well, but be sure the shampoo is safe for cats. Dog shampoos can contain certain harsh chemicals that are safe for dogs but very harmful to ferrets.

Choose only shampoos that are ferret-safe. If you're unsure, stick with the stuff that's made for cats or kittens. A tearless baby shampoo also works well on ferrets. Other shampoos may contain chemicals that are harmful to your fuzzy.

If your ferret is unfortunate enough to have fleas, be sure to read the section on fleas in Chapter 15 before bathing him.

Don't neglect the fuzzy's paws during the grooming routine. Some paws can get hard and brittle, especially during the colder seasons or as the ferret ages. After a good bath and drying session, apply a little Vaseline or Vitamin E to your fuzzy's pads. It should help soften the tough spots.

Choosing the crime scene

Where's the best place to bathe your ferret? Many people look at bath time as a great opportunity for the water-loving fuzzy snorkeler to play in the bathtub and get in some quality swimming time. This is okay, but allow the free swim before the water gets all soapy and yucky. Also, many ferrets get so excited at the thought of bathing (yeah, right) that they poop in the water.

Other people choose the kitchen sink to clean their smelly ferret and prefer using the sink's pull-out hose for easy rinsing. Some even let their fuzzies into the shower with them. Unless your ferret is comfortable with this and manageable in the shower — or you shower with your clothes on — I urge you to take extra precaution in the shower. A naked human is an extra-vulnerable human.

Doing the deed

The water should be a comfortable enough temperature for a human child. Remember, the ferret's body temperature is quite a bit higher than ours (100–104 degrees Fahrenheit). What feels warm to us may be a pinch too chilly for your ferret and cause fuzzy goosebumps. Keep the water warm but always test it before wetting your ferret down; you don't want to scald the little bugger.

Fill the tub or sink with warm water, just deep enough to submerge the ferret's body but allowing his feet to touch the bottom, which gives the anxious fuzzy a little extra security. Remember, swimming is only fun if you like water. If you were one of those kids who learned how to swim by being thrown in, you know what I mean. Being unable to feel solid ground beneath your feet can be a terrifying experience.

A ferret with water-soaked fur is slightly heavier than a dry ferret, so take extra care to support the full weight of the fuzzy during and after the bath. It can be tricky lathering the rascal up while he's trying to crawl up your arm. You almost need an extra set of hands — two to hold the ferret, one to pour the shampoo, and the other to lather. It's an art that's quickly mastered by the multiferreted human.

Wax on, wax off

I start by lathering the ferret's back because it's the easiest place to pour the shampoo. I spread it evenly across all parts of his body, including the top of his head (see Figure 11-2). Be careful not to get any soap in the eyes and ears. Some shampoos sting like heck, and the ferret will be sure to hold grudge for next time. If you do get soap in the ferret's eyes, using a cupped hand, flush his face gently with water.

Keeping the soap out of the ferret's mouth can be more of a challenge. Lots of fuzzies seem to enjoy the taste of soap. While this quirk may appear disgusting to some, I must fend for the ferret by saying I also enjoyed the taste of soap when I was a child. Unlike me, though, a ferret doesn't outgrow the taste. A little bit won't hurt him, but keep him from sneaking in a lick anyway because there's nothing nutritious in soap and too much can make him ill.

If you have several ferrets to bathe, invite a few friends over for a nice lunch. Once you get them over, ask them to participate in the bathing assembly line: One helps bathe and then passes the ferret to the towel dryer, who dries while another grabs the next fuzzy for bathing. Another keeps an eye on the ferrets as they finish drying in their own creative ways. And so on. It's great fun . . . . Well, I think so, anyway.

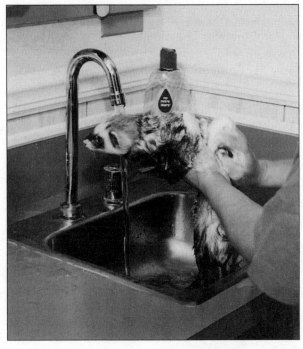

Figure 11-2:
Lather the entire body, being careful not to get soap in your ferret's eyes.

Rinsing thoroughly is as important as lathering the ferret up. Besides drying out the fur and making him itch more, any soap residue left on the fur attracts dirt and gunk, and you'll soon have a dirty ferret again. For this reason, I suggest that you drain the tub or sink and use fresh, warm water as a rinse. You can use a cup to pour the water over the ferret, or you can hold the ferret under the faucet as long as the water pressure isn't too hard. I enjoy using a hose that attaches right to the faucet. Some sinks already have hoses built in.

When you rinse, remember to make sure that you test the water temperature first. Water that's too hot scalds, and water that's too cold causes your fert to scramble for cover. Don't drown the poor bugger while rinsing, either. Don't pour water directly over his head. Use your hand to scoop water onto the ferret's head and as a sort of washcloth. Remember to rinse the hard-to-reach areas, like the armpits and throat. A well-rinsed furball is a squeaky-clean furball.

Drying out

If you think your dog makes a fuss after a bath, wait till you get a load of the ferret. Drying time is a major production, no doubt about it. This is happy, hopping, dooking time. It's a time for puffed tails and sideways sashays. The ferret's main goal now is to get as dry and as filthy as he possibly can in the shortest amount of time. This means rubbing up against anything and everything he can, from the couch cushions and the carpeting to the dust bunnies behind the sofa and that disgusting little spot that you can't reach behind the toilet.

Because you both probably went through quite a bit to get him clean, you'll want to prevent the fuzzbutt from undoing all your hard work. This means you must take it upon yourself to dry the ferret or allow him to dry himself in a clean, safe place. First things first: Towel-dry him as best you can, making sure that you're gentle yet thorough in removing as much water as possible (see Figure 11-3). Some people even use warm towels to dry the ferret. You can warm a towel in a clothes dryer or microwave. Don't burn your house down in the process and don't let the towels get too hot.

Figure 11-3:
Towel-
drying an
overly
excited
ferret
can be
challenging.

Some ferrets even allow you to use a hair dryer on them. (If you use a little round brush, you can give the fuzzy a little extra poof — just kidding.) Use the warm, not hot, setting and keep the dryer moving to be sure the warm air isn't aimed at the same part of the body for long. It can cause burns (and split ends). Also, keep the dryer at least 12 inches from the body to prevent burns.

If, after towel-drying or blow-drying, your ferret is still damp, you need to put him someplace where he can finish drying off. The best place is a warm place with no drafts. Obviously, unless his cage is clean, is filled with clean towels, and temporarily has the litter box removed, the cage is out of the question.

A great place for drying time is a bathtub filled with dry towels. Wherever you decide to let your ferret hang out to dry, keep in mind that he'll want to go to the bathroom soon after the bath, whether he did an oopsie poopsie in the bath or not. If he poops on the towels, he'll probably step in it, roll in it, and fall asleep in it. Drying time should be a supervised time. Besides, you wouldn't want to miss the drama for the world.

A bath alternative

Some ferret people claim that chinchilla dust powder is a great natural alternative to the traditional bath. Others think that the dust can be harmful, although it isn't to chinchillas. If you want to give it a try, pour some dust in a shallow pan or litter box and watch your ferrets dive in. As they roll around, the dust binds to the oils on their skin and fur, thus reducing odor. It also doesn't dry out their fur. This is a sneaky way to get them clean while they're thinking it's all fun and games.

Caring for Those Little Ears

The ferret's normal earwax is light brown or reddish brown. It's also pretty stinky, so cleaning regularly helps control odor problems. Some furballs need their ears cleaned more than once a month. Some can go for longer, and others get their ears clogged up again within a week of the last cleaning. Sometimes health, age, and season determine how much wax is produced. I use playtime as an opportunity to do a quick ear inspection. Follow your nose. What your eyes may miss, your nose may discover.

It's sometimes easy to forget about the ferret's ears, but regular cleaning can prevent many ear ailments, such as ear mites, infections, and even deafness. Dirty ears are warm and moist and attract undesirable bacteria and bugs, so this part of the grooming process shouldn't be overlooked.

Ear mites

Ear mites are characterized by a dark brown or black discharge accompanied by your ferret scratching relentlessly at his itchy, painful ears. Left untreated, ear mites can become serious enough to cause chronic ear infections or deafness. It's a pesty condition that'll bug you and you fuzzy right up the wall. Caught early, ear mites are easily treated with medication prescribed by your vet. See Chapter 15 for more information on symptoms and treating this problem.

To clean your ferret's ears, you need cotton swabs and a couple of other things before you begin:

- ✔ A good liquid ear cleanser. You can purchase this from most pet supply stores or even your vet. Make sure that the solution is safe for cats and kittens because then it'll be safe for your fuzzy, too.

- ✔ If you have a bunch of ears to clean (I currently have 46 fuzzy ears to clean), having a small dish on hand may be helpful. Pour a little ear cleaning solution into the dish so you can dip the clean end of a cotton swab into the liquid instead of fumbling around to squirt some on the tip. Some people even moisten down the tips of several swabs before they begin. If you do, place them on a clean surface to prevent them from getting dirty.

To clean the ear:

1. **Dip a clean cotton swab in the ear cleaning solution.**

2. **While your ferret's being scruffed or firmly held, hold the tip of his ear between your fingers. Using your other hand, use the moistened end of the swab to wipe the inside of the ear (see Figure 11-4).**

   Some experienced ferret humans feel comfortable scruffing the ferret with one hand and using the other to clean the ears. I prefer to have a helper hold each ferret. Besides the fact that my arms eventually begin to get sore from all the holding (especially in my multi-multi-ferret household), I like to have one hand free to hold the fuzzy's ear when I'm navigating with the cotton swab in the other hand. You should also make sure that the ferret's bottom is supported when he's being scruffed, especially if he's a big guy. If he moves too much, lessen the bottom support a little until he settles down a bit or try getting a better hold of the scruff before beginning.

   Always use the moistened end of the cotton swab first. It helps loosen and scoop up a lot of the ear gunk. Starting off with the dry tip can be too abrasive for the ferret's sensitive ears.

3. **Use a circular motion, making contact with the inner walls and crevices of the ear, to remove all the hidden gunk.**

   Never push the cotton swab into the ear canal. Doing so will hurt your ferret and possibly damage the ear canal. You can also pack the earwax deep into the ear canal, making it difficult to get out and making it hard for the ferret to hear.

   A good guide is to always make sure that you can see the tip of the swab. If you're uncomfortable doing this dirty deed, ask your vet to do it for you on your next visit.

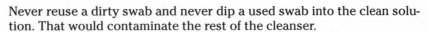

4. **Repeat with the moistened swabs until the tip comes out with little to no ick on it.**

   Some ears require a repeat of the process with two to three freshly moistened swabs.

   Never reuse a dirty swab and never dip a used swab into the clean solution. That would contaminate the rest of the cleanser.

5. **Use the dry end of the swab next and repeat the circular wiping process.**

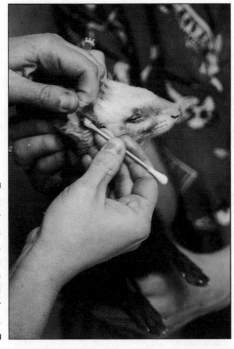

Figure 11-4: Clean your ferret's ears regularly, using a cotton swab and a good liquid ear cleanser.

Your ferret will probably squirm during the process. If you hit a particularly sensitive or itchy area, he may even jerk a leg back and forth the way a dog does when you find that perfect scratching spot. However, this isn't a feel-good reaction. Be a little gentler and pull the swab out in case you're in too deep. Don't forget a lick of Linatone when you're finished as a treat for a job well done. Make sure that your ferret gets a taste, too.

Routine ear cleaning can be tough for the beginner, so it's often a good idea to have your vet demonstrate the procedure once or twice until you feel comfortable. No matter how comfortable you become, your ferret will hate having his ears cleaned. Those cotton swabs may look tiny for our own ears, but for a fuzzy's ears, it's a pretty large wad of cotton. The key to preventing injury is gentleness. If you don't think you can handle ear cleaning, your vet will be more than happy to perform this necessary procedure for a minimal fee. No matter what, it must be done by someone.

Instead of digging out the gunk with moistened cotton swabs, you can place a few drops of ear cleanser in your ferret's ears and let it squish around for a moment or two. Your fuzzy will do half of your cleaning job by shaking out the partially dissolved wax and gunk with a violent head shake. This is another good way to clean ears, but wear goggles and keep your mouth closed.

Nailing Down the Manicure

Clipping your fuzzbutt's claws regularly helps lessen the severity of human scratches and damage from digging (see Figure 11-5). Trimming also makes the ferret more comfortable. Fuzzies need their claws for many things, from walking and balance to climbing curtains and counter cruising. Overgrown nails can hurt the ferret because long nails prevent the foot from resting flat on the ground. Trimming helps prevent the nails from splitting and getting caught on cage wires, carpeting, and even bedding.

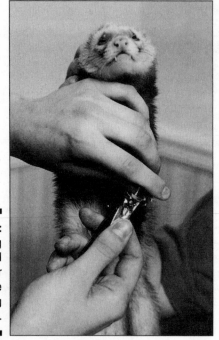

Figure 11-5: Clipping nails should be a regular part of the grooming routine.

You need to clip nails frequently because ferrets should *never* be declawed. Because the ferret's claws are nonretractable, like the claws on rabbits and dogs (cats have retractable claws), removing a ferret's nail would entail removing part of his toe, and most veterinarians find this mutilating surgery too inhumane to even perform, as do I.

The frequency of clipping claws, however, varies from ferret to ferret because nail growth rates vary. Also, the amount and type of exercise provided may wear down some nails. Strips of fine sandpaper in my ferret exercise wheel help wear down the nails on my ferrets that use it. On average, I find that I need to break out the nail trimmers at least every two to three weeks.

How you approach nail trimming depends on you and your ferret: You can use the scruff method, the distract method, or the sneak attack. The number of ferrets you have, the time available, the ferret's tolerance to nail clipping, and his distractibility are key factors in determining the method to use.

✔ Scruffing the ferret is probably the quickest way to trim nails. It steadies him, gives you a better grip, and lessens the chance of over-cutting. It's also a faster method for many people.

   If the scruffed ferret moves around a lot while he's having his nails clipped, allow him to lick Linatone while you scruff him. Just allow him to lick it from the bottle. You can clip the nails quickly and easily this way; however, this method does require two people.

✔ The distraction method can take a little more time but is a nice way for you and your ferret to spend some quality time together. The distraction method involves setting the fuzzy in your lap and placing a few drops of Linatone or Ferretone or another tasty substance on his belly. While he's busy licking it off, you dive in with the clippers and clip before he has a chance to object to what you're doing. This method doesn't work with all ferrets, but it's always worth a try. Either way, a treat should be given during or after the manicure.

✔ Another method that's worth a try is the sneak attack, which is performed while the ferret's in a deep sleep. Depending on the quality of his sleep and your talent, you may get all 20 nails clipped or just 1 or 2 before he wakes up.

Once you decide how you're going to approach nail trimming, take a good look at the ferret's nails so you know what you're dealing with. Most fuzzy nails are long, curving, and dagger-like. Some fuzzies get thicker nails as they age. The nails on the back paws are much shorter because they wear down more quickly. Those nail tips can be more difficult to clip. But unlike many dogs, whose nails are solid black, the ferret's nails are white. The *quick*, or vein, is easy to see, so you know exactly how much nail tip you can clip off.

Cutting into the pink or blood area is painful and causes the ferret to bleed and get really ticked off. Because accidents happen (either from you not paying attention or from your fuzzbutt suddenly moving), have some styptic powder on hand before beginning, to stop any bleeding that may occur. Bee's wax works just as well, but it doesn't sting like heck.

I use fingernail clippers designed for human babies. Regular size clippers work well, too. Some people like to use cat or dog nail clippers, but I find them too awkward to handle on such tiny nails. You also can't see what you're doing because of the shape of that type of clipper. Whatever clippers you find most comfortable, make sure that the blades are sharp. Dull blades can cause the nail walls to crush, leaving the edge rough. Also make sure that the lighting is adequate. Try cutting your own toenails in the dark.

To trim your ferret's nails:

1. **Take your thumb and first finger and hold the paw close to the toes with your thumb on the bottom of the paw.**

2. **Use the pressure of your thumb to spread the toes.**

   Doing so makes going from claw to claw easier.

3. **Clip as much of the white nail tip off as you can, leaving some white after the quick.**

   Even though it won't bleed, cutting too close to the quick can be painful, and your ferret will let you know. Take extra care with the back nails. Some have teeny-weeny little nail tips. Look closely before clipping them. If the tips are too short to clip, try filing them with a nail file, being careful not to scrape the fuzzy's sensitive paw pads.

If you accidentally clip a nail too short, apply the styptic powder or another blood stopper directly to the tip of the bleeding nail. If such a product isn't available, try dipping the bleeding nail into a bar of white soap, bee's wax, or flour. You can also try running cold water over it. And I suggest postponing the rest of the manicure until after your ferret has forgiven your dreadful deed.

If you let your ferret's nails grow for a long time in between cuttings, the quick will grow longer and longer into the nail, allowing you to cut less and less of the nail off. This isn't a good thing. Cutting frequently causes the quick to regress back toward the paw so that you can cut a good amount of the nail off.

If you can't manage to nail down the art of nail trimming, your vet will be more than happy to assist you for a minimal fee.

Chomper Maintenance

Most people neglect their pets' teeth, and the ferret is no exception. As a routine part of your ferret's grooming process, you should check out his teeth and gums regularly. A high-quality dry ferret or cat food, or a balanced alternative diet, helps keep your ferret's teeth in good shape, but as with all animals, tartar eventually begins to build up. In addition, teeth can go bad and/or chip, leading to abscesses that can seriously affect his health. Aging ferrets have more dental problems than younger ones. It's up to you to sink your teeth into this chore. Your fuzzy's health and happiness depend on it.

All children resist brushing their teeth in the beginning. A fuzzy isn't different. Most ferrets get used to having their teeth cleaned if you do so regularly and gently. This is an important part of ferret care that you don't want to neglect.

The dental checkup

The checking part is usually easy but can be quite a challenge with more difficult patients. Most of my carpet sharks sit in my lap with minimal fidgeting and allow me to lift their gums for a peek while I steady them gently with the other hand. Others need to be scruffed gently while I perform the dental inspection. I always like to use an extra pair of hands so that I can concentrate on my findings. No matter how you do it, be gentle. Ferrets don't understand why we're poking around in their mouths, so take that into consideration.

You have several things to look for when doing the checkup. First, take a peek at all the teeth. The grayish or greenish discoloration you may see is tartar. Buildup begins on the back teeth and works its way up to the canines over time. The buildup increases as ferrets age. A small amount is expected and not necessarily a cause for concern. However, it can be your ferret's enemy if not kept in check.

Tartar can lead to tooth decay, which is characterized by an icky brown buildup on the tooth close to the gum line. Decaying teeth can be painful, lead to serious infection, and cause the ferret to stop eating. Removal of the tooth by a veterinarian is usually recommended at this point.

Next, take a look at the gums. They should be smooth, moist, and pink. If they are very light in color (whitish/grayish), your ferret may be seriously ill, and a visit to the vet is a must. If you dare, stick your nose up to his mouth and take a whiff. Gum problems and ulcers result in a case of bad breath. Red, inflamed gums are a sign of gum disease and should be treated immediately by a vet. If you notice isolated swelling over one or two teeth, you can suspect a tooth abscess.

Ferret teeth versus rabbit teeth

Ferrets are not rabbits or rodents that may require an occasional tooth trim. In the case of rodents, it can be a medical necessity to cut overgrown teeth so that the proper chewing/eating function can be maintained. Ferrets have teeth like humans. Cutting them is a painful procedure and may lead to exposed canals and serious infections. Trimming or cutting a fert's sharp canine teeth to minimize the damage reaped from biting will only cause damage to his teeth. Therefore, unless your vet thinks there's a medical need, don't cut, file, or pull your ferret's teeth.

Ulcers on the gums or the inside of the lip flap are a common sign of the disease *insulinoma*. These ulcers are usually whitish in color, and sometimes they ooze. Sometimes a ferret points out these ulcers or dental problems by pawing at his mouth. Other signs may include drooling and a crusty bib. While insulinoma is not a dental problem, it's something to keep an eye out for as long as you have your eye in there. (For information on insulinoma, see Chapter 17.)

With the exception of small traces of tartar buildup, if you see something out of the ordinary in your furball's mouth, contact your vet and schedule a visit. Dental problems can be serious enough to cause death. Problems not related to dental hygiene but located in the mouth are almost always signs of an underlying illness. Regardless of whether you have a dental emergency, your vet should perform yearly dental exams and remove any excess tartar or decaying teeth.

 Sometimes it can be challenging for you to get more than a sneak preview in your ferret's mouth. But a full viewing is frequently needed. A popsicle stick, wooden chopstick, or even a piece of fluffed gauze can be gently sneaked across the back of the ferret's mouth during a fuzzy yawn. It helps keep the mouth wedged open while you do a thorough exam. Remember to be gentle and give your fuzzy extra treats for being such a good sport.

Brushing their teeth

After you do an exam and figure that everything is okay, what can you do to help prevent any future dental problems? First of all, unless medically necessary, keep your ferret on dry food or a varied alternative diet. Additionally, you can make cleaning the ferret's teeth a regular part of your routine. Invest in a cat toothbrush (don't use your spouse's) or use a piece of gauze and wrap it around your finger (which serves as your makeshift toothbrush).

Many ferrets get used to the unnatural practice of having their teeth brushed, especially if you do it often and make it worthwhile by offering a drop or two of Linatone on the gauze or toothbrush. There are toothpastes designed for use on cats, but I find that most ferrets find the taste equally disagreeable. The toothpastes may be worth a try, though.

Never use human toothpaste on your ferret. The ingredients in human toothpaste are thought to be poisonous to fuzzies, and ferrets don't know the meaning of "rinse and spit."

To brush your ferret's teeth:

1. **Lift the gum and gently wipe the teeth with the dry gauze or toothbrush.**

2. **Gently go over the gums, too.**

3. **Pay particular attention to the gum line (where the teeth disappear into the gum).**

Patience and gentleness are the keys to successfully brushing your ferret's teeth. After all, you're not sanding down old paint.

The rough pattern of the gauze is usually enough to wipe off the surface gunk. You can use your fingernails to pick some of the hardened tartar off. If you're queasy about messing with your ferret's teeth, and he gets his needed regular checkups, dirty teeth can always wait until the next visit. You'll never be able to top a veterinarian's professional cleaning, but it's necessary that you perform the critical dental checkup at least every two to three weeks. And never forget the treat afterward. That would be almost as negligent as not performing the checkup itself.

Breaking Out the Hairbrush

Ferrets go through two seasonal coat sheds, at which time they lose a great deal of fur. The sheds happens during the spring and fall months. Some people choose to brush their fuzzies as they would a dog or cat. Brushing does have some advantages. Besides helping to keep your ferret's coat clean and free of debris, it also removes loose fur — an especially important thing since fuzzies are prone to hairballs, and hairballs can be fatal.

Giving your ferret a hairball preventive several times a week is a good practice. Even if you're a little lax on giving this preventative to your ferrets, be sure to change your habits during the shedding seasons, when ferrets are more prone to hairballs. (For information on hairballs and how to prevent them, see Chapter 16.)

If you decide to brush your fuzzbutt, stick with a soft brush designed for kittens or rabbits or other small mammals. They are generally shorter bristled and just hard enough to remove loose fur, but gentle enough to not irritate sensitive skin. Stroke the brush in the same direction as the fur. I've found that most furkids don't want to remain motionless for very long, and brushing can be a small adventure. A few ferrets, however, enjoy this part of the grooming process and come to look forward to it.

Chapter 12

Traveling (or Not) with Your Ferret

- -

In This Chapter

▶ Taking your fuzzy on vacation

▶ The do's and don'ts of traveling with furballs

▶ Alternatives to taking him with you

- -

Some people think a vacation is time away from the kids and pets. Others wouldn't dare leave their ferrets behind. For me, however, lugging 23 fuzzbutts to my dream destination just doesn't seem feasible or relaxing. It's difficult enough taking a spouse along for the trip. (Of course, you can always decide to leave the spouse behind and take off with the fuzzies.)

This chapter deals specifically with the sensitive subject of traveling with your ferrets or leaving them behind in someone else's care. You should take certain things into consideration when doing either of these things. Much of it depends on where you're going and for how long.

Fuzzy's Going on Vacation

If you decide that your fuzzy deserves a vacation too, or you just can't bear to leave him behind, you need to do some pretrip investigating as well as preparations. Depending on how you're traveling and where you're traveling to, taking your ferret may be a (somewhat) simple task or it may be a major ordeal. No matter what, the health and safety of your ferret should be your utmost concern.

No matter where you go or how you get there, your vacation should be as relaxing as possible. That's true for your fuzzy as well. This means giving him ample playtime and attention as usual — if not more. It also means a comfortable cage to live in while away from home. Don't keep him in a tiny carrier. After all, if it isn't going to be a vacation for your ferret too, then leave him at home where he'll at least be in familiar surroundings.

Checking ahead

If you're staying in a hotel, make sure that your fuzzy's welcome *before* you get there. Sneaking a ferret into a ferret-free hotel may mean an extra financial charge for you or being booted out with nowhere to go. Be smart. Likewise, don't show up on your Aunt Mary's doorstep with ferrets in hand without getting permission first. A call from the car phone a mile from her house is not what I have in mind, either. Being considerate of other people helps ensure that your ferret is treated well on his vacation.

If you're staying at a hotel that does allow ferrets (and other pets, for that matter), you may be required to pay a little extra for the room or put down a refundable deposit to cover possible damage.

Many people forget that their beloved fuzzies aren't currently welcome in all cities and states. If your destination is a ferret-free zone (see Chapter 3 for info on these places), leave the fuzzy behind for his own well being. If you're only passing through a ferret-free zone to get to your destination, consider what would happen if you were pulled over for a traffic violation or were in a car accident or if your ferret suddenly required medical treatment. The penalty could vary from a simple warning to the confiscation of your beloved pet. While the odds of being discovered on a simple journey through the ferret-free zone are remote, some people check the ferret laws of the towns they pass through just to be sure. It's up to you to chance it or drive a different route. In either case, keep a health certificate and proof of rabies vaccination on hand.

Packing the necessities

Traveling with a ferret is relatively easy as long as you pack the necessary items to make his journey comfortable. Wherever you're traveling, whether you're going across the state line or heading to the other side of the country, you need these basic things:

- ✔ Your ferret's first-aid kit (see Chapter 13 for a list of what should go in this kit). Be sure to include an appropriate supply of medication that your fert may need.

- ✔ Proof of current rabies vaccination and a current health certificate issued by your veterinarian.

- ✔ A lasting supply of ferret food and a water bottle.

- ✔ A pet carrier or travel cage to keep your ferret safe. The bigger, the better — especially if it's a looooong trip. (*Note:* If you travel with a small carrier, bring along a decent-sized cage for the duration of the vacation. Don't keep your ferret cooped up.)

  ✔ A harness and leash.

  ✔ A litter box and litter.

  ✔ Fluffy, snoozy bedding (don't forget to pack a change of bedding, too) and toys, toys, toys.

Road trip!

To prevent accidents or injuries, keep your ferret in the carrier or cage when you're driving (see Figure 12-1). Make frequent rest stops. During rest stops, you should take the time to dress your fuzzy for a walk and allow him to do a little sight-seeing with you safely in tow. Resist the urge to let strangers handle your already stressed-out and excited fuzzy during stops. Stress is one of the conditions that can lead to unpredictable fuzzy behavior.

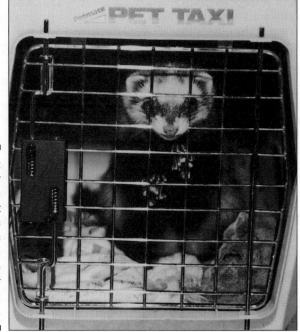

Figure 12-1:
No matter how much your ferret protests, his antics should be confined to a pet carrier during road trips.

Frequent stops are also good times to offer water to your ferret. While he should have plenty of food in his carrier during the road trip, the water bottle should be removed while you're driving because it will continually leak from the jostling.

If you're crazy enough to make a long, hot, summer road trip in a car without air conditioning, bring along a cooler with several 2-liter plastic bottles of frozen water. Always keep one wrapped in a towel and in your pet's travel carrier to help keep him cool.

Following are some No No's for road trips:

- Don't leave your ferret in the car unattended when the temperature is extremely warm or cold. And don't leave him in the car overnight while you snooze comfortably in a stopover motel.

- Don't pack your ferret in the trunk of the car. Besides being cruel, the temperature is unstable and carbon monoxide can kill him. Similarly, don't fasten your caged ferret with the rest of your luggage on top of your vehicle. You'd think common sense would prevail here . . . .

- Don't travel with very sick, old, or pregnant ferrets. The stress of traveling may jeopardize the already stressed fuzzy's health.

- Don't take your ferret camping. While the playtime may be new and interesting, you know darn well that he'll spend most of the time unattended in a cage. Also, a ferret inside or outside of a tent may attract other predators who may end up eating both you and the ferret.

Ferrets are master escape artists. Take into consideration that your ferret may be able to get out of his cage or carrier in the car. Or a child or spouse may let the ferret out without anyone knowing. This is particularly scary if you drive with windows down. And before slamming that car door shut, be sure your ferret is safe in his carrier where he belongs. In a car door versus ferret situation, the car door always wins.

Remember that traveling, even comfortably, is very stressful on your fuzzy. As a responsible fuzzy human, you must see to it that your ferret's needs are met at all times while he's away from his familiar home. Provide lots of favorite toys to keep him amused and preoccupied when he's not sleeping. As an extra bonus for keeping him busy, he won't be dooking, "Are we there yet? Are we there yet?"

Taking to the friendly skies

Some extra requirements and considerations go along with traveling by air. In addition to packing the first-aid kit, medications, toys, harness, leash, and extra bedding in your suitcase (see the section "Packing the necessities"), you need to do some preflight tasks. First, check with the airline to find out about any specific rules and regulations regarding traveling with pets. While each airline has its own set of rules about flying with pets, here are some typical requirements (be sure to follow all rules, including any that I may not cover here):

✔ A prior reservation must be made for your pet. Be sure to confirm the arrangement a couple of days before takeoff. (*Note:* There is an additional charge for in-cabin travel — that is, under-the-seat method — as opposed to cargo.)

✔ A health certificate must be issued by a veterinarian no more than ten days before takeoff, indicating that the ferret is current on vaccinations and is healthy and fit for travel. (Keep proof of current rabies vaccination on hand.)

✔ The pet must be in an airline-approved carrier. If traveling in-cabin, the carrier must be small enough to fit beneath the seat. Also, the pet must remain in the carrier while on board.

✔ Some food should be available to the pet during flight, and the carrier must contain comfortable bedding — fuzzy snoozy stuff.

For health reasons, USDA regulations stipulate that airlines cannot transport most animals via cargo during extreme hot or cold conditions. If you must transport this way, be sure to take temperature into consideration. Also, most airlines have guidelines to make sure that your pet's carrier is properly labeled for identification. At minimum, do the following:

✔ Attach a label that clearly provides your name, address, and phone number, along with the same information for an alternate contact from home.

✔ Have a carrier label that states "LIVE ANIMALS" with an up arrow for the directionally challenged cargo handlers.

✔ Include information about the pet's final destination, such as city/state, hotel name, and phone number, in case you need to be contacted about your lost pet.

✔ Because ferts are the Houdinis of the animal world, consider adding an ID tag to the fert's harness and leaving it on him while he's traveling. If he does escape, an ID increases the odds of a safe return.

When you're traveling with more than one small pet, some airlines (not all) require that the pets travel in separate carriers. Three ferts may mean three carriers, which means more money for traveling. Also, in-cabin traveling isn't possible with three carriers, unless you have two other family members traveling. If you must fly your pets via cargo, check with different airlines to see whether you can check your ferrets in at the ticket counter or have to make an additional stop at the cargo terminal. Try to choose an airline that allows checking pets in at the ticket counter. Doing so decreases the odds of the ferrets being sent on a different flight.

Always book nonstop flights whenever possible, especially if your ferret isn't traveling in-cabin with you. A change of planes is an added stress, and you run the risk of having your ferret get lost in the shuffle between flights. Nonstop flights are also shorter, thus minimizing the length of an already wearisome situation. If your fuzzy will be changing planes, find out what precautions are taken by the airlines to ensure a safe and timely transfer of your pet.

Going via cargo

Even though many airline cargo handlers are only minimally trained in animal transportation, I've had many animals shipped *to* me with only three bad incidences. Each time, the animals being shipped were not put on a nonstop flight, and the cargo handlers failed to get them on the connecting flight. These mishaps are probably infrequent, but I have heard of pet deaths occurring from being left in extreme cold or heat by careless cargo handlers. One death I know of personally was attributed to the carrier being hit by a luggage truck. Also consider what would happen if your fuzzy was temporarily lost and couldn't be given his daily medication if necessary. Even though my airline experiences have been for the most part very positive, I advise pet owners to always try to take their pets in the cabin whenever possible.

Going international

Traveling abroad with pets, whether moving permanently or vacationing, can go quite smoothly if you follow the guidelines of the airline (see the preceding section) and destination country. In addition to the airline regulations, there are additional things to research:

- ✔ Does the destination country have a quarantine requirement?
- ✔ Does the health certificate need to be translated into the appropriate language?
- ✔ Does the destination country require that you obtain an import license?
- ✔ Does the paperwork need to be mailed or faxed prior to you leaving the country? (Always keep copies on you.)
- ✔ What's required to get through customs? Usually, the proper documents get you right through.

Most international flights have layovers before continuing on to the planned destination. Almost all airlines allow you to visit your pet during layovers if prior arrangements have been made. During this time, you can check on how the fuzzy is doing and give him water, food, or medication if it's required.

Ferrets should not be given sedatives or tranquilizers of any sort while traveling. If you think your ferret *must* have one, either leave him at home or take a sedative yourself and continue on with your travel plans.

Unless you're traveling abroad for a very long period of time, I suggest you leave fuzzy at home. I've heard of many international trips that went smoothly but also of several that were a nightmare for everyone involved.

Leaving Your Fuzzy in Good Hands

Aaaaah, now this is a vacation. As much as I love fuzzies, I just have to get away from time to time with no one to take care of but myself for a change. Don't get me wrong — I always buckle with anxiety over finding the right person to watch my babies or the right place to take them to. And, of course, while I'm supposed to be relaxing on vacation, I'm wondering how all the kids are managing without me. Usually, when I get home, I must face the reality that there are people out there who can play Fuzzy Mom just as well as I do. It's quite an ego smasher.

No matter who takes care of your ferrets while you're gone, make sure that you've educated him or her on ferret basics. Give your fuzzy sitter a good book on the subject — this book, for instance — to help the sitter along with his or her education. Also provide at least the following:

- ✔ The phone number where you can be reached and the name of the people you're staying with.

- ✔ An emergency phone number (or two) of someone close to home, such as a friend or relative.

- ✔ Your veterinarian's phone number and address, as well as the emergency clinic's phone number and address.

- ✔ An adequate supply of any necessary medication, as well as exact instructions on how to medicate your ferret. If you can, demonstrate the procedure (especially dosing) before you leave.

- ✔ A written description of each ferret and each ferret's personality (attach a photo next to each description to be extra helpful), and include do's and don'ts if necessary.

- ✔ An adequate supply of food and precise written and demonstrated instructions on feeding, especially if a varied diet is used or you have a ferret that requires assisted feedings.

- ✔ In addition to the basic information, provide detailed instructions on how to clean up after your ferts, supervise safe playtime, and watch for signs of illness or injury.

The perfect pet sitter

Many people laugh at the idea of paying a stranger to come to the home to visit with and care for pets while they're away. But more and more people choose this option as reliable pet sitters gain experience and good reputations. Often, pet sitters come highly recommended by previous clients, veterinarians, friends, or neighbors. And pet sitters aren't just for vacationers anymore. Many people who work long hours choose pet sitters to assist in the routine care of their pets.

Many pet sitters are more familiar with dogs, cats, and birds. It's up to you in some cases to educate the pet sitter on how to properly care for fuzzies. A good pet sitter will be willing to stop over once or twice to get acquainted with the fuzzbutts and the routine prior to your "abandoning" them.

If at all possible, pick a pet sitter who comes highly recommended by someone you trust. Request and carefully check out the sitter's references. This person will have a key to your house and access to your belongings, not to mention the fact that this person will be entrusted with the complete care of your fuzzies. Trustworthiness, reliability, and honesty are all musts. Find out if the pet sitter also has a reliable and trustworthy backup in case of an unforeseen emergency, such as an accident or sudden illness.

The National Association of Professional Pet Sitters is an organization dedicated to promoting high standards for pet sitters nationwide. For a pet sitter referral, call 1-800-296-PETS. If you'd like more information about the organization itself and its goals, you can contact the organization as follows:

> National Association of Professional Pet Sitters
> 1030 15th St., NW, Suite 870
> Washington, DC 20005
> Phone: (202) 393-3317
> Fax: (202) 393-0336
> Web site: www.petsitters.org

Depending on how much money you're willing to spend, a pet sitter can make a daily visit or stop by several times throughout the day. The sitter may clean daily or every other day or however often you request. The arrangements are usually based on a fee schedule. Discuss your options with the pet sitter before you leave; also get everything in writing.

Another possible pet sitter can be a trusted neighbor or friend. I know with all the animals at my home/shelter, it takes several people to come in on a daily basis to help with their upkeep when I go away. I feel like I'm leaving a 100-page manual behind. But I always feel better knowing the people in my home.

A paid pet sitter will usually do a good job because his or her reputation relies on it. A friend will usually do a good job because a friendship depends on it. On the other hand, having friends watch your pets can be tricky and awkward if you're not happy with the job they did. Every situation is different. Go with what makes you feel most comfortable and works best for your ferret.

Going away to camp: Boarding your ferret

If you can't find a reliable person to care for your fuzzy in your own home, boarding him while you're away will be necessary. You have several options:

- Some veterinarians board pets for a fee.

- Some ferret shelters will watch ferrets temporarily for a fee if you promise to pick them back up within a designated period of time.

- A friend may agree to having a fuzzy houseguest temporarily.

- Some professional boarding facilities board animals other than dogs and cats.

Again, if you choose an unfamiliar person or place to watch your fuzzy, get references and check everything out. Visit the home, shelter, vet clinic, or boarding facility to evaluate its overall condition. Don't leave your ferret there unless you're completely comfortable.

In addition to having to provide emergency numbers, explicit instructions, ferret education, and such, you may face a few more hurdles if you board your ferret while you're gone:

- You may have to transport the ferret's condo to the facility.

- You may be required to provide proof of current vaccinations or a health certificate. (Actually, if this isn't required by a boarding facility, I'd avoid that facility altogether. If the facility doesn't ask you for proof of your pet's health, it probably doesn't ask other boarders for proof, either.)

- Many facilities are not properly prepared to allow your ferret his daily freedom and exercise. Same goes for the homes of friends, unless you've taken the time to educate them on ferret-proofing and they're willing to go that extra mile while you're away.

When sending your ferret to a boarding facility, shelter, or animal clinic while you're away, you run the risk of your fuzzy catching a disease or an illness from another animal. A friend's home isn't always safe either, especially if the home contains other ferrets or animals. Make sure that your ferret is always up to date on shots.

Whenever you leave your ferret in the hands of other caretakers, risk is involved. Nothing is foolproof. All you can really do is prepare your ferret's temporary caretaker as best you can and hope for the best. The more you educate, the better off everyone will be. More often than not, you'll arrive home to a happy, healthy ferret who's just darn glad to see you.

Part IV
Health Issues, Concerns, and Treatments

The 5th Wave   By Rich Tennant

"Let me guess—the vet's analysis of the ferret's fleas showed them to be of the 100 percent fresh ground Colombian decaf variety."

In this part . . .

*I*t's important that you prepare ahead of time for minor catastrophes by having the best vet picked out and your first-aid kit stocked because every pet owner will face an emergency at one time or another. Nevertheless, this part is not meant to take the place of a veterinarian! It merely helps guide you through administering basic first aid until your ferret can be taken to the vet. In addition, it covers the more common diseases and illnesses our ferrets face — what to look for and when you need to seek expert advice.

This part also takes an in-depth look at knowing when to say good-bye to your ferret and what sort of things to expect after he's gone. There's so much more to think about than you might realize.

Chapter 13

Vets and First-Aid Kits: The Basics

In This Chapter
▶ Finding a good ferret vet
▶ What to expect during routine checkups
▶ Doing preventive maintenance
▶ Preparing for emergencies

*I*t's inevitable. You'll go through all the trouble to safeguard your ferret, and something's bound to happen anyway. Sometimes the mishap is preventable; other times it's not. Often, what has you running for the first-aid kit is an illness or an age-related problem. The bottom line is that if the situation is something you can learn from, please do so you can prevent the episode from happening again.

In any case, there are certain things you need to know and have on hand at all times for those "just in case" situations. That's what this chapter is about. After all, it's better to have an unopened bottle of hydrogen peroxide sit for ages in the medicine cabinet than to get caught in a situation where you desperately need it but don't have it. And finding a good ferret vet at the very last, desperate moment can be difficult — if not life threatening. Even if you're not facing an emergency, your ferret still needs routine checkups and vaccinations to ensure good health.

Selecting Your Ferret's Veterinarian

At some point in time, all responsible pet owners venture into a veterinarian's office, whether for routine care or an unforeseen emergency. Knowing what to look for is important when you're searching for your ferret's doctor (see Figure 13-1).

Figure 13-1:
A good
veterinarian
is essential
to your
ferret's
health and
well being.

The most fancy, expensive veterinarian facility is not always the best veterinarian facility. The modest, single-doctor practice around the corner may be the best veterinarian for your ferret. Don't judge on looks alone. Go by reputation, recommendation, and your gut feeling. Swing by for a visit before entrusting your pet to a particular vet or clinic. Your veterinarian can and should be your friend in the office.

Vet schools and ferret doctors

The few veterinary schools that exist in the United States have very few or no courses at all relating to the treatment of ferrets. Students are usually offered only brief overviews of what is considered nontraditional medicine, and the ferret is too often left by the wayside. Good ferret veterinarians learn what they know by attending continuing education lectures and conferences, talking with other ferret vets, and researching, researching, researching — because they like fuzzbutts.

The fact that a certain veterinarian may know little about the care of ferrets may say nothing at all about his or her talent for treating more common pets, such as dogs and cats. Usually, it only means the vet has had little exposure to these wonderful animals.

Ask questions

In your search for a vet, don't be afraid to ask questions. In fact, insist on quizzing the candidate. Begin by asking if the doctor even treats ferrets. Some do not and will refer you elsewhere. A good, professional veterinarian and staff will recognize your valid concerns and won't hesitate to answer your questions as completely as possible. Once you find a candidate, do a little more investigation:

- Ask how long the doctor has been practicing ferret medicine and ask how many ferrets are encountered in a typical day or week.

- Ask if the facility stocks vaccinations for ferrets, such as the approved Imrab rabies vaccine and Fervac for canine distemper.

- Make sure that the facility is capable of properly housing ferrets that may need to be hospitalized.

- Ask about fees for routine care, such as checkups and vaccinations. Does the veterinarian perform routine surgeries (such as spaying and neutering) on ferrets? Can the vet handle and treat common diseases of the ferret?

- Inquire if the vet is experienced at the more difficult surgeries such as splenectomies, adrenal surgery, or other tumor removals.

- How does the vet stay up to date on the latest developments in ferret medicine and surgical techniques?

The answers, and the general tone of the answerer, should give you a sense of whether or not this person is a ferret-friendly veterinarian. Do you feel comfortable with this doctor? If you don't, chances are your ferret won't either.

Word of mouth is another wonderful way to find a good ferret vet. Talk to other ferret owners. Ask where they take their babies and what kind of care is received. Call your local ferret shelter to see who it recommends. With so many ferret-crazed people out there today, you're bound to find a good veterinarian.

Go for a visit

Once you've chosen your vet, pay the doctor a visit. If you already have your fuzzy, he's probably due for a checkup anyway. First appearances are usually a good indication of how the practice is run. Is it clean? Does it smell clean? Are you greeted in a friendly manner by the staff? Are the exam tables sanitized after each use? Do technicians and vets wash their hands after handling animals?

See if this doctor is all he or she appeared to be on the phone or as described by other clients. Does the vet talk to your ferret in a calming way? Does the vet handle the ferret with loving care and show genuine concern for both you and your pet? Does the doctor explain what's being done in a concise and clear manner? Are your questions answered in an understandable fashion? Does the vet seem rushed and preoccupied with other goings-on in the clinic, or is he or she focused on your pet?

It's equally important that your new veterinarian listen to and acknowledge your concerns. You are the ferret's mom or dad. If you've had him long enough, you know what's normal for your ferret. A vet who is unwilling to listen to you and learn from you may also be too presumptuous to give your ferret the care that may ultimately save his life.

A good vet will also refer you to a more experienced vet if he feels it necessary in certain circumstances. Remember that no veterinarian is perfect. But one who is willing to recognize his or her limitations and seek out someone with more knowledge for the sake of your pet is usually a keeper.

Vaccinations and Checkups: What to Expect

I'm one of those fanatical people who thinks that no matter where or when you get a new pet, a visit to the vet within a day or two of his homecoming is a must. I'm also an advocate of regular vaccinations. This section covers what you can expect for your little fuzzy (you can find information on the unexpected in Chapter 14).

Kits

Baby ferrets receive some protective antibodies from the mom. These eventually start to wear away in stages as the kit ages, so you must vaccinate them to counteract this gradual loss of protection. Most farm-raised babies receive their first ferret-approved canine distemper shot (Fervac or Galaxy) at 4 weeks old. Private breeders usually give the first canine distemper shot at 6 to 8 weeks.

Distemper vaccine

Depending on your veterinarian, your ferret kit may be vaccinated for canine distemper according to vaccine protocol (United Vaccine) at 8, 11, and 14 weeks of age. Other vets prefer to vaccinate for canine distemper at 8, 12, and 16 weeks of age. Ferrets over 16 weeks of age with *unknown* or *no* vaccination history only need two distemper shots, three to four weeks apart. At this age, they'll receive the same protection as the kits that receive the full series of distemper vaccinations.

Although uncommon, some ferrets have allergic reactions to the distemper booster (see the section "Recognizing allergic reactions" for the signs). The allergic reaction may happen only once, or it may happen repeatedly. Some reactions can be life threatening. If your ferret has a history of allergic reactions, your vet may pretreat him with an antihistamine before the vaccination to offset any reaction. I know a couple of fuzzies that still have bad reactions to the vaccine despite pretreatment. If your ferret has a history of severe life-threatening allergic reactions to the distemper vaccine *and* he is strictly an indoor pet with no other contact with strange ferrets, you may want to consider skipping the distemper vaccine. (Do *not* skip the rabies booster for any reason.)

Rabies vaccine

The ferret-approved rabies vaccine (Imrab 3) is labeled for use after the age of 12 weeks old. Some vets wait until the ferret is 14 to 18 weeks old in case the ferret's birthday is recorded incorrectly somewhere along the way.

The timing of the rabies shot can be an issue for you, your vet, and your ferret! Many experts believe that the rabies and distemper shots should be given at least two weeks apart to prevent any potential allergic reactions. Keep that in mind when scheduling your ferret's vaccinations.

Other stuff

The vet should also test your kit for internal parasites, so remember to bring in a poop sample on your first visit. This sample also gives your vet an idea on how your ferret's digestive tract is doing. An overall checkup should, at the very least, include weighing, listening to the heart and lungs, checking for fleas or other external parasites, and checking eyes, ears, and teeth.

Adolescents and adults

If you get an adult with a questionable background, vaccinate him just in case. While you won't need to make the four to five trips to the vet like you would with a kit, you will need to make at least two. Your new fert should receive a canine distemper shot along with his initial physical. Don't forget a morsel of poop to make your vet's day and rule out parasites.

Bring the ferret back in about three weeks for a second distemper shot as well as a rabies shot (assuming he's over 3 months old). Often a vet will have you come in a third time for the rabies shot instead of giving it along with the final distemper shot. Many experts believe that doing so minimizes the chance of a bad reaction. Discuss this important option with your vet.

In addition to doing a regular exam like a ferret kit would receive, your vet should also do some extra palpating (touchy-feely stuff) to rule out enlarged organs, particularly the spleen, or suspicious lumps. If you know your ferret is an oldie (5+ years old), yearly blood work along with the annual booster shots is a great idea. Catching and controlling illness early can prolong your furball's life and possibly minimize suffering.

You'll also want to broach the topic of the dreaded heartworm disease. If you're a responsible dog owner, you should already know about it. Just like dogs and cats, ferrets are susceptible to this mosquito-delivered disease. Don't forget that even if you don't take your ferret outside, mosquitoes can get into your house. For information on heartworm — getting it, recognizing its symptoms, and treating it — head to Chapter 15.

Recognizing allergic reactions

Sometimes a ferret has a reaction to a vaccination. This allergic reaction, called *anaphylaxis,* almost always occurs within 30 minutes of the vaccination injection. Anaphylaxis is not very common but can present itself as either a slight reaction or, at worst, a life-threatening one.

Here are the signs of an allergic reaction:

- ✔ Swelling around the eyes or nose (a tiny lump where the needle went in is not a reaction; a tiny lump is very common)
- ✔ Vomiting
- ✔ Diarrhea
- ✔ Seizures
- ✔ Lethargy (usually, another sign should accompany the lethargy because a trip to the vet can be exhausting for all involved anyway)

The first 24 hours after the vaccination is the most crucial period. After that, your baby should be in the clear.

It's not unusual for a ferret's owner to wait around the clinic during the immediate waiting period (the first 30 minutes after the vaccine) just to be safe. In fact, I recommend that you *do* remain close to the vet clinic after the vaccination because it's important to immediately treat a fuzzy suffering from anaphylaxis. If you're already home when you notice the signs, pack right up and head back to the vet. Keep the ferret warm (he may be experiencing the beginning signs of shock).

Your vet will most likely treat your fuzzy with an injection of an antihistamine and/or cortisone. (**Note:** Some vets like to pretreat a ferret with a history of vaccination allergy with an antihistamine and/or cortisone just to be on the safe side.) Sometimes fluids will also be administered. This course of action treats the allergic reaction *and* heads off shock, which can be deadlier to your ferret than the allergic reaction itself.

Does injection location matter?

Some ferret experts believe that the place of injection may reduce or increase the chances of an adverse reaction to the distemper shot. They further suggest that most reactions occur when the injection site is on the ferret's neck or shoulder, as opposed to the flank (hip or leg). My personal vet always administers distemper vaccinations on the ferret's flank, and my fuzzies have never (knock on wood) encountered an adverse reaction. Always wait at the vet's office for at least 30 minutes after the vaccination before heading home, just to be safe.

A ferret that exhibits signs of vaccination allergy may not have a reaction to every single shot. Likewise, just because your ferret has never shown signs of anaphylaxis doesn't mean he never will.

Your Ferret First-Aid Kit

Your household should be equipped with a first-aid kit whether you own ferrets or not. A lot of what you might put in your own first-aid kit is also useful for the ferrets, but I recommend that you put together and keep one aside strictly for the ferts.

Always consult your vet before using any over-the-counter product, medication, or supplement with your ferret. Using some common items in your ferret's first-aid kit may actually aggravate certain illnesses or diseases. Also, you'll need to get the proper dosage amount from your vet. It's easy to overdose a ferret on medication.

Your ferret's first-aid kit should include the following items (if you use something, be sure to replace it as soon as possible):

Emergency phone numbers:

- ✔ Your veterinarian's number
- ✔ The number to a 24-hour emergency clinic
- ✔ The number for the National Animal Poison Control Center

  To reach the National Animal Poison Control Center, you can call 800-548-2423; this service costs $30 per case — credit cards only. Or you can dial 900-680-0000; this service costs $20 for the first 5 minutes and $2.95 for each additional minute — applied to your phone bill.

Health records (include the following for each of your ferrets):

✔ General health records with a corresponding identification photo of the ferret

✔ Rabies certificates

✔ A list of prescription medications your ferrets are currently taking

Foodstuffs:

✔ Jars of meat baby food - chicken or lamb (for the sick kids)

✔ Light Karo syrup or Nutri-Cal (for a quick calorie boost)

✔ Pedialyte or Gatorade (to rehydrate the dehydrated ferrets)

✔ A can of prescription feline A/D (you can get this from your vet) (easily digested food for the sickies)

✔ A can of strawberry or vanilla Ensure (a high fat supplement for the sickies)

✔ Canola or olive oil (sometimes helps to move bad ingested stuff through)

✔ Petromalt or Laxatone (hairball preventives)

Cleaning solutions:

✔ Hydrogen peroxide (for cleaning cuts)

✔ Betadine solution (for cleaning cuts)

✔ Ear cleanser (for routine grooming)

✔ Eye wash/rinse (for flushing foreign bodies)

Bandages and such:

✔ Gauze pads

✔ Gauze wrap

✔ Washcloths

✔ Adhesive bandage tape (cloth tape holds the best)

Other health aids:

✔ Styptic powder or bee's wax (for bleeding nails)

✔ Antibiotic ointment such as Neosporin (for soothing and protecting cuts and scrapes)

✔ Bene-Bac (for replacing beneficial bacteria in the digestive tract after illness or diarrhea)

✔ Desitin (for rash and burn relief)

- ✔ Petroleum jelly (to help move a blockage through and for easing in the thermometer)
- ✔ Kaopectate or Pepto Bismol (for diarrhea and soothing the tummy)
- ✔ Immodium liquid (for diarrhea)
- ✔ Ferretone/Linatone (for mixing with medicine)
- ✔ Pediatric Liquid Benadryl (for counteracting allergic reactions)

Miscellaneous stuff:

- ✔ Heating pad (to help maintain body temp in a young or sick ferret)
- ✔ Chemical heating pack (portable heat for the young or sick ferret)
- ✔ A small plastic atomizer to spray cleaning solutions such as Betadine (allows coverage of a larger area using the least amount of solution)
- ✔ Nail clippers
- ✔ Tweezers (to remove foreign bodies)
- ✔ Cotton balls and cotton swabs
- ✔ Ice pack (to reduce swelling or slow bleeding)
- ✔ Rubber or latex gloves
- ✔ Scissors
- ✔ Pen light (to see wounds and foreign bodies better)
- ✔ Pill crusher
- ✔ Rectal thermometer (the normal temperature for a fert is about 102 degrees Fahrenheit)
- ✔ Tongue depressors (for immobilizing injured limbs)
- ✔ Baby wipes (for general clean up)

At my house, I have many types of critters to deal with, so I have a pretty large first-aid cabinet. I keep a printed list (from the computer) taped to the front of it. When something is used or needs replacing, I put a check mark next to it. This way, I run little risk of being unprepared in an emergency. I also add things that I hadn't previously thought of to the list for the future. Write down the expiration dates of foods/medications on the same list so that you'll also know when to toss and replace them.

Providing first-aid for your ferret does not mean foregoing a trip to the vet if the situation warrants it. Use your best judgment and keep your ferret's health and happiness in mind at all times.

Chapter 14

Ferret First Aid

*L*et's face it. We already know ferrets are trouble magnets. No matter how much we love them or how much money we spend on preventive care, ferrets will eventually test our first-aid knowledge and our ability to work under severe emotional duress. Even if you kept your ferret confined to a cage all day and night (the fert patrol and I would hunt you down and pummel you if you did), you'd still have a misfortune here or there. The odds increase as the numbers of fuzzies increase. Even the sweetest, most innocent ferret may have a mishap through no fault of his own.

This chapter covers immediate first aid only, whether to fix an easy problem or to control a difficult one until a medical professional can be sought out. The following chapters explain the serious diseases and illnesses.

Things You Don't (Generally) Need to Worry About

You'll be happy to know that some funky behaviors are normal. Like a grown man scratching his belly after Thanksgiving dinner and falling asleep during a football game, ferts also have a few peculiar behaviors that you can predict. Do not be alarmed. They're usually harmless.

Shivering

Ferrets shiver for many reasons, but most reasons are simple and harmless. They all shiver to raise their body temperature after sleeping more than half the day away. It's a natural and effective method. Many shiver when being scruffed. You may want to give a little bottom support to these shivering scruffers. Frightened ferrets rarely shiver, but excited ferrets often do. If you suspect your ferret's shivering is due to something other than body temperature or excitement, consult a veterinarian.

Itching and scratching

Ferrets are itchy critters, plain and simple (see Figure 14-1). It's annoying for the fuzzy and makes most people paranoid about fleas. Ferrets will sometimes awaken from a deep sleep just to feverishly scratch a sudden itch; then they roll over and fall back to sleep. Or they stop in the middle of a mad dash across the room to scratch an itch. If you watch a ferret itch and scratch long enough, you'll begin to itch and scratch, too.

If you do notice a rash or missing fur, take into consideration the ferret's environment, such as his bedding and what it was last washed in. Skin, both a human's and an animal's, tends to dry out a little during the colder months. Although uncommon, fuzzies can also have allergies. Sometimes too much scratching can lead to raw spots that may need to be topically treated. If this is the case, see your vet. If fleas have been ruled out and no fur is missing, then you can probably chalk it up to a typical fert quirk.

Figure 14-1:
Ferrets are itchy critters. Here, Cookie gets to those nasty itches her paws can't quite reach.

Yawning

Yawning is such a common ferret quirk that ferret enthusiasts even have yawning contests (see Figure 14-2). I don't know why our furkids yawn, but they do, and they do so frequently. Maybe it has something to do with how much sleep ferrets indulge in. Ferrets being scruffed are particularly vulnerable to yawning attacks. While the effect on them seems unlasting, people watching can be enveloped in their own yawning attacks. I yawn as I write this.

Excessive sleeping

Sleeping excessively is common in ferrets (so don't take it as a sign that you're a complete bore). Sometimes they can sleep so hard it appears that they're in a coma or even dead. They're warm and breathing, but they just won't wake up.

If you're being an over-concerned mom or dad and insist on making sure that fuzzball is alive, lift him up and call the ferret's name loudly. Give his back or belly a few good rubs (*don't* shake him violently). Scratch the ferret between the ears. Scruff and wiggle him a bit if he still hasn't responded. Sometimes a dab of his favorite treat on his nose is enough to jostle him awake. (The smell should get his little brain going. If it doesn't, he's probably sick.) As a last resort, rub a small amount of Nutri-Cal or Karo syrup on the ferret's gums.

Figure 14-2:
Yawning comes naturally to ferrets, especially when they're being scruffed.

Usually, this deep, deep sleep (referred to as "SND," that is "Sleeping Not Dead") is normal. After the ferret finally raises an eyelid to inspect the rude gate-crasher, you can usually be assured he's okay. Play with the fuzzy a bit if you still feel the need to reassure yourself. It's taken almost a full minute to wake up one or two of my guys on some occasions. And it still scares the beans out of me. If this situation occurs frequently with the same ferret, a trip to the vet may be a wise idea.

While ferrets do sleep quite a bit, and some even enter the deep SND mode, be aware of sudden changes in your furkid's sleeping patterns. If he starts to sleep more often than usual, it may be a sign of an underlying medical condition such as insulinoma or another illness. Don't ignore this sudden change in behavior. He made require immediate medical attention.

Sneezing, hiccuping, and coughing

With all the maladies fuzzies can get, you'd think sneezing and hiccuping would be just two more things to worry about. Not so. Fuzzballs get around by sense of smell. If you watch closely, you'll see that the exploring ferret has his nose to the ground almost all the time. He's inhaling everything, from dust bunnies to carpet fibers. He's bound to snort up bits and pieces of all that junk, and sneezing is the only way to clear his nose of it. Once the sneezing attack is over, it's nose to the ground again.

Coughing is usually a sign of a minor irritation to the throat, or a piece of kibble swallowed too quickly and coughed back up. If coughing persists, contact your vet. After all, your ferret can even catch the common cold. *Persistent* coughing, however, is also a sign of several illnesses, including cardiomyopathy, so do take note of how much coughing your fuzzy does. It's always better to be safe than sorry.

Ferrets sometimes cough or hack as though they have something stuck in their throats. It's common and, more often than not, harmless. If you're concerned, offer a little Laxatone (or another cat hairball remedy) to see if that helps. If something is stuck, the Laxatone will give it a lube job and may help it through. Never try to force an object through. Doing so only makes matters much worse.

I've only seen a hiccuping fuzzball once, and that was my old fert Goomer. It's actually a common and harmless fuzzy condition that results from a spasming of the diaphragm. In ferrets, hiccuping seems random and more of a bother to them than a condition at all. In humans, it's often a result of too much beer. Try giving the ferret a little lick of Ferretone or Nutri-Cal. This remedy can sometimes shorten the duration of the hiccuping.

A suckler

Some fuzzies, like many cats and kittens, find comfort in sucking on something soft (since their thumbs have sharp nails at the end), especially when they're falling asleep. This behavior is seen frequently in any animals separated from Mom at an early age. Cats usually choose fabric (called wool sucking) or fingers. Some ferrets view the ears of other ferrets as pacifiers. If the recipient of the ear sucking doesn't mind and the ear doesn't become raw and irritated, then it's not a problem. You should, however, offer an alternative, such as a safe baby toy or Nylabone.

Drinking urine

No one knows for sure why some of our adorable little fuzzies engage in the obnoxious practice of urine drinking. Maybe it's to gross us humans out. Some fuzzy experts believe that drinking urine is just another way for a thirsty ferret to consume liquid, so make sure that enough water is always available. Honestly, while it seems disgusting to us, it's common for a ferret to drink his own urine. It's a harmless act, unlike drinking too much beer.

Handling Emergencies

Ferrets hide pain and illness too well. Sometimes by the time you recognize a problem, it has become severe. Some ferret problems may be an indication of more severe problems. Therefore, unless the situation is as simple as a toe-nail cut too close to the quick, a visit to the vet as soon as possible is always the safest measure.

- ✔ Ferrets are tiny. They need to eat frequently. They dehydrate quickly. They don't have very much blood, so they can't afford to lose much. Know your ferret's body language and behavior well. In any case, never panic. Your preparedness can save your furkid's life.

- ✔ If he's in pain or scared, the ferret may bite. I'll assume that your pet knows and trusts you. Your soft, reassuring voice may help comfort him and calm him down. But you should still exercise caution.

- ✔ Familiarize yourself with an after-hours emergency hospital that is ferret-knowledgeable, in case your ferret needs care when your veterinarian is unavailable.

Bleeding

Fuzzies don't have very much blood in their bodies. Any wound that bleeds profusely requires immediate emergency medical attention. All other wounds or injuries should be looked at by a veterinarian as soon as possible, no matter what the degree of injury.

Bleeding from the ears, nose, mouth, rectum, or vaginal area is usually a sign of serious illness or injury. No matter the source of bleeding, visit your vet immediately.

Treating injured nails

The most common source of bleeding is a toenail cut too close to the quick. It's quite painful, and your ferret will let out a series of small screeches to let you and all the other ferrets know you screwed up. Talk to him softly and hold him cautiously to inspect the damage.

To stop the bleeding, always have a small jar of styptic powder on hand when doing nails. Apply a small amount with your finger to the tip of the bleeding nail. Press hard for a moment and release your finger. If it's still bleeding, apply the powder again. Styptic powder burns, and you may tick off the ferret, so be careful. Get the powder off your finger quickly because it will burn you, too.

A painless alternative to styptic powder is bee's wax. Some people suggest pressing the nail into a bar of white soap (preferably a mild one). Others use cornstarch or flour to stop nail bleeding, but these remedies may take longer to work.

If the nail has been torn off, do not use the powder. Rather, apply pressure to the top of the toe. Do not apply pressure directly on the toe tip. The blood will eventually clot on its own. Seek veterinary care as soon as possible if it's more than just a closely clipped nail. Otherwise, it may become infected. Torn claws may need to be removed completely and require stitches, but that is a worst-case scenario.

Treating cuts

Gently wash lacerations with cold water; then apply gentle but firm pressure on the wound. Using something clean and dry is important — gauze or a clean washcloth. If you can, wrap the area. Make sure that the wrap's not too tight. Depending on the cause of the cut, your ferret may also be suffering from internal injuries that you can't see.

Regardless of its size, any laceration can be serious. Your ferret may need a more extensive exam, stitches, and/or antibiotics. Remember, ferrets don't have a lot of blood to lose.

Heatstroke

Ferrets are extremely susceptible to heatstroke, especially in temperatures above 80 degrees Fahrenheit, and a heatstroke can quickly kill your ferret if he's not treated immediately. Signs of heatstroke include heavy panting, mucous coming from the nose or mouth, extreme lethargy or limpness, seizures, and loss of consciousness.

The main objective is to lower the ferret's body temperature slowly. The *gradual* decrease in body temperature is necessary to prevent shock. (A rapid decrease in body temperature can be as deadly as heatstroke.) You can slowly lower body temperature many different ways.

- First, get the ferret out of the sun and heat and give him water to drink. If you have an electrolyte replacer, such as Pedialyte or Gatorade, use it if the poor ferret will drink it. (**Note:** If your ferret is unconscious, *do not* try to get any liquid or food into his mouth. He can choke.)

- Apply cool (not cold) water to body areas where there is less fur — the groin and lower stomach areas, as well as the feet, for example.

- You can either place the ferret directly in shallow room-temperature water (keep his head and the top half of his body above water) or place a wet washcloth on the key areas. The evaporation of the water on the skin cools the body and lowers the temperature. Do *not* submerge the ferret in cold water. The shock of doing so could kill him.

- You can apply rubbing alcohol to the feet only, making sure not to miss the paw pads. Or rub ice cubes on the ferret's feet.

- Another option is to place the ferret in front of a fan. This last method isn't as effective, but it's better than nothing in an emergency situation.

No matter how you think your ferret weathered the situation, get him to the vet immediately. Often, the vet will want to give him additional fluids to make up for those lost during the heatstroke. The vet may also recommend additional medications or other home support.

Take extra precautions in the warmer months. Do not leave him in a closed-up or hot car. Keep your ferret and his carrier out of direct sunlight and be sure to give him extra water. If you do take your ferret out during very warm months, a great way to keep him extra cool is to bring along a bottle or two of frozen water. Even a frozen hot-water bottle works. Just wrap the bottles up in towels and keep them in the carrier or cage. This is a wonderful and easy solution to a deadly problem.

Fractures or spinal injuries

Ferrets are extremely flexible and resilient, but occasional bone injuries occur. Sometimes it's hard to recognize a break without an actual x-ray. The best course of action is to keep your ferret immobile and quiet. Don't try to fix anything. If your ferret has a broken bone or an injured spine, he may exhibit limping or resistance to moving, or he may drag a leg or hold one up.

If the injured part is a paw, wrap it in a towel to steady the limb. Place the ferret in a small carrier and keep him warm. Get to a vet immediately.

Spinal injuries can be devastating, if not fatal, and can be the result of a fall, getting pounced on by a dog, or getting folded up in a piece of furniture. Keep the ferret as still as possible by placing him in a small carrier or wrapping him in a towel and get him to the vet immediately.

Vomiting

Vomiting can occur for several reasons, ranging from bad food to an intestinal blockage (vomiting is actually a primary sign of intestinal blockage). Sometimes a small piece of ingested material comes up with vomit, and then the vomiting stops. But keep a close eye on the vomiting ferret. If your fuzzy vomits repeatedly and either can't hold down his food or shows no interest in food, he possibly has a blockage. The only way to treat a blockage is to remove the offending factor. Not doing so may spell death for your ferret. So get to a vet as soon as possible.

Diarrhea

Diarrhea can be very difficult to treat because it can be a symptom of so many other diseases or illnesses. The cause can be as simple as having indulged in one too many treats (we've all been there). The condition may be easy to correct (internal parasites, for example) or difficult to correct (intestinal obstruction, for instance). Diarrhea can also be a sign of fatal diseases, such as distemper or liver disease. But no matter what the cause, diarrhea can quickly become life threatening because your fuzzy is losing precious fluids and not absorbing all his food.

If diarrhea persists for more than half the day, take the ferret and a sample of the poop to the vet immediately to rule out all the other nasty things he may have. The treatment may be as simple as daily doses of Kaopectate and electrolyte replacer, but let your vet decide.

Dehydration

Dehydration occurs from extreme fluid loss, which can happen when your ferret stops drinking or has severe diarrhea. Except in cases of neglect (complete lack of water, for example), dehydration is almost always a symptom of an underlying illness. Regardless of the cause, it can be fatal if not addressed immediately.

How do you know if your ferret is dehydrated? Scruff your ferret and then put him down. Does the skin stay in the scruffed position for a while, or does it quickly flatten to its original elasticity? Lack of fluids and dehydration cause the skin to stay pinched up for a while and not flatten. The longer it takes the skin to flatten out, the more dehydrated your ferret is. The immediate solution is to get fluids back into your ferret.

Encourage your fuzzy to drink extra water. Sometimes ferrets enjoy the fruity taste of Pedialyte or Gatorade while getting the added benefit of extra electrolytes. Sometimes warm chicken broth encourages drinking. If the fuzzy refuses to drink at all, use a feeding syringe or an eyedropper to feed him the liquid. Be careful not to force too much liquid or feed too quickly because he can choke.

Note that getting enough fluids into a dehydrated ferret this way is difficult. Often, it's necessary for you to have your veterinarian administer extra fluids subcutaneously (under the skin) or intravenously (through an IV directly into the vein). Remember, dehydration is a symptom of something else. Take your ferret to the vet so that you'll know what's making your fert ill. Treating the underlying illness oftentimes prevents future bouts of dehydration.

Poisoning

The world is a scary place for ferrets. Even your own home can be a source of harm to him. Most homes contain an unusual amount of funky chemicals and cleaners, half of which we don't remember where we stored. The most commonly encountered ferret poisonings are from rat poison and Tylenol. When your ferret finds these things — disaster. Poisoning can also occur from accidentally overdosing your ferret on prescribed medication.

If you see or suspect that your ferret has ingested something poisonous or has been given too much medicine, take him and the suspected substance to the vet immediately. Try to figure out how much was ingested and how long ago, as well.

Treatment depends on what the ingested substance was. It can range from induced vomiting to medication. You may want to consider having a supply of Vitamin K soft gel caps on hand (you can get them from your vet and add them to your first-aid kit) to use as an antidote for rat poisoning if you can't get to the vet immediately. Only your vet will know the proper course of action.

Keep the number to the National Animal Poison Control Center closely on hand and also make sure that your vet has it for reference. You can reach this nonprofit agency at 800-548-2423 ($30 per case/credit cards only) or 900-680-0000 ($20 for the first 5 minutes and $2.95 for each additional minute, with the cost applied to your phone bill).

Animal bites

People with ferrets often have other animals in the home. You need to limit and monitor pet interactions closely to avoid aggression. If your ferret gets bitten by a household pet, wash the wound lightly with cold water and gently dab the area with hydrogen peroxide. If the wound is bleeding, apply pressure. Then get him to the vet immediately. Cat bites are particularly dangerous to both people and other animals due to the amount of bacteria in cat saliva. Often, cat bites require special antibiotics.

If your fert is bitten by a stray or wild animal, take your poor fert to the vet right away. If you know the animal that bit your fuzzy, make sure that it's up to date on its rabies vaccination. While the incidence is extremely low and unlikely, your ferret can still contract rabies from an infected animal. Prevention is the key. Watch your ferret closely for changes in behavior and report any to the vet.

Electric shock

An electric shock can be severe enough to kill your little fuzzy. There's very little you can do for him except keep him warm and quiet until you can get him to the veterinarian. Electric shock is usually the result of chewing on electrical cords, which is why you need to keep them far out of your ferret's reach (see Chapter 7 for info on ferret-proofing your house). If he's lucky enough to survive, you can be almost certain he'll suffer damage to the teeth, gums, and mouth. Be aware that chewed cords can also cause a fire. Check for and replace any frayed or bitten electrical cords immediately.

Burns

Sometimes our carpet sharks get into things they shouldn't. The reason is usually because we aren't paying close enough attention or we allow them to venture into unsafe territory. Burns can come from fireplaces, cigarettes, ovens, and even pilot lights. If your ferret suffers a burn, apply cold water immediately to the burned area. If you can, apply an ice pack for no more than five minutes. Get your ferret to a vet immediately.

Eye injuries

Ferrets can get very rough with each other and get into a lot of trouble on their own. Eye injuries and foreign matter in the eyes are not beyond the ferret realm. If your ferret receives a scratch to the eye, flush it out with cool water. If you suspect foreign matter, such as kitty litter or sand, *do not* apply any pressure to the affected eye. Doing so can cause the particle to further damage the eye by scratching it or getting more deeply lodged. Any eye injury requires the attention of an experienced ferret vet quickly.

Seizures

A seizure is a scary thing to witness. It occurs when the electrical brain impulses misfire. Lasting from seconds to a few minutes, seizures can be a symptom of many different underlying conditions from *hypoglycemia* (low blood sugar) to a severe ear mite infestation. Some seizures can occur very quietly and go unnoticed, but the majority involve the involuntary thrashing about of the limbs in combination with any of the following: loss of bladder/bowel control, salivating, vomiting, and involuntary vocalizations.

The only thing you can do for your ferret during a seizure is move him to a soft, cushioned place so that he doesn't suffer any injuries during the seizure. Also keep your fingers, pens, wallets, or whatever else you might grab away from the ferret's mouth when he's in the middle of a seizure. Keep him away from other ferrets and pets. If you have the wits about you, time the incident for future reference. In the end, you'll have a very wiped-out fert. (By the way, neither people nor ferrets have the ability to swallow their tongues. That's only a myth.)

Don't try to hold your ferret down during a seizure. Restraining him can cause further injury to him — and to you. He may inadvertently and seriously bite you without even knowing what's going on around him. Because the jaws of a seizuring animal/person clamp tightly shut, anything that gets in the way is bitten severely.

When your ferret's seizure ends, keep him calm, warm, and quiet. He'll be confused and shaken. To give him a needed boost to recovery, rub a little Karo syrup on his gums. Repeat every five minutes or so until your fuzzy starts coming around. Also offer a little soft food, such as prescription feline

A/D (available from your vet — check your ferret's medicine cabinet) or another high-protein canned food, to stabilize his blood sugar. If the ferret's not up to licking from a spoon or off a plate, offer it from a feeding syringe.

From start to finish, the ferret needs about 30–40 minutes to recover from a seizure. *Always* seek veterinary help immediately following a seizure. You need to find the underlying cause and prevent future seizures.

Shock

Shock is usually a common aftereffect of injury, illness, or severe fright. It can cost your ferret his life. Prevention and supportive therapy are essential to helping your fert through the crisis. Recognize the big signs of shock:

- Rapid breathing
- Lethargy
- Shivering
- Fast heartbeat
- Pale nose, skin, ears
- Cool to the touch
- Bluish gums
- Unresponsiveness
- Diarrhea

To help the fuzzy pull through, keep him warm and quiet. Cover his body with a towel (you can even warm the towel up in a microwave but don't make it too warm). Leave the ferret's head exposed so he can get the air he needs. Talk softly and reassuringly to him and dim the lights if possible. Sometimes a little dab of Karo syrup on the gums is helpful.

Do not attempt to get a ferret in shock to eat or drink. Your fuzzy is having a hard enough time breathing, and his swallowing reflex just isn't there.

Make sure that the car is warmed up inside and ready to go; then get him to a vet immediately. Let your vet know what measures you've already taken and how your fert has responded to them. Often, additional fluids given subcutaneously by the vet help speed the recovery. If your ferret's in shock due to blood loss, sometimes a blood transfusion from a big healthy fuzzy can be lifesaving. It sounds extreme, but it has been done with great success.

Feeding the Sick or Debilitated Fuzzbutt

Most fuzzy humans, at some point, need to assist a ferret in keeping his belly full of good stuff. The assistance may be needed for the old fert, the toothless ferret, the sick ferret, or the fuzzy recovering from surgery. No matter what the reason, the feeding method is basically the same.

The recipe

You need to make a very special food mixture to feed to your sick or debilitated fert. Some people call it Duck Soup, but I prefer to call it Fert Soup, and it's relatively simple to make. The only requirements are that the concoction be soft, easy to digest, full of energy-boosting calories, and hopefully yummy enough so that your fert is less likely to resist eating it. To make the soup:

1. **Take what your ferret was used to eating before he got sick or debilitated (provided that it was a good meal) and grind it up.**

2. **Moisten it with water or Pedialyte (an electrolyte replacer).**

3. **Toss in some other good-smelling stuff.**

   Canned A/D from your vet, meat-based baby food, and a tad of Nutri-Cal are all good for this purpose. If you want to add some extra calories, add a teaspoon of a soy-based product such as Ensure or Prosobee.

4. **Mix the whole batch up until it's smooth and creamy.**

5. **Find a comfy place to sit, grab a few towels or rags, and get ready to feed.**

   If you're a fuzzy chef extraordinaire, your ferret will lick this concoction right from the spoon or bowl with little hesitation. If you're a disaster in the kitchen, you may have to use a feeding syringe to get the stuff into his mouth. Expect a little ptooeying in this case. And see the next section for suggestions on how best — and how often — to get the food down.

The method

If your ferret is strong enough and finds the soup appetizing, present it to him in a shallow bowl or allow him to lick it one spoonful at a time. Don't just place him in the cage with the bowl. Watch him and make sure that he's doing more eating than spreading it around his cage. Also, if he has cage mates, they will probably get to the food before he gets his share.

If he's not strong enough to feed himself, you'll have to feed him. If you do need to force-feed, first take the word *force* out of your vocabulary. It's bad enough that the poor guy is sick. Don't make feeding an unpleasant experience as well.

You can obtain a feeding syringe (it has no needle at the end) from your vet or use an eyedropper (plastic, not glass). Eyedroppers can be a bit more time-consuming because they're smaller. Suck the liquid soup up into the syringe and squeeze a small amount into the corner of the ferret's mouth. Feed slowly and in small amounts. Give him time to swallow. You don't want to choke him. He may crinkle up his nose and eyes with displeasure or surprise, but don't give up until you know he's had enough. Take the time to wipe his mouth and, if needed, your face should the stuff go airborne during a violent ptooeying.

Way too often, fuzzy humans are in a hurry to feed their sick babies. Forcing large amounts of food into the ferret's mouth can cause him to aspirate or choke. Feed slowly. Feed small amounts. Let him set the pace. It may take him awhile just to get used to your cooking.

Don't ever give up on a stubborn fert who refuses to eat. You may end up with a ton of gunk in your hair, on your face, and in your mouth, but make sure that your sickie gets several cc's of good stuff 4–6 times a day. The feeding frequency can be less often if he's eating a little on his own in between feedings. Providing good nutrition and preventing dehydration are crucial to healing and/or prolonging the life of your ferret.

Help in the Bathroom

Both older and ill ferrets need special help (and consideration) in the poop department. Older and sick ferrets, for example, tend to forget where the litter box is, and some older ferrets will poop whenever and wherever the urge strikes, sometimes as you are picking them up. If the fert is tiny, sick, or old, make sure that the box has a low side or is small enough for him to easily get in and out. For other tips and suggestions on how to help your ferret find and use his litterbox, head to Chapter 20.

Chapter 15

When Bugs Get You Down

Simply put, a parasite is an organism (or person) that feeds off of another organism (or person) without giving anything back. You may even know one or two personally. Every living thing is host to a parasite party or two — or maybe a hundred. Parasites come in all shapes and sizes. Some are internal. Some are external. Some are harmless and hardly noticeable, while others can be quite damaging and not difficult to miss.

This chapter deals specifically with internal and external pests that can bug the heck out of both you and your fuzzy. It also sheds some light on parasites, diseases, and germs that can be passed back and forth between humans and their better halves, the carpet sharks.

Things That Go Bite in the Night

They are ruthless and always hungry. Under the microscope, they look a bit like creepy prehistoric monsters. Can anything be more annoying to the pet and pet owner than external parasites? These incredibly sturdy little ectoparasites need little to survive. Unfortunately, you and your ferts can be hosts to these ungrateful diners.

Fighting fleas

Living on your pet only part-time, fleas spend most of their time building flea resorts in your rugs and couches and any other cozy place they find. Ferrets are just as prone to flea infestations as Fido and Tabby. So what can you safely do to rid your domain of these blood-sucking pests and prevent them from turning your frisky ferrets into illing itchies? First, you need to know what army you are dealing with:

✔ Fleas are rude guests. They invite themselves over, and then they eat and run. The act of feasting on your pet's warm blood triggers the female flea to lay thousands of eggs all over your home. Sometimes you may observe a flea scurrying across its dinner table, your pet. More likely, you'll only see the end results of their wild flea parties — usually, the "flea dirt" left on the skin of your pet. Only it's not dirt at all but rather flea waste, which looks like tiny specks of reddish black sand.

✔ Fleas are opportunistic little buggers. Where there is wildlife, there are fleas. And lots of them. They hitchhike right into your home on other pets, such as dogs and cats. While fleas can't live on humans, they can be carried in via clothing or perhaps a picnic blanket. And don't forget about the greatly appreciated, supervised trips your ferret takes to the wonderful outdoors. Through no fault of his own, the fert may be the one to bring them into your house.

✔ Fleas love warm, humid places. They love all warm-blooded victims. While it may be warm and humid only several months a year where you live, the battle against fleas lasts year round.

Fleas can be more than a mere nuisance: A severe infestation can cause life-threatening anemia in your ferret. Fleas also carry parasites such as tapeworms and can pass them along to both you and your pet. So if your ferret has fleas, you need to get rid of them.

Checking for fleas

To check for fleas, ruffle back the fur with your hands and examine your ferret's skin, particularly the belly, closely. Also, inspect your ferret's bedding and change it often. You can shake out his towels or other sleeping bedding onto a white floor or paper; it's easy to distinguish specks of kitty litter from flea dirt. If you want to be really sneaky, place a shallow bowl of soapy water outside of the fert's cage (out of paw reach) and place a lamp on the floor directly over it. The light and warmth will attract the fleas to the sudsy pool, where they'll quickly jump in and drown.

Poor fur quality, thinning patches of fur, and fur discoloration can sometimes be an indication of a flea infestation. You may find yourself suffering some of the same ill effects; don't be surprised if you encounter some bites around your feet and ankles if the infestation is severe (remember, fleas can jump over 100 times their body length). Herein lies one of the biggest problems with fleas: Their tiny bites are painfully itchy. To the flea-allergic pet, the situation can be almost unbearable and even unsightly as hair falls out and is replaced by a raw rash.

Because ferrets are obsessive scratchers, this act of relieving an aggravating itch doesn't always mean fleas are present, so check your pet carefully, using the suggestions in this section.

Don't be embarrassed if your house has fleas. Most pet owners encounter this situation at one time or another. You *do* have control over how severe the problem becomes, however, so be ready and willing to take appropriate action.

Getting rid of fleas

If one pet has fleas, all your pets have fleas. If you have several pets in the family, you must treat all of them, whether or not you see evidence of fleas on them.

Before you treat any of your ferrets for fleas, however, keep the following points in mind:

✔ Use only products made specifically for the type of pet you have. What is safe for your dog can kill your ferret or cat. Controls such as sprays, dips, and flea collars may work for your other pets, but they *are not* meant to be used on your ferret. Ferrets are hypersensitive to most of these products, particularly organophosphate pesticides. Even ferret-safe products can be harmful to the sick, geriatric, young (under 12 weeks old), or nursing ferret.

   With the exception of flea collars, here is a good rule to follow: If it's safe for a cat, it's safe for a ferret.

✔ It is essential that you see a veterinarian before applying any flea product on your ferret — or any pet, for that matter. Your vet will make sure the product you use is safe and that your pet is healthy enough to withstand chemical treatment.

✔ Prepare to follow these steps again in 7-14 days to catch the hatchlings that were missed the first time around.

Step 1: Treating your ferret

To rid your ferret and home of fleas, you begin by tackling all of your warm-blooded furry pets with safe flea shampoos. Once you have a ferret-safe flea shampoo in hand, preferably one made with pyrethrins or other natural ingredients, follow these steps:

1. **Gently bathe your ferret from head to toe and remember the tail (tails have fleas, too).**

   Refer to Chapter 11 for detailed information on bathing your ferret. Here are some highlights: Don't forget your goggles, snorkel, and shoulder-length rubber gloves, and remember to prevent the shampoo from getting into the eyes, nose, mouth, and ears.

2. **When your ferret is dry, use a flea comb to remove any flea corpses from your pet.**

3. **Move the fuzzy to a warm, dry, and flea-free place while you tackle his cage.**

   A travel carrier works well in times like these. After all, putting a squeaky-clean furball into a flea-infested cage doesn't make much sense.

While you're treating your ferret, invite all your friends over for a barbecue. Under this guise, you can gather a few extra hands to tackle the other pets and knock out all flea baths and bedding washes. All your efforts will go unnoticed if you only temporarily chased the fleas onto Fido, Tabby, or Bun Bun. So do the job completely.

Step 2: Treating the ferret's cage, bedding, and other stuff

When your ferret is flea-free, you're ready to take on the cages and bedding (remember, you have to do the same with your other pet stuff, too):

1. **Remove all bedding and machine-wash it in hot water. Or place it in a sealed plastic bag and throw it away.**

   Chances are, the bedding is harboring flea eggs left behind to carry on the nasty flea tradition.

2. **Scrub the cage thoroughly with hot, soapy water.**

   If possible, take the cage apart before scrubbing it.

3. **Spray the cage with cat-safe flea spray and allow it to thoroughly dry.**

Do not neglect toys, dishes, litter boxes, and water bottles. They probably need cleaning anyway. Empty all litter boxes, scrub them with hot soapy water, and refill them with fresh litter before returning them to the cage.

Step 3: Treating your home

Once your pets and cages are clean and flea-free, you must tackle an even bigger undertaking — your entire house. This third step is probably the most inconvenient and time-consuming of all. You may have killed the fleas on your pet and the eggs on his bedding, but thousands of eggs are just getting ready to hatch all over, including in baseboards, carpeting, and furniture. Because most commercial products do not successfully kill all eggs, larvae, and pupae, you need to repeat this step 7–21 days after the first treatment, depending on which product you use.

There are several ways to go about treating your home and basement. The easiest is to hire a professional exterminator. Other methods are foggers, sprays, and powders. As you decide what method to use, keep in mind that ferrets are remarkably sensitive to chemicals, so the safest and most natural method should always be chosen whenever possible. And *always* follow product directions.

Chigger bug

Chiggers, members of the dreaded mite family, are very common in the warmer states. The bites from these nasties cause itchy, burning swellings on the skin of the victim. These swellings can last for weeks. Not only are humans targets of these attacks, but ferrets are, also. At the turn of the century, large numbers of fuzzies were released into the Caribbean to control rabbits and rodents. Reports indicate that one of the reasons they failed to survive was because the chigger infestations they encountered produced debilitating mange-like symptoms in the poor guys.

It's very helpful to have a flea-free friend take your ferrets and other pets for the day while you treat the interior of your home.

Step 4: Treating your yard

If you have made it to Step 4, pat yourself on the back, take a deep breath, and head outside for the final step in eradicating your current flea infestation. The yard cleanup has probably been on your list of things to do for several months, and now is your time to do it. Mow that grass, rake up leaves, and clean up the garbage that has blown in between bushes and other shrubbery. Afterward, treat the yard and plants with an outdoor flea-specific spray. Don't forget the garage.

You can do this stuff yourself (be sure to read product directions before and after treating your yard) or hire a lawn care company for the yard and an exterminator for the pesticide application. Whichever you choose, don't allow pets or children to play on the grass until it has been dry for several hours. To be completely safe, wait a day or two before allowing the grass to be enjoyed as usual.

Step 5: Stopping fleas from coming back

Care must be taken regularly to prevent reinfestation. Here are some general suggestions: Keep your pet's environment clean. Vacuum and sweep regularly. Inspect and de-flea all incoming pets *before* they enter your home.

There are a few relatively new spot-on liquid products on the market that, when properly applied, kill the fleas shortly after they get on your pet. Sometimes the products work so fast that the fleas can't even bite your pet. They're made in different formulas for either cats or dogs; ferrets do well on most products made for cats. However, neither the makers of these products nor the FDA has approved these products for use on ferrets, although most have been found to be safe by many, many veterinarians and ferret owners all over. One of these products is called Advantage, and it's made by Bayer. The other, made by Meriel, is Frontline Top Spot.

✔ **Advantage:** Made with the ingredient imidacloprid, the product is said to kill 98–100 percent of the fleas on your ferret within 24 hours of initial application.

Applying a small amount of the liquid directly on the skin at the base of your pet's skull provides up to 28 days of protection. The liquid spreads evenly across your ferret's skin to provide full body coverage. Monthly applications are advised to protect against newly hatching fleas from the original infestation. Because shampooing your ferret may shorten the length of effectiveness of Advantage, reapplication is recommended after bathing, but your ferret should receive no more than one application per week.

✔ **Frontline Top Spot:** Made with the active ingredient fipronil, this product targets both fleas and ticks. It is designed to bind to the natural oils of the skin and hair follicles, which allows the active ingredient to be continually released onto the ferret's skin and fur for at least one full month after initial application. Frontline Top Spot becomes waterproof two days after being applied; therefore, don't bathe your ferret during this period. Likewise, due to the way the product works with your ferret's natural oils, don't apply Frontline immediately following your ferret's bath (bathing strips the hair and skin of oils, making the product ineffective). If you must bathe your ferret before applying the product, then wait at least five days after the bath before applying Frontline Top Spot.

One reason Frontline Top Spot is deemed so safe for mammals is because it is not absorbed into your pet's bloodstream. Like Advantage, Frontline should be applied monthly but no more frequently than that.

The wonderful thing about these products is that they kill the fleas before eggs are laid. If you stick with a spot-on product with all your pets, chances are you won't often (if ever) need to go through the frenzied treatment process described in the first four steps. Currently, these types of products can only be purchased from your veterinarian, but most are well worth the cost, considering the alternative consequences to fighting an infestation.

If you think you have won the fight against fleas with all this ammunition, you are sadly mistaken: To be truly effective, you must remain vigilant and act quickly whenever you see signs of fleas. The war against fleas is seemingly unending at times, but your efforts will be well rewarded by a healthy and happy ferret companion. And your ankles won't itch.

Ticked off by ticks

Ticks look like tiny, tiny brown crabs. When filled with blood, they resemble a raised mole on the skin. Fortunately, ticks are relatively easy to deal with if you find one hitched to your fuzzy's skin: Using a pair of tweezers or forceps, grab the tick as close to the ferret's skin as possible. Gently pull it off, being sure not to leave the tick's barbed mouth parts still attached to the fuzzy. You can also apply a small amount of mineral oil on the tick to make him loosen his grasp a little. Once removed, crush or burn the tick.

Here are a couple of things to know about ticks and getting rid of them:

✔ Finding ticks can be difficult. You must feel beneath the fur for the tiny lumps. Ears are also great hiding spots for ticks.

✔ Ticks can harbor some diseases, including Lyme disease, which can affect both humans and other animals. Some spot-on products (like Frontline Top Spot) used to control fleas are also effective in killing ticks.

✔ Do not burn the tick off of your ferret. Although many people suggest this, you run the risk of seriously burning your little fuzzy.

Ear mites

Common in ferrets, blood-sucking ear mites can be identified by the brownish-black gunk in the ear canals. Ferrets with ear mites may scratch feverishly at their ears, walk with a slight head tilt, and shake their heads due to the extreme discomfort. Their ears may also stink and be slightly discolored.

Ear mites can be passed between fuzzies and other household pets, such as cats and dogs, so it's important to treat all animals and wash all bedding during treatments.

Treatment is relatively easy (if you stick with it) and necessary to prevent secondary infections that can be extremely painful and even result in deafness. Some vets may prescribe an ear ointment such as Tresaderm. Others may use injectible ivermectin. Ivermectin (same as injectible ivermectin) mixed with propylene glycol or used by itself and applied directly into the ear canal also works. There are other ear ointments that work just as well when used as prescribed by your vet.

Before applying ear mite medication directly in the ear, place a few drops of ear cleanser into the ear, wait a moment, and then swab it out. If you're lucky, and you probably will be, your ferret will do a nice head shake and spray the partially loosened wax and mite gunk all over you. Consider yourself baptized.

Ear mites aren't eradicated with one application of medicine but rather over a series of applications, so it's crucial to be painstakingly thorough.

Cows and your ferret

Cattle are prone to a specific type of ringworm that can also be passed to ferrets. So, if you live on a farm or ranch, don't let your fuzzies snooze with or kiss the cows. Speaking of cows and parasites, ferrets are also highly susceptible to a form of bovine tuberculosis. Fuzzies are also prone to avian tuberculosis and human forms of tuberculosis (a bacterial affliction). And by the way, you're vulnerable to all these things mentioned, too.

Sarcoptic mange (scabies)

As one who's suffered from this dreadful pest, I can testify that the condition is unbearably itchy and definitely no fun. This external bug is actually in the mite family and passes quite easily from animal to animal or to human. Depending on your fert's case, he may have itchy patches of hair loss on the belly, face, or legs. The skin may also be crusty with oozing, pimple-like sores.

Sometimes the infestation attacks only the feet and toes, causing *foot rot*. Marked by scabby, swollen, and red feet, foot rot often results in the claws falling out if left untreated. Diagnosis can sometimes be made by skin scrapings. For treatment, you can choose really, really stinky vet-prescribed lime sulfur dips and shampoos, or you can go the safe and simple oral or injectible ivermectin route.

Ringworm

Technically, ringworm isn't a parasite but rather a fungal infection, but it affects the skin like many external parasites do. Fuzzies are highly susceptible to ringworm, as are humans. This infection passes easily from animal to animal or animal to human through contact with infected hairs. Identifying this itchy pest is relatively easy because it causes a red, inflamed rash that spreads outward in a near perfect circular form. Hair loss is always noted, with flaking or oozing skin. Your vet may prescribe a topical or an oral medication or even a shampoo to combat this irritating problem.

Use care when handling a ferret with ringworm because you can get it, too.

The Internal Buggaboos

It's bad enough that pests invade the outside of our little fuzzbutts, but they also can take over the fuzzy's insides. Some of the many intestinal parasites your fuzzbutt can contract are roundworms, hookworms, tapeworms, coccidia, giardia, and toxoplasma. Another deadly internal parasite rarely discussed in ferrets is heartworm.

Some internal parasites can be life threatening and require immediate attention. Watch for the warning signs and always take your little guy to the vet if you suspect something's wrong. And *never, ever* take on the role of doctor and medicate your ferret without your vet's guidance. Ferrets are tiny and can overdose very easily. Some medications can be lethal in combinations. Also, you may run into problems or cause more harm if you misdiagnose or fail to see other underlying health problems in your kids. Don't be stupid. Always get help from an experienced ferret vet, who will be able to diagnose and come up with the proper course of action.

Intestinal worms

Some intestinal worms are passed from one animal to another or to a human through the animal's infected poop. Others, like the tapeworm, are passed through fleas or other intermediate hosts. And yet others can get into your system just by having the tiny larva burrow through the skin. Ferrets are prone to many intestinal worms, including roundworms, hookworms, tapeworms, flukes, and lung-worms. Almost all intestinal infestations harbor the same symptoms:

- ✔ Diarrhea, mucousy or bloody poops, and/or worms in the poop
- ✔ General weight loss
- ✔ Abdominal bloating
- ✔ Dry, brittle fur
- ✔ Weakness or lethargy
- ✔ Itchy heinie
- ✔ Increased appetite
- ✔ Increased gas (imagine)
- ✔ Tender belly

If you have more than one ferret and one of them has internal parasites, chances are you have more than one wormy fuzzy. Treat all ferrets thoroughly, according to your vet's instructions. Don't forget to change litter boxes and clean cages to prevent reinfestation. If you have dogs and cats, check them, too. Animals just love to get into poop.

Although the symptoms are generally the same, treatment of intestinal parasites can vary depending on the organism you're dealing with. Some require oral medication, either in liquid or pill form. Others can be taken care of with an injection, often ivermectin. Whatever the case, intestinal parasites left untreated can cause your fert to have chronic intestinal problems and be prone to poor health. In rare instances, severe cases can cause death.

Giardia

This lovely protozoan can get into you or your ferret via a water source (streams, lakes, ponds, and infected tap water, for example) or through the ingestion of infected poop, which can happen through routine licking and grooming the fur and feet. Once inside the intestinal tract, these buggers attack the inner lining of the intestine, causing an uncomfortable inflammation. Signs include weight loss, bloating, diarrhea, and mucousy poops.

Giardia can be difficult to find under the microscope, and it's sometimes misidentified. Yeast cells from ferret food that come out with the poop can almost pass for giardia's twin.

While some people believe giardia is rare in ferrets, others believe it's very common and only shows its ugly warning signs when the fuzzy's stressed out. This is one parasite that's still being investigated. Treatment is usually Flagyl (metronidazole). Some vets suggest Panacur (fenbendazole) as another option, although this medication isn't made specifically for this parasite. In healthy fuzzies, some experts think that the symptoms may go away without treatment. I always suggest getting help. It may take up to a month to cure your furball, but it's well worth it.

Some medications, especially Flagyl and Pepto-Bismol, are *so* offensive to fuzzies that they projectile-ptooey them all over you. This is where treats such as Nutri-Cal or Linatone can come in handy. Mixing the medication with a yummy-tasting supplement can save you a laundry bill. It also causes less of a rebellion on the fert's part. Keep in mind what you're medicating the fuzzy for in the first place before mixing meds with a food or supplement; for example, ferrets with insulinoma shouldn't have sweet stuff.

Coccidia (Coccidiosis)

This is a protozoan infection that is common in ferrets as well as other animals. As usual, it's picked up through the ingestion of infected poop and can be diagnosed by your vet, using a stool sample. However, this isn't always a fail-proof test. The *oocysts* (eggs) may be shed only periodically, which means you may test a poop on a day when no oocysts were shed. For the most accurate results, pick a poop that is bloody and mucousy.

Severe infestations can cause diarrhea, lethargy, dehydration, weight loss, loss of appetite, and, in severe cases, death. Kits are most susceptible to severe coccidia infestations and may have thin, brittle fur and a sparse coat. Whiskers are stubby and broken off. In prolonged conditions, the heinie may be red and swollen. Treatment is usually successful if caught early enough. Many vets prescribe Albon (sulfadimethoxine) to treat coccidia.

Helicobacter mustelae infection

Helicobacter mustelae is a nasty bacterial gastric infection that attacks the stomach lining in fuzzies. It's extremely common, and almost all ferrets eventually get it. Like most of the intestinal parasites, poop has a lot to do with it. And, actually, so does mama fuzzy. This bacterial disease is invited in when the fert ingests infected poop. It can also pass congenitally from Mom to kit.

Serious bouts of Helicobacter mustelae infection may result in gastric problems because the bacteria can cause a decrease in the production of stomach acid. Some ferret experts believe that this little bug can be serious enough to cause gastric ulcers, although this theory still hasn't been proven (in fact, almost all fuzzy ulcer patients are infected with Helicobacter mustelae). In any case, ferts with gastric ulcers are almost always harboring Helicobacter bacteria. Experts also think that this ongoing infection can cause enlarged spleens and chronic gastritis. Here are the symptoms of this infection:

- ✔ Vomiting
- ✔ Loss of appetite
- ✔ Diarrhea
- ✔ Dark, tarry stools
- ✔ Teeth grinding
- ✔ Weight loss

It seems as though the ferret's own system can control this bacterial invasion under normal circumstances. Unless your fuzzy is extremely stressed out or already weakened by disease or illness, symptoms may not appear at all. Although the relationship between stress, disease, and illness hasn't been proven to cause the bacterial rebellion, once symptoms appear, your ferret should be treated. Medications that have been successful in treating Helicobacter mustelae are Amoxicillin, Flagyl, Pepto-Bismol, and Biaxin (in combo with Amoxy).

Heartworm

Where there are lots of mosquitoes, there will be lots of cases of heartworm, and ferrets are just as susceptible to this deadly disease as Fido and Tabby. In fact, all carnivores are. Even if ferrets don't go outside, mosquitoes can come in. We're all familiar with the annoying buzzing made by the elusive mosquito invader in the middle of the night while we're trying to sleep.

Infected mosquitoes inject the parasite into the fuzzy with a single piercing bite. The loathsome parasite then develops and migrates to the fuzzy's heart where the adult worms reap cardiac havoc. It only takes a single worm to produce devastating results.

Symptoms of heartworm include the following:

- ✔ Constant hacking
- ✔ Lethargy
- ✔ Fluid buildup in abdomen
- ✔ Labored breathing
- ✔ Pale lips, gums, and tongue
- ✔ Passing out
- ✔ Heart murmur
- ✔ Muffled heart sounds
- ✔ Enlarged heart

The best course of action, naturally, is prevention. Many vets prescribe the small feline Heartguard chewable treat or ⅛ of the small canine Heartguard chewable treat once a month. Most fuzzies don't like the stuff, but you can try to disguise it in a yummy. Some vets prefer giving ferrets ivermectin orally on a monthly basis. Monthly injections of ivermectin may also be used.

Note: Meriel, the maker of Heartguard, advises against splitting the pills or chewables. The company claims that the effective ingredient (ivermectin) is not evenly distributed throughout the pills or chewables. So you don't know if the fuzzy's really getting an effective dosage. Ferrets can handle large dosages of ivermectin, and a whole feline chewable Heartguard has less ivermectin than the dosage a fuzzy would receive for some parasites.

Before beginning any heartworm prevention, your ferret should test negative for heartworm, if possible. Fuzzies can sometimes be tested for heartworm with the same in-clinic test that dogs get, although accuracy isn't guaranteed, and positive cases often yield negative test results. Rarely does a blood smear reveal the baby worms swimming around because ferrets harbor only a few worms that rarely mature. Another method of detecting heartworm that's sometimes successful is a cardiac ultrasound.

Heartworm is on the rise, and infected ferrets die without treatment. Although still relatively new to ferrets, treatment does exist with reports of a 60- to 75-percent survival rate. Unfortunately, treatment is costly, and often the treatment itself can cause the death of your fuzzy.

Heartworm and humans

Humans can also get heartworm but certainly not from infected fuzzies or other heartworm-infected critters. Incidences are rare and only occur when an infected mosquito bites a person who has a severely impaired immune system.

Toxoplasmosis

Toxoplasma is a parasite that gets into you or your pet through the ingestion of infected cat poop, undercooked meat, or the flesh of infected animals. Mom ferrets can also pass it to their kits.

Currently, experts believe that cats are the only definitive hosts for toxoplasma. The parasite undergoes sexual reproduction in the cat, and the oocysts (eggs) are shed in the poop. Then the poop becomes infective and dangerous if ingested at this stage. Toxoplasma has been known to cause miscarriages in humans during early pregnancy, which is why pregnant women often pass the pooper scooper to the guy. This parasite can also be hazardous to young children and people with already weakened immune systems.

Take care when changing *any* critter's litter box. Even though it's not been proven that fuzzies pass the oocysts (eggs) in their poop like cats do — and experts believe that they *don't* — take precautions anyway. If you're pregnant and you can't sucker someone into cleaning all the litter boxes, at least use gloves and wear a mask.

Symptoms vary according to the degree of infestation and which organs have been attacked. Diagnosis is usually made by a blood test. Treatment for your infected ferret can be long and involves combinations of oral medications such as sulfadiazine and pyrimethamine. Sometimes, supplementing the ferret's diet with baker's yeast and folic acid is helpful in combating the effects of the medications themselves.

Blood transfusion, anyone?

Ferts don't have blood types like humans do. While they also don't have that much blood to begin with, large healthy ferrets can often be used as blood donors for ferrets that need transfusions. Transfusions may be necessary during big surgeries or even some debilitating diseases. Question: If a human received some fuzzy blood, would he have an even smaller attention span?

Chapter 16

Viruses, Cooties, and Other Problems That Afflict Ferts

*N*o matter how hard we try to stay healthy with good eating, exercise, and proper immunizations, millions of humans always manage to get the worst viruses, colds, and flus every year. So why would your fuzzy be any different?

Entire books have been written on the diseases and illnesses ferrets can get. This isn't one of them. Here, you get the basics on what you need to know about these diseases and what you can do about them. This chapter deals with the most common diseases and conditions, from the simple (flu) to the deadly (rabies) and from the serious (cardiomyopathy) to the not so serious (mouth, tooth, and eye problems). As I make clear throughout this book, recognizing changes in your ferret's appearance and behavior can mean the difference between life and death. Even some of the presumably innocent conditions described in this chapter can take a turn for the worse or be indicative of another, more serious condition.

A handful of symptoms seem to show up with almost all fuzzy ailments. That's just one more reason to leave the diagnosing and medicating to your experienced vet. In some cases, your ferret may be suffering from more than one malady. Also, be aware that symptoms are not set in stone. Your ferret may exhibit one symptom or a combination of several. He may show none at all, especially in the beginning of an illness. The symptoms listed in this chapter are the most common ones for each illness described and are for reference only. Don't wait until more signs appear before hauling your fuzzbutt to the vet.

Canine Distemper

Canine distemper is an unforgiving and miserable disease that is 99.99 percent fatal. In extremely rare instances, there have been reports of survivors, but all have suffered neurological impairments. Since no treatment is available, prevention is critical. For information on the distemper vaccine, go to Chapter 13.

This virus is extremely contagious and can be transmitted to your fuzzy via other infected animals. If you think your fuzzy is safe from canine distemper because he never leaves the house, you're *dead* wrong. This virus can be carried into your household on your shoes and clothing. The distemper virus can also live a long time outside of the victim's body. So be careful and vaccinate your fuzzy.

The incubation period (the time it takes from the day of infection to the onset of symptoms) in your ferret may be as little as 7 days or as long as 21 days. Once symptoms appear, death usually occurs quickly because the virus attacks many fuzzy organs all at once. On rare occasions, the fuzzy may suffer a longer, more miserable death. If a positive diagnosis is made, your ferret should be humanely put to sleep as soon as possible. The extremely rare survivor suffers severe neurological damage.

Symptoms of distemper include

- Eye infection/discharge
- Severe lethargy
- Loss of appetite
- Rash on chin, lips, and nose
- Rash on belly and heinie
- Hardened/thick paw pads
- Diarrhea
- Vomiting
- Seizures
- Coma

Because the prognosis is hopeless and symptoms are unbearably miserable, humane euthanasia is preferred once distemper is diagnosed. Also, note that humans can't catch this disease from the poor victims.

Cardiomyopathy

Cardiomyopathy is rather common in ferrets, particularly those over the age of 3. It is a heart disease that causes a deterioration or hardening of the lining of the heart muscle. Eventually, the heart enlarges and weakens. Muscle is replaced by scar tissue. Inevitably, there's a decrease in blood flow through the heart, and the heart is rendered less efficient.

The cause of cardiomyopathy may be congenital, result from viral infections, or stem from other factors. Some experts have even suggested that a lack of taurine in the fuzzy's diet may contribute to this heart disease (the relationship has already been proven in cats). For diet information, see Chapter 9.

Cardiomyopathy is generally irreversible and has no cure. However, there have been some scattered reports of the disease actually reversing itself. But even if your ferret is diagnosed early and the symptoms are managed properly, how long your big-hearted fuzzy will live ultimately depends on how fast his heart is deteriorating. If you're lucky, he can last up to 24 more months.

Depending on the severity or progression of the disease and which part of the heart is affected, cardiomyopathy may be managed with medication. Some medications that are commonly prescribed by vets to manage cardiomyopathy are Digoxin (Digitalis), Vasotech, and Furosemide. Only your vet will be able to determine which medications (if any) and dosages will possibly work for your ferret.

Symptoms

This disease usually begins long before a diagnosis is made. However, diagnosis may also be made before the onset of symptoms. EKGs, x-rays, and ultrasounds have proven to be reliable diagnostic tools. Following are the symptoms of cardiomyopathy (heartworm disease shares many of the same symptoms):

✔ Labored breathing

✔ Hacking or coughing

✔ Irregular or rapid heartbeat

✔ Lethargy

✔ Frequent rests during play

✔ Hypothermia (cold)

✔ Fluid buildup in the chest area

Normal heartbeat

The average heart rate of a healthy fuzzy is an amazing 215 to 260 beats per minute. No wonder they fly around like crazy. Some experts suggest that this normal rate is actually a little high because of the stress of having a cold stethoscope pressed to their little chests by strange humans. The average heart rate detected by my vet is 200 beats per minute. A fuzzy with cardiomyopathy can have a heart rate exceeding 300 beats per minute. Try to count that.

Ferrets with cardiomyopathy often have enlarged livers or spleens, as well. Frequently, the suffering fuzzy also has a swollen belly. In this case, he has congestive heart failure, and the swollen belly is caused from a buildup of fluid in and surrounding the lungs and in the abdomen.

What you can do for your ferret

A fuzzy cardiac patient needs extra care. A cardiac fuzzy is often put on a low-sodium diet and ordered to take it easy. Ferrets with heart disease should embark on a gentle exercise routine and not be allowed to roam and play freely. Overstimulation may worsen the condition. Of course, common sense also dictates that frightening or startling these little heart breakers isn't a good idea. No barking dogs, firecrackers, or tuba playing, please.

If your heart patient is housed with a hyper fuzzbutt, consider separating them and housing the fragile critter with an older, less crazy fuzzbutt.

Common Cold

Don't sneeze on the fuzzy and don't let him sneeze on you, either. Your ferrets are highly susceptible to these bothersome bugs. The influenza virus is the most common respiratory infection in ferrets. In normally healthy ferrets, recovery takes about five days. In weak or old ferts, the sickness can be a little more serious and last several weeks. Here are the signs (ones we all, unfortunately, know so well):

- ✔ Sneezing and coughing
- ✔ Runny nose and eyes
- ✔ Fever over 104 degrees Fahrenheit
- ✔ Lethargy

A flu bug is a flu bug is a flu bug, right?

Wrong. Many, many types of influenza viruses exist. Some of them include human (types A and B), avian, equine, swine, and seal influenza viruses. Your ferret can catch all of these diseases. Ferrets only exhibit symptoms when infected with the human or swine strains. Don't kiss your fuzzy when you're sick and keep the pigs outdoors.

> ✔ Wheezing
>
> ✔ Diarrhea
>
> ✔ Loss of appetite

Unfortunately, these symptoms are so general and so common to other conditions that it's sometimes difficult to identify the common cold or flu. A little tender, loving care is usually all it takes to get the ferret through. However, sometimes antibiotics, fluids, and tummy-coaters may be necessary for severe bouts of the flu. For severe sneezing, some vets recommend the antihistamine Chlor-Trimeton at one-quarter pill twice a day.

If the symptoms persist for longer than a week or your fuzzy shows signs of refusing to eat at all, you may not be dealing with the flu or common cold. Get to a vet immediately. A ferret with the flu is crabby and tired but not knocked completely on his butt. Also look for abnormal discharge from the nose. A flu discharge is clear. Remember to wash your hands frequently after and in between handling your sickies. They don't think twice about sharing their miserable virus with you or other ferrets.

Bacterial pneumonia can bubble up for several reasons, but often it's due to a flu gone from bad to worse. In addition to having flu-like symptoms, pneumonia also causes open-mouthed breathing or labored breathing and severe, sometimes discolored, nasal goo. Bacterial pneumonia can kill your fuzzy quickly. Treatment depends on the type of bacteria producing the pneumonia. Your vet can culture a fuzzy throat loogie (or phlegm) before making the diagnosis and prescribing the defense. Depending on the type of bacteria present, your vet will probably prescribe the correct dosage of penicillin, sulfadiazine, or trimethoprim.

Dental Disgraces

Lots of things go wrong with the teeth. It's a fact of life that no toothy critter can hide from — not even fuzzbutts. Some fuzzy dental problems are genetic.

Others can be related to overuse and misuse of the chompers. Diet and physical health can also play a major role in the decay and destruction of the fert's teeth. Make sure that your ferret gets a dental checkup during his routine exams at the vet's office (see Figure 16-1).

Faulty teeth

If you spend enough time with your fuzzies, you'll see them rough and tumble pretty hard with each other and their imaginary fuzzmates. They fall and crash into things. When they're cage crazy, they may gnaw frantically at the cage bars until someone rescues them. Most ferrets are fed mainly a hard kibble diet, too. Fuzzy teeth endure a lot of wear and tear and abuse.

Chipped, broken, and worn teeth aren't necessarily things to gnash your teeth over, unless there's an obvious problem. But always let an experienced vet make that decision for you if you have any doubt. A vet can smooth out a chipped tooth if the surface is rough and irritating the inside of the fert's lip.

Worn teeth are facts of life and worsen as your ferret ages. Chewing hard kibble into manageable sizes for swallowing may be more difficult, so older fuzzies with worn teeth may need a softer diet. Breaks can be a little more serious. Exposed tooth pulp is painful and can lead to infections. Usually, a root canal or complete removal is warranted.

Figure 16-1:
Buster's getting his teeth checked for any problems that may exist. Your ferret should have his teeth checked during routine exams.

Your ferret may possibly end up looking more like a Bulldog than a fuzzy weasel. Some poor kids have teeth that protrude outward — usually, the canines. Because these teeth prevent the lip flap from resting against the gums, the gums may become dry. And the inside of the lip gets irritated from the constant irritation of the rubbing teeth. I've only had this situation happen to one ferret, and the offending teeth were two lower canines. The problem was fixed by surgically clipping the teeth as far down as necessary and filling them with a safe, hardening substance (acrylic is commonly used). If a tooth is severely deformed, completely removing it may be necessary.

Some furkids actually grow extra baby teeth. Albino kids are notorious for this condition. Usually, all baby teeth are pushed right out when the adult teeth come in. Other times, they linger for several days before finally being squeezed out. If you notice a baby tooth that overstays its welcome, you probably need to have the vet uproot it to prevent problems down the road. Some adult ferrets have an extra incisor tooth (called a *supernumery tooth*); this condition is harmless.

The dreaded dental disease

Gum disease, or periodontal disease, occurs with great frequency in fuzzies, especially ones that are over 5 years old. Come to think of it, it happens in humans with even more frequency. Humans are poor tooth brushers; that's a fact. And if we can't take care of our own teeth, we're probably not going to spend a lot of time on our pets' teeth.

Some experts argue that the main cause of periodontal disease is a canned or wet diet. Other diseases, such as lymphoma, can also play a role. Experts also agree that the severity can be greatly reduced by regular monthly cleanings by the human and more extensive cleanings by an experienced vet as often as needed.

The three biggest problems our ferrets face in terms of periodontal disease are lack of roughage to help scrape off the plaque (which is why most people recommend hard diets), eating fine particles of carbohydrates, and changes in the oral pH. My answer to combating periodontal disease is to opt for the alternative diet, which offers various food items with varying degrees of texture. (See Chapter 9 for details about diet.)

The signs of periodontal disease include

  ✔ Loose teeth

  ✔ Discolored teeth

  ✔ Stinky breath

  ✔ Red, inflamed, or receding gums

Medications and teeth

Some medications can cause dental problems in humans and animals. I had a friend whose teeth permanently turned greenish gray from a really nasty long-term medication. Diphenylhydantoin (that's a mouthful), a drug that's used to control epilepsy in humans and companion pets, has been reported to cause a dental disease called gingival hyperplasia.

✔ Drooling

✔ Mouth ulcers

✔ Difficulty eating

✔ Tartar and plaque buildup

✔ Refusal to floss (just kidding)

At the very least, you should add dental checkups to your weekly or monthly grooming habits. In addition to checking for lumps, bumps, bruises, and other abnormalities, stick your head in fuzzy's mouth and look for dental problems. For more on general care, head to Chapter 11.

ECE — Epizootic Catarrhal Enteritis

ECE is an inflammation of the mucous membranes in the intestines. Ferrets with ECE can't absorb food and water properly. The fuzzies most at risk are older carpet sharks or very young snorkelers. Also at high risk are ferrets already battling other illnesses, such as lymphosarcoma, adrenal disease, and/or insulinoma. Healthy young and middle-aged furkids seem to get over ECE fastest with the right support, almost as if it were the flu. In multiferret homes, you can expect most, if not all, of your fuzzies to get this disease at some point once it enters the door.

This nasty virus can last anywhere from several days to several months, and it is transmitted through bodily fluids, feces, air, handlers, or direct contact with another ferret. So watch your ferret closely and get him to a vet the moment symptoms become apparent. Unfortunately, no reliable fail-proof test for ECE is available. ECE is diagnosed based on the process of elimination of other illnesses or diseases.

While many other illnesses can cause ECE-like symptoms, true ECE can kill your fuzzy quickly. So be on the lookout for sudden changes for the worse and be ready to act.

> ## More about ECE
>
> Infamously known to the ferret community as "the Greenies" or "Green Slime Disease," this virus didn't rear its ugly epidemic heinie until 1993 when it hit fuzzies in the mid-Atlantic states. It quickly spread from ferret to ferret and state to state like wildfire. In the beginning, mortality rates were extremely high, with sudden, severe symptoms baffling vets as everyone scrambled to figure out the best methods of treatment. While the disease is still running rampant, ferret humans and vets have a better understanding of what to do, and mortality rates have dropped considerably. Although the initial mass panic has somewhat faded, the risk is still very real.
>
> A great place to get up-to-date information on treating ECE and other illnesses and diseases is right on the Internet. The Ferret Mailing List (FML) is a huge support/informational group of fuzzy humans, veterinarians, shelter operators, and other ferret fans. Get answers to your questions from knowledgeable ferret owners and share some stories of your own. To join this great list, simply go to `ferret-request@cunyvm.cuny.edu` and subscribe. You won't be sorry.

Symptoms

Some typical symptoms of ECE follow:

- Diarrhea that is neon green to yellow, bubbly, foul-smelling, or slimy
- Seedy poop, often yellowish in color (indicating undigested food)
- Dehydration, often severe
- Lethargy and sleepiness
- Extreme weight loss (up to 50 percent in severe cases)
- Vomiting
- Oral and stomach ulcers
- Coma and death

Treating ECE

There is no cure for ECE at this time. Also, currently no vaccine is available to protect against ECE, although experts are working diligently to develop one. Because ECE is viral in origin, medications only help to relieve symptoms and fight secondary infections that almost always invade the already weakened fuzzy. In healthier or younger ferrets, the disease should be treated like the flu unless symptoms become severe.

Theories about ECE

Many theories exist regarding the dynamics of this virus. Some experts believe that it is constantly mutating, making firm treatment plans difficult. Some believe that it's like chicken pox: Once your ferret's had it, he won't get it again. With that thought, some have suggested purposely exposing younger, healthier furkids to it just so they can get it over with and develop an immunity to it. However, the Greater Chicago Ferret Association has reported that many of its shelter ferrets and personal ferrets have had this disease several times after appearing to have made a full recovery from a previous episode.

Another theory is that ferrets can be carriers of ECE for six to eight months. However, having seen a case where a healthy ferret was moved to a new home and immediately came down with ECE, I believe that ferrets can be carriers of the virus for longer than the currently held belief of six to eight months. This ferret hadn't been exposed to the virus in well over a year. This case also strengthens the belief that stress possibly plays a role. Healthy carriers of the virus may exhibit symptoms only after being subjected to stress (illness, a move, loss of a cage mate, etc.). From what other fuzzy humans have experienced, we know that ferrets can pass on the virus to other ferrets before or after showing the classic symptoms themselves. And some exposed fuzzies may never exhibit signs but still be capable of passing the virus on.

Serious bouts of dehydration must be combated with subcutaneous fluids and/or electrolyte replacers, such as Pedialyte or Gatorade. Supplemental feedings with Feline A/D, Ensure or Sustecal, chicken baby food, and Nutri-Cal have proven very helpful. Once your ferret is back on his paws again, be aware that his intestinal lining will be abnormal for some time even after symptoms seem to go away. He may suffer from periodic bouts of diarrhea and dehydration. Monitor recovering fuzzies closely and for several months.

Several medications and supportive measures have been successful in multiple combinations (see your vet). Treatments vary by degree of illness and should only be administered under the guidance of a veterinarian. Not all medications work for every ferret. You may find, through trial and error, the perfect combination of medication and support to get your fuzzy through his ordeal. Some medications that have been successful (in certain combinations) in treating ECE are Pepto-Bismol, Kaopectate, Amforol, Liquid Immodium AD, Pepcid AC, Carafate, Amoxidrops, and Prednisone.

ECE is an extremely contagious disease that spreads from ferret to ferret very quickly. To safeguard your ferret, clean, clean, clean. Do not let other people handle your ferrets without taking precautions. Wash thoroughly before and after handling any ferrets. Change clothing before handling your own little guys after visiting with strange ferts. Quarantine newcomers who may be healthy carriers. Until this thing is figured out, always take the safest route.

Enlarged Spleen

The spleen serves as a blood purifier. An enlarged spleen, or *splenomegaly*, is extremely prevalent in fuzzies, and no one really knows why for sure. This problem often appears by itself with no other underlying diseases. The spleen normally gets larger with age, but sometimes this growth is accelerated. For example, the use of certain anesthetics is known to rapidly cause this condition.

Diagnosing an enlarged spleen is relatively easy. Most experienced vets should be able to feel the large organ just by simply squishing around the ferret's abdomen (see Figure 16-2). Care should be taken not to apply enough pressure to rupture a severely bulging spleen. An x-ray often confirms the size and condition of the organ.

The shared expert opinion regarding this beefed-up organ is to leave it in if it isn't causing discomfort or other problems in the ferret. In other words, "If it ain't broke, don't fix it." Fuzzies can generally live long, healthy lives with big spleens. Removing a spleen unnecessarily can put your baby in more jeopardy. On the other hand, if the oversized spleen is obviously causing discomfort, lethargy, or loss of appetite, removal is necessary. Surgery to remove the spleen is actually quite easy, and the survival rate is extremely high — especially when no other illnesses are present. Some vets send a piece of the spleen to a pathologist to rule out cancer. I recommend you spend the extra money to do this if you can.

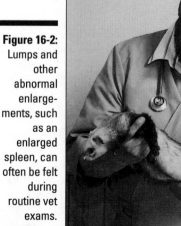

Figure 16-2: Lumps and other abnormal enlargements, such as an enlarged spleen, can often be felt during routine vet exams.

Many of the common fuzzy cancers and diseases frequently have an enlarged spleen listed as a prevailing symptom. No one knows why this is so prevalent in ailing ferrets. While an enlarged spleen doesn't always mean there's a dreadful disease lurking around the corner, when a cancer accompanies an enlarged spleen, removal of the spleen is highly recommended. (For info on cancer in ferrets, turn to Chapter 17.)

Eye Problems

I believe that every living thing with eyeballs is prone to cataracts and other afflictions of the eye. Naturally, ferrets are no exception. I have several fuzzies with cataracts. Some of these furballs are completely blind. Others have partial vision. Two of my special fuzzies have completely different eye problems: *luxated*, or displaced, lenses (see the sidebar "Are you lookin' at me, kid?" for info on this condition).

With the exception of eye infections, which I haven't seen very often, most eye problems in ferrets aren't correctable. Don't worry. A blind ferret can find trouble as well as or better than a seeing carpet shark.

Following are signs of eye problems that affect your ferret's eyesight:

- ✔ He's more cautious about moving around.
- ✔ He startles and backs off or snaps at you when you reach in to grab him.
- ✔ He walks into things.
- ✔ Cataracts are visibly present.
- ✔ He places a call to your health insurance carrier to see if laser surgery is covered.

You can also do the *finger test.* All of my sighted ferrets rapidly chase, follow, or watch my finger as I move it from side to side. My blind guys just pop their heads up and listen to figure out what everyone else is doing. I love them. They're so cute.

Cataracts

Most of us know someone who's had cataracts removed from their eyes so that they can see better. Ferrets are also prone to this eye disorder, but they can't have their cataracts removed. This condition is easy to spot because the eye becomes opaque or filmy across the pupil (see Figure 16-3). Cataracts eventually cause blindness because they prevent the light from reaching the retina.

Are you lookin' at me, kid?

I have two unrelated ferrets at home with an eye problem that's actually pretty bizarre looking. They each arrived with one *luxated*, or out-of-place, lens. They looked as if someone had dropped a tiny white dot into the bottom of their eyes — almost a 3-D image. I thought it was due to injuries, but over time the other lens in the other eye also became luxated and dropped to the bottom. Both fuzzies eventually went completely blind. Experts don't know much about this odd condition. But I know that both of my ferrets are doing just fine.

If your ferret has cataracts and is under 1 year old, the problem is probably genetic (that is, the result of poor breeding). Sometimes cataracts can be caused by an injury (even while the furkid is inside his mom), a disease, and even an improper diet. Cataracts can also be a developing sign of old age.

No treatment is available for cataracts. But what the heck — ferrets don't see well anyway. Blind ferrets adapt very well, as long as you're careful not to startle them or move the furniture around.

Figure 16-3: The cataract in Goomer's left eye has left him partially blind, but you'd never know it.

Tiny eyeballs (Microphthalmia)

Some ferrets are born with itty-bitty eyeballs. The cause is genetic. The eyes on these kids are noticeably smaller than those on the average ferret, and they may even appear sunken. You can also see tiny white crystal deposits in the lens, like the snowflakes in a shaken-up snow globe. However, these deposits don't sink to the bottom. They stay fixed in the lens. What you're seeing are actually white crystal-like deposits that may or may not be trying to form into cataracts.

Sometimes instead of the eyeball being small, the eyelid is small. In this case, the resulting appearance is small eyes. Sometimes this can be corrected by surgery. Although this condition is not usually physically irritating to the ferret, in some instances the eyelashes point downward and rub on the eye itself. This condition is also considered genetic in origin.

Ferrets with tiny eyeballs often have *hypermature* lenses. It's like having the eyes of an 80-year-old person when you're only 20 years old. In tiny eyeballs, the distance between the lens and cornea is shallower than normal, and this situation impairs vision. The extent of vision impairment often depends on how narrow the distance is. Also, the iris is thicker and spongier than in normal fuzzy eyes. To give you an idea of why the thickness matters, consider what the iris's function is. The iris dilates and constricts, causing the pupil to open up or close down, thus controlling the amount of light that reaches the retina. A defective iris leads to a failing pupil. Good thing a ferret doesn't need his eyes to pass carpet shark tests.

Hairballs

Ferrets are extremely prone to hairballs, and hairballs can lead to intestinal blockages. Unlike cats, ferrets can't leave colorful wads of urped-up fur on your newly shampooed carpeting. Ferts are capable of throwing up, but usually the fur accumulates until it becomes a large mass — too big to go either up or down. Hairballs and other blockages (see the section "Intestinal and Stomach Blockages") cause ferrets to become seriously ill — and often cause death.

You can find hairball remedies or preventives at many pet stores and certainly the larger pet supply stores. Some ferret shelters and veterinarians also carry these products. You absolutely must always have a tube of this type of product on hand (see Figure 16-4).

You should give your ferret a hairball product such as Laxatone, Petromalt, or Laxaire on a regular basis to help clean out his system. I give each of my ferrets ¼ teaspoon of a hairball preventative a few times a week. Most ferrets like the taste of the stuff. Some need to get used to it. With others, you need to insist that they take it — by squeezing it directly into their mouths.

Figure 16-4:
Hairball preventives should be given regularly. Most ferrets, like Dook, enjoy the taste.

If you think your fuzzy ingested something that can cause major damage, increase the hairball remedy to ½ teaspoon twice a day to help pass the object through. Monitor his health and behavior closely and get him to the vet immediately if his health deteriorates. If you don't have a yummy tasting hairball preventative on hand, a good substitute is petroleum jelly (Vaseline). You may need to mix a little Ferretone or other liquid treat in it to help the ferret swallow it.

Intestinal and Stomach Blockages

The leading causes of death in ferrets under 2 years old are intestinal and stomach obstructions. Youngsters mouth and taste everything from fingers to foam rubber. But older kids aren't immune to this affliction. Blockages can occur when your overzealous carpet shark eats something that's too big to keep passing on through. Hairballs are frequently the cause of clogs (see the "Hairballs" section for things you can do to take care of hairballs). No matter what the cause, if the blockage can't be pushed out the other end, everything backs up.

Blockages can occur anywhere in the digestive tract, from the throat to the stomach to the small intestine. It all depends on where the object gets hung up. Stomach blockages may move around and cause symptoms to appear and subside. A clog in the belly can last a long time and cause a slow wasting away. If it's a hairball, the mass slowly grows.

Symptoms of a blockage

Here are some signs that your fuzzy may be blocked up:

- Constipation
- Tiny poop (looks like string cheese) or black, tarry poop
- Bloating
- Painful belly
- Loss of appetite
- Loss of weight
- Vomiting
- Mouth pawing
- Dehydration
- Teeth grinding
- Face rubbing
- Lethargy

If you suspect that your fuzzy ate something he shouldn't have, start giving him Laxatone a couple times a day. Watch for foreign objects in anything that comes out the other end (if anything poops out). *Hint:* Poop mixed with water makes identifying foreign bodies quite a bit easier.

Keep in mind that it often takes more than Laxatone to fix a blockage problem. Left untreated, a stopped-up fuzzy dies an agonizing death. Don't wait until the last minute to go to the veterinarian.

Diagnosis and cure

Diagnosis by feeling around the ferret's belly isn't fail-proof. Sometimes large tumors cause similar symptoms and feel like an obstruction. Often, the vet confirms suspicions with an x-ray.

Stomach surgery cures this ailment. Once the blockage moves into the small intestine, surgery is imperative, or painful death can occur within a day or two. A soft diet for several days following the surgery is recommended.

Because dehydration from failure to eat and drink is a serious problem, administering oral fluids every few hours is imperative.

Rabies

Rabies is a subject that every human should know about. While our ferrets are highly unlikely to ever contract rabies, the possibility is not nonexistent. And rabies is one fatal disease that mammals can pass to humans. Rabies, caused by a rhabdovirus, is passed through the saliva of an infected animal, most frequently through a bite that penetrates the skin. Once inside the body, the deadly virus attaches to nerve bundles, reproduces, and migrates to the vicitm's brain. Then the virus travels along nerve bundles until it reaches the salivary glands where it can then be passed to another victim through biting.

There are many different strains of the rabies virus, including rodent, raccoon, fox, and skunk strains. Studies suggest that our fuzzies are most susceptible to the raccoon strain, which they also can pass on before death.

Don't start foaming at the mouth just yet!

Before you panic with the rabies scare, keep the following things in mind:

✔ Studies indicate that ferrets (and their family members) have an incredible natural immunity to rabies, even when bitten by a rabid animal.

✔ Studies also show that it's highly unlikely that even an infected fuzzy will pass on the virus because the virus rarely reaches the salivary glands before the ferret's death. If it does hit the salivary glands (in cases of the raccoon strain), experts suggest that the virus is in such a minimal amount that it's not enough to infect another animal or person.

✔ The rare rabid ferret doesn't become aggressive, anyway. He has *dumb rabies*, so he doesn't attack others.

✔ There has never been a documented case of rabies being passed from fuzzy to human.

✔ The USDA-approved Imrab-3 rabies vaccine for ferrets proved almost 95 percent successful in tests where vaccinated ferrets were purposely infected with the rabies virus.

✔ The Centers for Disease Control has documented fewer than 20 ferrets infected with rabies since 1954.

✔ Your fuzzy is an indoor pet (supervised when outdoors) with minimal exposure to rabid animals.

Keeping score

In six years, 1989 through 1994, there have only been four cases of ferrets with rabies. Compare that number to our companion dogs and cats, whose rabies incidence numbers were 928 and 1,425, respectively. That's a lot of rabid poochies and kitties. Raccoons came in highest with 21,447 cases, and skunks took second place with 10,733. Only 15 rabid people were reported, but that's still more rabid people than rabid ferrets.

Rabies can manifest itself in one of two ways: *furious rabies* and *dumb rabies*. With furious rabies, the infected animal exhibits intense aggression, biting, and foaming at the mouth. With dumb rabies, the animal becomes lethargic and deathly ill and wants little to do with people or other animals. Animals with dumb rabies don't attack and usually die quickly. Although ferret infection is extremely rare, studies indicate that ferrets exhibit dumb rabies, with death occurring seven days (on average) after the ferret has been infected.

While these symptoms can indicate a host of problems, they can also suggest rabies:

✔ Disorientation

✔ Loss of coordination

✔ Lethargy

✔ Muscle spasms

✔ Difficulty breathing

✔ Drooling

✔ Nervousness

✔ Hind leg weakness

✔ Passiveness

✔ Hind end paralysis

Many years ago, no approved vaccinations were available to protect fuzzies against viral diseases, such as rabies and distemper. Today, we're a lot more fortunate. Today, you have a choice on how much life "insurance" you're willing to buy for your lovable fuzzbutts. While some people weigh the pros and cons of vaccinating (the only viable con being a history of life-threatening allergic reactions), the pros weigh heavily on the scale. Failure to vaccinate your ferret can lead to a miserable disease and death. To the true fuzzy human, the emotional cost of losing a ferret to a preventable disease is immeasurable. Proof of vaccination may also calm the fears of people who might get bitten or scratched — and perhaps prevent confiscation of your pet. For information on the rabies vaccine, head to Chapter 13.

Ulcers

By the time you're done reading about all that can go wrong with your fuzzy, you yourself may be suffering from an ulcer. While you may think caring for a ferret can cause ulcers, the ferret is more apt to be the ulcer victim. The causes are just about the same for both fuzzies and humans:

- ✔ **Stress, stress, and more stress.** It can be from illness, disease, grief (loss of a cage mate), low quality food, injury, or even anxiety over the environment (overcrowding, abuse, small cage, poor husbandry, no exercise).

- ✔ **Possible bacterial invasion.** The bacteria Helicobacter mustelae is found in almost all ferts. My thought is that stress can allow the resident bacteria to take advantage of the weary ferret and rapidly multiply to harmful levels, thus causing an ulcer.

- ✔ **Ulcer-causing substances.** These substances include alcohol, aspirin, and certain medications.

Having an ulcer diagnosed as soon as possible is important because it's a painful condition that can lead to death. Besides being unable to adequately digest their food, ulcer patients bleed internally from oozing blood vessels. For some reason, ulcer symptoms are often misdiagnosed as another intestinal or stomach problem. A good diagnostic tool is a barium x-ray, which shows any signs of burned-out bellies or intestines.

If an ulcer is allowed to progress without proper treatment, it may become so deep that it hits a major blood vessel and causes the suffering fuzzy to bleed to death internally. (The black, tarry stool associated with ulcers, for example, is actually digested blood and a sign of bleeding somewhere in the digestive tract.) If your ferret doesn't bleed to death, anemia may result from the constant rupturing of small blood vessels in the belly.

The symptoms of an ulcer include the following:

- ✔ Lethargy
- ✔ Tender belly
- ✔ Face rubbing
- ✔ Black, tarry stools
- ✔ Teeth grinding
- ✔ Loss of appetite
- ✔ Vomiting (may be bloody)
- ✔ Weight loss
- ✔ Pale gums
- ✔ Bad breath

Stomach acid and ulcers

Stomach acid is much stronger than battery acid. That's a burning fact. When an ulcer begins, the stomach secretes more acid than normal and the stomach lining is unable to protect itself from the acid. The result is tiny burns in the stomach wall. The reason for the failed balance between stomach acid and the stomach's protective lining isn't clear.

If you notice these symptoms, take your ferret to the vet for an exam and diagnosis. Treatment usually begins with antibiotic therapy with medicines such as Amoxicillin and Biaxin to combat Helicobacter. Some veterinarians use Flagyl. A tummy coater such as Pepto-Bismol, Carafate, or Tagamet is a must to relieve the burning and nausea that accompany ulcers.

A bland diet is recommended during treatment. Because stomach acid is always being secreted to help break down food, treatment can be long and tedious. It can take over a month for a ferret's ulcer to heal.

Urinary Tract Problems

Several urinary tract problems can pop up in carpet sharks. Many diseases and problems have similar symptoms, so a trip to the veterinarian is advisable — especially if you consider that urinary tract infections can become serious enough to cause kidney damage and even death in ferrets. It's imperative that the correct diagnosis be made and treatment begun as soon as possible.

Bladder or urinary tract infections

Bladder infections are most often caused by that irritating resident poopie bacteria, E. coli (found in poop, so keep that litter box clean). Staphylococcus is another bacteria that can be the evildoer. While both males and females are susceptible to this type of infection, it seems more common in females in heat and females with adrenal disease (see Chapter 17 for info on adrenal disease).

Symptoms of a bladder or urinary tract infection include

- Straining to urinate
- Painful urination
- Frequent piddles
- Discolored or smelly urine

If you notice any of these symptoms, take your critter to the vet immediately. Bladder infections can travel to the kidneys and cause major damage, and even death. By the time a kidney infection is detected, your fuzzy may be so gravely ill that treatment can prove futile, so correct and early diagnosis is imperative.

Most experts agree that treatment with the proper antibiotics should continue for a minimum of two weeks, and some opt for a three-week course. Stopping the medication too soon may cause the infection to flare up again soon down the road. Also, the bug may be even stronger and more resistant to medications the next time around.

Prostate problems

Although male ferrets can get urinary tract infections — they can exhibit similar symptoms — the vet should first rule out a prostate problem, such as inflammation, cysts, tumors, or abscesses. Prostate woes can sometimes be diagnosed just by feeling for an enlargement. If you're really lucky, you may also get to see a little pus ooze out of the fuzzy when you squeeze an infected prostate. Eeeeew. Since this male condition is often a result of adrenal disease, it may go away when the other condition is treated.

Stones and blockages

Bladder stones aren't that common in fuzzies, and the cause is still not fully understood. Some experts speculate that a poor diet high in ash or plant-based protein plays a major role. Other ideas include bacterial or viral infections and even genetic links. Whatever the cause, this is a painful condition that causes symptoms like those of a urinary tract infection. Other symptoms may include bloody or gritty urine (the grit or sand is actually mineral deposits).

If the stones get big enough or collect in the same area, blockages occur. Your fuzzy will no longer leave piddle puddles at this point. This situation is deadly.

Because stones and blockages mimic infections, diagnosis can be difficult. Often, your vet will be able to feel the large, urine-filled bladder or even the stones themselves. Use of x-rays has also been successful in identifying stones in the bladder.

Treatment depends on the severity of the situation. Treatment may be as simple as a change in diet, or more drastic measures — such as surgery — may be needed. The ferret is always put on a regimen of antibiotics to help combat the problem.

ADV: A Killer Among Us

ADV, or Aleutian Mink Disease Virus, is a parvovirus which has been on the rise in pet ferrets throughout the world. Still somewhat of a mystery in the ferret community, every effort is being made to learn more about this devastating infectious disease. Your ferret could already be infected or be at risk and you might not even know it! Arm yourselves with information and protect your lovable ferrets. For more information on ADV, visit the following sites: `www.geocities.com/russiansmom`, `www.geocities.com/wolfysluv/adv-straight.html`, and `http://groups.yahoo.com/group/advferret`.

Chapter 17

The Big C and Other Lumps

• •

In This Chapter

▶ The three biggie ferret diseases: adrenal disease, lymphosarcoma, and insulinoma

▶ Other common ferret conditions: skin tumors and chordomas

▶ Treatment and manageability options

• •

*W*hether you own one ferret or ten, you're likely to run into one or two of the ferret cancers or conditions talked about in this chapter. The three most prevalent conditions are adrenal disease (which may or may not be cancerous), lymphosarcoma, and insulinoma. These types of cancers or diseases are quite common in ferrets. Symptoms and treatments vary, as well as prognoses. As you see in this chapter, the Big C diagnosis isn't always an immediate death sentence. Some cases are treatable. Others are manageable, and your ferret may still live a few more quality years after the diagnosis, with or without ongoing medical intervention. However, early detection and treatment are often instrumental in adding quality months or even years to your fuzzy's life, so watch for changes in your fuzzy's appearance, habits, and behavior. A good vet will trust your judgment that something's not quite right with your fuzzbutt.

Adrenal Disease (Hyperadrenalcorticism)

Everyone has adrenal glands, including carpet sharks. These tiny organs are located very close to the kidneys. In a nutshell, these glands produce extremely important hormones that increase blood glucose levels, regulate electrolyte levels, increase musculature, and produce adrenaline. (So that's where the "get up and go" comes from.)

Adrenal problems are extremely common in ferrets, but no one knows why for sure. Some suspect the problem has a lot to do with early neutering. Others believe it's caused by prolonged exposure to light. Yet others believe being subjected to prolonged stress may also be a factor. Maybe it's a combination of all these things.

Hyperadrenalism, an overproduction of adrenal gland-produced hormones, in dogs and cats is almost always due to the pituitary gland mistakenly telling the adrenal glands to overproduce. This condition is called Cushing's disease. Cushing's disease in ferrets is extremely rare. The overproduction of adrenal gland hormones is almost always caused by a tumor, a lesion, or an enlarged gland.

Symptoms of adrenal disease can vary depending on the location of the tumor because different parts of the adrenal glands are responsible for different hormone production. Most common is the disease in which estrogen is the overproduced hormone. An adrenal ferret may have lesions or tumors on one or both of the tiny glands, which doesn't necessarily mean adrenal cancer. Lesions on the adrenal gland produce almost identical symptoms and problems as adrenal gland cancer. This condition usually hits furballs that are 3½ years old or older. Fortunately, in most cases, the tumors or lesions remain localized on the adrenal glands. Occasionally, they spread to other organs, such as the lungs or liver, but it's uncommon.

Symptoms of adrenal disease depend largely on which hormones are being overproduced and may include the following:

- Hair loss on tail/body (most common symptom but not always a symptom)
- Thinning hair or patchy fur loss
- Loss of appetite
- Lethargy
- Red, flaky skin
- Thin skin
- Excessive itchiness
- Swollen vulva (in spayed girls)
- Aggression and sexual acting out (in neutered boys)
- Weakness in back legs (in extreme cases)
- Increased thirst and urination
- Enlarged prostate
- Weight loss despite a pot belly appearance
- Osteoporosis (has been reported)
- Enlarged spleen
- Anemia
- High blood pressure
- Rapid heartbeat

Making the diagnosis

Diagnosing adrenal disease can, at times, be pretty easy just by looking at the ferret. If he's got some of the typical symptoms along with the massive balding (see Figure 17-1), he's probably got adrenal disease. However, a fuzzy can be suffering from adrenal disease and show no symptoms for a very long time.

Currently, no blood test exists that is 100 percent infallible. You and your vet may opt to send the fuzzy's blood to the University of Tennessee. There, they can perform an adrenal gland panel to evaluate the levels of hormone and steroid production. This is one more way to help zero in on a diagnosis. However, many vets will, with just cause, suggest surgically removing the affected adrenal gland without going to such diagnostic measures if the major signs are already there.

If you have a baldy ferret, your vet will sometimes be able to feel an enlarged left adrenal gland (the right adrenal gland is hard to locate). Exploratory surgery should yield a no-brainer diagnosis to any experienced fuzzy vet. So will an ultrasound, in many cases.

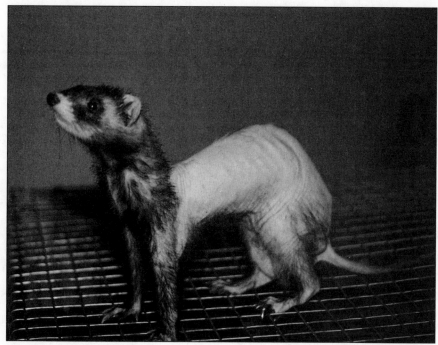

Figure 17-1: Although this ferret is as lovable as ever, advanced adrenal disease is not pretty.

Courtesy of Jean Caputo-Lee

Is adrenal disease gender-biased?

Some people believe that this disease is more often seen in the girls. Could this belief really be true? Probably not. Most likely, what's happening is that the classic swollen vulva (seen in most female adrenal patients, but also a sign of an unspayed female in heat) has more humans running to the vet, fearing that their baby girl is unspayed even though she's supposed to have been spayed already. Because the boys don't have this obvious warning sign, they may go for longer periods without being diagnosed — or miss being diagnosed altogether if no extreme hair loss is noted.

My fur! My beautiful fur!

Don't get all freaked out over a ratty-looking tail. Many fuzzies lose most or all of the fur on their tail during seasonal shedding. Sometimes it can take up to three or four months for the fur to grow back. It's not *the* sign of adrenal disease. However, *do* worry about patches of missing fur on other parts of your ferret, especially on the lower back and top of the buttocks. That can be a sign of many illnesses, including adrenal disease. Hair loss caused by adrenal problems is the result of extreme hormonal changes, particularly the overproduction of estrogen and corticosteroids. Unlike seasonal shedding, hair loss caused by adrenal woes begins at the base of the tail and spreads up the body. Sometimes ferrets lose all but their socks and hats.

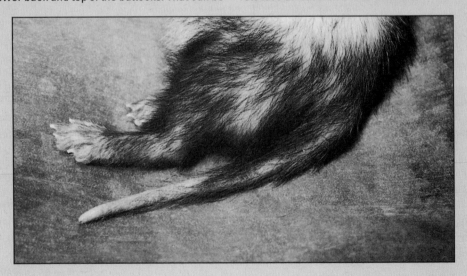

Removing both glands

Only a short while ago, your fuzzy would've been a nonsurgical candidate if the tumor resided on the right adrenal gland. Removal of this gland can be extremely dangerous because it resides close to the biggest blood vessel in the body, the *vena cava*. However, new surgical procedures have been developed, allowing both adrenal glands to be removed successfully if necessary. It's still extremely risky to remove the right adrenal gland, and the vet must *really* know the procedure well.

Yes, a ferret can have both adrenal glands removed. Some ferrets even manage okay without hormone supplements after the surgery. The reason is that some functioning tissue may be leftover after the surgery, which secretes a satisfactory amount of the good stuff.

Not all ferrets can have both adrenal glands removed without needing post operative medications. Sometimes removal of both glands causes Iatrogenic Addison's disease (not enough hormones produced), which will kill your ferret if your vet is unaware of this. All bilateral adrenal ferrets should have their cortisol level checked within three days of surgery. The normal value of cortisol in a ferret is 25.9 – 235. If the level is not within this range, your ferret will need injections of Percorten every three weeks and prednisone twice daily to survive.

Treating the disease

The treatment most often opted for is surgical removal of the affected adrenal gland. Some vets choose to also supplement the ferret with a steroid, such as Prednisone, after surgery for an extra pick-me-up. Postoperative prognosis is pretty high but can depend on where the tumor is and what else is going on inside.

What causes adrenal disease: One theory

One theory on the cause of adrenal disease is the extended unnatural periods of light ferrets are exposed to in our homes. Breeding is linked to photoperiods, and most fuzzies are altered. Experts suggest that lots of light may cause the adrenal and pituitary glands to "think sex" and function improperly, causing an outpouring of hormones. This confusing hormonal attack on the altered furball's tissues may eventually cause tumors or lesions. While the lighting theory hasn't been proven, and changing the lighting schematic won't cure a ferret who's already sick, some fuzzy owners opt to turn lights on and off in the fuzzy area in accordance with the natural outside lighting. (Some people have claimed complete recovery, but again, the lighting relationship hasn't been proven.) Experts suggest that ferrets should receive 14 hours of total blackness during every 24-hour period. By the way, all of my 4-foot light fixtures contain full spectrum bulbs. This type of bulb replicates natural, healthy sunlight.

Fortunately, tumors tend to occur more frequently on the left gland, which is easier to remove than the right. Also, while it's still uncommon, tumors that spread to other organs usually start on the right adrenal gland. Once the diseased gland is removed, symptoms gradually disappear. The fur usually grows back, although it can take many months, but sometimes the fur is thinner; it may even be a different color.

Anytime your vet performs an invasive surgery on your ferret, it's a good idea to have him or her also rule out common cancers and diseases while he's in there poking around. Besides doing a thorough internal checkup, the vet should also check the adrenal glands for tumors and lesions and the pancreas for insulinoma tumors. By doing this "auto check," the vet may diagnose a condition in its early stages, before symptoms appear. Early detection can prolong your fuzzy's life and make medical management more successful.

What if your ferret is a nonsurgical candidate? The reason may be because of the his age or other medical conditions (often, lymphosarcoma is also present). Or maybe your own fears are preventing you from going the preferred surgical route. Well, fuzzies can live up to three years completely untreated. Sometimes the fur grows back at the next seasonal coat change. But they usually lose more hair the next time around. And it may not grow back at all.

You do have other medical options that have been used, some with great results. But not all adrenal ferrets are candidates for alternative treatments. Speak with your vet about what's right for your furkid.

✔ The medication Lysodren works by lowering hormone production as it attacks and kills off excess adrenal cells. Unfortunately, this medication may also be detrimental to the insulinomic ferret because it also causes a decrease in blood sugar.

✔ Lupron and Tamoxifen are two new drugs that are still in the early stages of testing, but they show some promising signs in the fight against adrenal disease. Experts agree that, for the most part, medications may cause some symptoms to go away, but they aren't cures. They can also come with many side effects.

Prostate problems in the male ferret are often associated with adrenal disease. The overproduction of testosterone causes the prostate to swell and sometimes interfere with the urinary tract. Full or partial blockage of the urinary tract may occur. Lupron, in high doses, inhibits the production of testosterone, thus causing the prostate to shrink back down to normal size.

Chordomas

It's difficult to explain these icky tumors without first giving you a simple lesson on a complex matter of development. All developing embryos have certain tissues that develop to form the basic support system, such as the spine (including the tail). Leftover embryonic tissues that don't develop into the skeletal structure rest in between the vertebrae. These remnants sometimes continue to grow, causing the formation of chordomas, which are tumors. They're typically diagnosed in fuzzies over 3 years old.

The most common chordoma seen in the ferret is located on the tip of the tail (see Figure 17-2). But in some rare instances, the chordoma grows in between the vertebra near the head, a tumor called a *cervical chordoma*. This more serious tumor can cause compression of the spinal cord, and the ferret becomes physically impaired. Cervical chordomas are also more apt to spread and cause severe pain and neurological problems.

Chordomas are easily diagnosed and can present more than just cosmetic problems for your ferret. The mass grows slowly at the tip of the tail, eventually giving the tail a club-like appearance. The tumor itself is made up of a bony center beneath a layer of cartilage and rough cells that resemble red, raw elephant skin. For the Herculean fuzzbutt, this tumor can be quite a weapon.

There's frequently hair loss on and surrounding the tumor. Often, the mass becomes ulcerated and oozy. Because of its vulnerable location and the probability of trauma to the tail, removal is generally recommended.

Figure 17-2:
Chordomas usually show up at the tip of the ferret's tail.

Insulinoma

Insulinoma is one of the most prevalent cancers diagnosed in ferrets. A ferret with insulinoma has cancer of the pancreas or tumors of the insulin-secreting pancreatic cells. One of the main roles of the pancreas is to release insulin as needed to regulate the ferret's blood sugar levels. In ferrets with insulinoma, the tumors cause an overproduction of insulin, which in turn causes bouts of rapid drops in blood sugar, or *hypoglycemia*. (Diabetes in ferrets is the exact opposite of insulinoma. In the case of diabetes, too little insulin is produced. The blood is then unable to properly use the glucose, making the blood sugar dangerously high. This condition is called *hyperglycemia*.)

Insulinoma can hit fuzzies as young as 2 years old but more often strikes after the age of 5. Interestingly, not only is insulinoma one of the most common cancers afflicting our furkids, but it's also more commonly seen in the boys. Sometimes this disease goes unnoticed for a long time as the ferret's system fights to regulate its own blood sugar levels, and symptoms may not be overly apparent. Some of the symptoms may include

- Weakness
- Salivation
- Pawing at the mouth
- Dazed and confused look
- Mouth ulcers
- Lethargy
- Tremors
- Seizures
- Loss of coordination
- Rear leg weakness
- Enlarged spleen
- Vomiting
- Weight loss
- Coma

With insulinoma, symptoms may come and go unexpectedly in the ferret. Things that can trigger and aggravate symptoms are exercise, stress, and diet.

What causes insulinoma?

As with many things relating to ferrets, there's no identified or proven cause of this cancer. Of course, I must mention a couple of the popular theories that are floating around the ferret community. Some believe that diet, mainly kibble, is a great contributor to insulinoma. Kibble contains a lot of starch. In brief, a lot of starch means a lot of glucose production to break down the starch, which in turn means constant production of insulin. European ferrets that are fed meat or more natural diets have low insulinoma incidence rates. Others believe that some fuzzies are genetically predisposed to this cancer. Again, perhaps it's a combination of both and other things not yet considered.

Making the diagnosis

Diagnosis is usually obtained by drawing a fasting blood sugar level. That means the fuzzy goes 4–6 hours without food before the blood is drawn. Normal blood glucose levels are between 90 and 120. Having a fasting blood glucose of less than 60 is generally considered diagnostic for insulinoma. I've had a couple of ferrets with levels as low as 10 pull through and survive. Exploratory surgery, x-rays, and ultrasounds are also helpful in detecting these tumors.

Treating the disease

Unfortunately, pancreatic tumors can be small and seedy nodules, located throughout the pancreas, making the condition inoperable. In some cases, the tumors are isolated nodules that can be successfully removed. Although surgery is frequently an option and can stop or slow the progression of insulinoma, it's rarely a cure. Tumors frequently return at a later date. Your vet will be able to help determine the best course of action, based on your ferret's history and current condition. Once diagnosed, your fuzzy may live an additional ten months or even longer with a lot of tender, loving care and a consistent management program. Some of the medications that vets have found to be successful in managing insulinoma are prednisone, diazoxide (Proglycem), and dexamethasone. Only your vet will be able to determine what's best for your ferret.

You may want to seriously consider changing your ferret over to a diet higher in animal protein. Bob's Chicken Gravy (see Chapter 29) is very high in protein and is closer to what the ferret evolved eating. While it's not a cure, I've read — and many people have told me — that this formula has helped regulate and raise insulinomic ferrets' blood sugar to near normal levels. Some have even been told by their vets to cut down the medication. Hey, it's worth a shot.

It's often recommended that you add Brewer's yeast to the insulinoma patient's diet. I suggest you *do not* do this. The chromium in Brewer's yeast has been shown to actually lower blood sugar as opposed to stabilize it, as once thought.

Always keep some Karo syrup or honey on hand, especially if you have a ferret with insulinoma. If your fuzzy crashes (shows extreme lethargy, weakness, or has seizures) due to low blood sugar, take a cotton swab and dab a little honey or Karo syrup on his gums. The sugar helps to stabilize the ferret until you can get him to a vet. Follow up with some high-protein food like chicken baby food. Use the sugar boost in emergency situations only, to bring your ferret out of a hypoglycemic episode. Too much sugar can be dangerous for a fuzzy with insulinoma.

Lymphosarcoma

Very common in our beloved furballs is lymphosarcoma, a cancer of the lymphatic system. A fuzzy suffering from this type of cancer normally has a severely impaired immune system. The cause of lymphosarcoma still remains a bit of a mystery. Environmental and genetic influences are possible factors. Some experts are convinced that this cancer is linked directly to some type of virus. Lymphosarcoma sometimes shows up in multiple cage mates, reinforcing the viral idea by implying some sort of transmission of the cancer between fuzzies. Although the viral connection hasn't been proven, you may want to take extra precautions when housing a fuzzbutt with lymphosarcoma.

The two types of lymphosarcoma that are most often identified in ferrets are *juvenile lymphosarcoma (lymphoblastic form),* which hits young furkids typically under the age of 14 months, and *classic lymphosarcoma (lymphocytic form),* which is generally diagnosed in middle-aged and older ferts.

Lymphosarcoma is not always easy to recognize, but some of the signs include

- Lethargy
- Wasting away
- Diarrhea
- Labored breathing
- Loss of appetite
- Enlarged spleen
- Enlarged lymph nodes

Lymphoma and lymphosarcoma: What's the difference?

Lymphoma and lymphosarcoma are inter-changeable words in the ferret world. While lymphoma is a general term that encompasses many types of cancers, both words describe the proliferation of abnormal lymphoid cells some-where in the body. The disease can involve one organ or many organs or an entire system. The most commonly seen lymphomas in fuzzies are juvenile and classic lymphosarcoma. Some other lymphomas are gastric (intestinal tract), orbital (eyeball), and even cutaneous (skin). There are many others.

Making the diagnosis

In the juvenile version, death usually occurs suddenly and often with no symptoms, as the disease raids many organs at once. Any warning symptoms that do exist in the youngsters are often misdiagnosed as pneumonia or cardiomyopathy — due mainly to respiratory and circulatory distress resulting from large, fast-growing tumors that invade the chest cavity and squish the lungs.

Classic lymphosarcoma is more commonly recognized by vets. In the older fuzzies, this cancer is often accompanied by tumors of the pancreas and/or adrenal glands. Because of the frequent presence of other underlying condi-tions and their symptoms and diagnoses, lymphosarcoma often goes undiag-nosed for quite a long time. Many vets attribute new or worsening symptoms to the already existing illnesses. In other cases, where no other abnormalities exist, your ferret may exhibit no outward signs until the disease has become fairly progressed.

Unlike with the juvenile version, classic lymphosarcoma frequently causes enlarged lymph nodes that are easily felt under the armpits and on the neck. Diagnosis should be confirmed by a biopsy of a lymph node, bone marrow, the spleen, or chest fluid. Often, irregularities in the complete blood count raise a red flag, but that's not always the case. It's always best to send out biopsy samples to a pathologist.

Treating the disease

Some fuzzy cancers, including lymphosarcoma, respond pretty well to chemotherapy. For many fuzzies, chemotherapy provides a decent remission rate, with life prolonged 6–36 months from treatment. However, treatment can be very expensive, and not all cancer patients are good chemo candi-dates. Talk to your fuzzy vet about all your possible options.

Some symptoms can be alleviated temporarily with steroids, but this treatment is not a cure.

Seriously ill ferrets and fuzzies recuperating from surgery should be kept in intensive-care cages away from other carpet sharks. This arrangement helps the fuzzy regain his strength. It's hard to heal when you have other fuzzies crashing into you and trying to engage you in play. Temporarily isolating sickies in intensive-care cages also makes assisted feedings and medicating easier on you. The cage should be small — preferably single level — but comfortable. It should be placed in a safe, ferret-comfortable, and convenient spot.

Skin Tumors

Skin tumors appear in all shapes and sizes on our fuzzy friends. The good news is that the majority of skin tumors seen on carpet sharks are *benign*, or noncancerous, although all are capable of becoming *malignant,* or cancerous. Removal of the lump, bump, or ugly formation is usually recommended. Although the most common ferret skin tumors rarely develop into cancer, the possibility that they will always remains if the tumors aren't removed. Also, several types of skin tumors are itchy and easy to rub and irritate. Removing them eliminates the risk of secondary infections from open sores. Be sure to send a tumor biopsy to a lab for analysis, just for peace of mind.

Many types of skin tumors can afflict fuzzbutts. The following sections touch on the most common ones.

Mast cell tumors

Mast cells are directly related to the immune system. These cells produce histamines to combat foreign bodies in the ferret's system. For reasons unknown, sometimes these cells migrate and form small tumors on the skin. They can appear anywhere on your fuzzy as a single tumor or multiple tumors.

Mast cell tumors are often round, slightly raised red lumps — button-like in appearance. Sometimes they're flat and scaly in appearance. Because of the constant production of histamines, this type of tumor is extremely itchy. You may witness your poor ferret scratching feverishly at the tumor, causing excessive bleeding and oozing. The site usually shows some hair loss and may be scabbed over from the constant irritation.

While mast cell tumors are often malignant in other animals, they rarely become cancerous in ferrets. Nonetheless, because of the risk of infection and the obvious discomfort your fuzzy exhibits, be a nice human and have mast cell tumors removed. Have a biopsy done, just to be sure, but don't fret while waiting for the pathology report; you can assume that the tumors are benign. Expect more, too, because they frequently recur.

Basal cell tumors

Basal cell tumors are slow-growing, wart-like nodules with a little crater in the middle of each tumor. They pop up anywhere on the ferret. They're loose on the skin and move freely when you push on them.

Because of their raised presentation and mobility, these types of tumors are easy to rub or scrape. For these very same reasons, basal cell tumors are easy to remove and should be removed, because of the possibility of infection. If removed properly, they shouldn't recur in the same place.

Sebaceous cell tumors

These are generally tumors of the skin's oil glands or hair follicles. Sebaceous cell tumors are really funky in shape, sometimes branching out like cauliflower. Sometimes they appear as bluish colored lumps just under the skin. Like the other skin tumors mentioned in this chapter, these tumors can appear anywhere on the fuzzy body. They're usually firm tumors that range in color from tan to brown to blue.

Removing these tumors is important because they often grow rapidly and can become cancerous. Besides, no one likes sporting a vegetable-shaped mass for all the world to see.

Chapter 18

When It's Time to Say Good-bye

. . . .

In This Chapter

▶ Knowing when to let go

▶ What to do with your deceased pet's body

▶ Grieving for a lost pet

. . . .

*W*ell, it was inevitable that this chapter had to come up — death, the taboo and rarely talked about subject. Naturally, we're never quite able to prepare for the death of a greatly cherished pet. The end always seems to come way too soon. And what's so unfortunate is that many humans don't know what they have until it's gone. Other humans cherish every breath their pets take, knowing all too well that it could be the last breath.

It's so difficult to watch a beloved pet suffer. And for the true animal lover, it never seems to matter how long the pet's been with us. Whether the critter was just recently left on our doorstep or was a longtime resident that was hand raised with TLC from infancy, the pain can be just as great. I can still remember and feel the passing of every single fuzzy that has died in the 10 years since they first graced me with their presence. And with each death came the same questions over and over and over again: Did I do something wrong? Was there anymore I could have done? Was this the right time to let go? Why this little guy? Why now?

This chapter deals specifically with death — a subject most people don't want to talk about. In this chapter, I talk about knowing when to put your pet to sleep and what your options are for humanely and compassionately taking care of your deceased pet's body. And what about all those unanswered questions?

Saying Good-bye

Sometimes the only way we can truly show our love for our pets is to let go of them. They count on us day after day to make the right decisions for them — to ensure that they lead a fun and healthy life, full of love and affection. But the day will come when they'll count on us to make that final, heartbreaking decision — to be selfless instead of selfish and end their suffering and allow them to leave this world with a little dignity. In their eyes we'll see. In our hearts we'll know.

You know it's time to let go when the fuzzy no longer enjoys life. His illnesses or injuries have been treated as well as they possibly can be, and yet he continues to suffer. Little hope exists, and the few months that have been cautiously promised will be filled with pain and misery.

Stop. Look. Listen. Your fuzzy will tell you if you're willing to listen closely. As hard as it may be for you, it will be comforting for him to hear your soothing voice and feel your touch while he leaves this world.

Humane euthanasia is painless to your fuzzy. It involves overdosing the ferret on an anesthetic, either by gas or injection. Your baby will slowly fall to sleep. For the first time in a long time, he'll feel no pain and be free from the suffering. In only a few short moments, he'll pass over the *Rainbow Bridge* — a term, which comes from a poem by the same name, that refers to an animal's passage from life to death — and be greeted by all the other pets that went before him. He'll once again romp and play and watch you from afar until the day you join him again.

Learning from Death

It seems an impossible thought. No way will you allow some vet to cut open your newly deceased baby and poke around in there just out of curiosity. Well, you may want to think twice about that. *Necropsies,* or postmortems, are done shortly after the death of an animal and serve many important functions:

- ✔ The procedure may shed light on sudden, unexpected deaths. Not all animals give lots of warning signs before leaving this world. Some die quite unexpectedly and throw their humans into emotional tailspins. Wouldn't you want some answers and relief to the questions buzzing around in your head?

- ✔ Should you and your other pets have something to worry about? I mean, let's face it — the fear of something contagious enters everyone's head at one time or another. If your ferret's death was a surprise, wouldn't you want to know if you could expect more or prevent other surprises? And remember, animals can pass some icky cooties to humans, too.

✔ What experts know about fuzzy diseases and treatments is based mainly on the findings of postmortems. Your fuzzy's death can assist other ferrets by providing precious data to veterinarians. This data can strengthen or weaken theories relating to diseases and illnesses. The postmortem can also give clues as to what does and doesn't work in terms of treating fuzzies. The more a vet sees, the more the vet learns, and the greater benefit the vet will be to your ferrets in the future.

✔ Many theories exist regarding how and why certain diseases exist. Postmortems may reveal internal genetic abnormalities, which are sometimes the result of poor breeding. Sometimes they reveal diseases or illnesses that hadn't been identified in your ferret. As horrible as this may sound, if your ferret was a new purchase, you may be able to use this information to get your money back or to get a new fuzzy.

✔ Another thing a grieving human doesn't want to hear is that husbandry may have played a role in the ferret's death. Diet and environment play big parts in the health of your fuzzy. Don't let this fact stop you from having a necropsy performed. Experts aren't the only ones who can learn from their mistakes. I know I'd want to correct any deficiencies on my part and prevent future losses.

Your vet may or may not charge you for this service. Most usually charge a fee. It depends on their own curiosity and desire to learn more. Some vets do the gross necropsy (dissecting and evaluating) for free and charge you only for samples sent to pathologists. While whole-body necropsies are sometimes performed, often vets opt to focus only on the known problem area or cause of death.

To perform an accurate and complete postmortem on an animal, the body must be fresh. So what should you do if your pet passes on at home? Place his body in a bag or container and put him in the fridge. Don't freeze him. Freezing damages tissues. Likewise, when a body is left for more than an hour or so in temperatures over 70 degrees Fahrenheit, rapid deterioration of the organs and tissues occurs, which also yields bad results.

If you choose to have a necropsy performed, your vet will, on request, stitch up any incisions once the postmortem is completed. Your ferret won't look exactly like your little baby, but he won't look like Frankenfert, either. Keep in mind that the body is only the package that your fuzzy was delivered in. He's no longer in there. He opted for the superior package deal over at the Rainbow Bridge.

Having a necropsy performed is a difficult decision. I've always been told never to make a decision when I'm Hungry, Angry, Lonely, or Tired (HALT). You should probably throw Grieving into that mix, too, but then it wouldn't spell a nice word. Chances are, you aren't reading this material because you're trying to figure out what to do at this very moment. So think about it now, before you're too emotional, and make a decision about what you'll do when your beloved ferret dies. The future of ferret medicine may depend on it.

A dedicated scientist

I have a paleopathologist friend who has vets and pet owners send him the bodies of deceased pet ferrets and ferret relatives so that he can study them extensively. Whenever possible, he's provided with the age of the animal and the suspected or known cause of death. He then removes the entire skeleton and collects data based on what he's been told and what the skeleton reveals. From this procedure, he's been able to come up with many fascinating theories and discoveries that have already helped us — and will help us in the future — to better understand the needs of our precious fuzzies.

What's After Death

Grieving, sadness, emptiness, anger, fear, loneliness. The list goes on and on. An important part of grieving is putting some closure on the loss. A necropsy that yields some answers is a great start. But once you've got the answers, then what do you do with your little deceased pet? You have several options. It's no longer just a choice between burying him in the backyard, tossing him out with the trash (it happens a lot), or leaving him at the vet for convenience.

- ✔ Some people have their pets cremated.
- ✔ Some people have elaborate funerals with caskets and everything for their recently departed pets.
- ✔ Others are even a bit more eccentric and have their pets freeze-dried or stuffed.

Choosing cremation

Whether your pet dies at home or at the veterinarian's office, your vet will, upon request, properly store your deceased pet and arrange for the pet crematory to pick up the body for cremation. Each option is offered for a different price and varies from vet to vet and from crematory to crematory. If you choose this route, you'll usually only have two options in terms of cremating your pet:

- ✔ Mass cremation without the return of your pet's ashes — crematory disposes of all ashes according to the law.
- ✔ *Special* cremation with return of your pet's ashes — guarantee (including a certificate) that your deceased pet was cremated completely separately from any other animals, assuring that all ashes are returned and are your pet's and only your pet's.

Your vet should also be able to give you prices for these services, as well as show you several urn styles, should you choose to have your pet's ashes returned. Urns are available for an additional fee. Some urns are simple. Some are elaborate. The style to choose depends on your taste and your budget. You can add an engraved nameplate or simply have the pet's name etched in wood. Some people even add a little picture of the pet to the container. This is a time for creativity and celebration of your pet's life (see Figure 18-1).

If you choose to receive only the ashes back, without a special urn, be prepared for what you may get. Most of my pets' ashes were returned in small, white, plastic bottles or decorative tins. Once they came back in a clear plastic bag, which was both startling and disturbing to me.

Finally, think about what your options are with the returned ashes:

✔ Some people keep each pet separated in special containers. They keep these containers on special shelves or other special places of honor.

✔ Other people have one big urn in which they keep everyone together as a family.

✔ Still others bury the ashes or spread them in the pet's favorite *outdoor* place. I emphasize *outdoor* because your fuzzy's favorite hidey-hole in the play area probably isn't a good idea. Nor is under the couch cushions. Your guests would question the rising dust as they plopped down for a relaxing chat.

Figure 18-1: Urns can be simple but still creative and attractive, like this one for Dusty.

Just recently, a local news station did some investigating and found that not all pet crematoriums were up to snuff. People were, in some cases, getting back way more than just their pet's ashes. In other cases, it was apparent that not all the ashes could have possibly been returned. Be careful which crematorium you choose. Speak with your vet about the crematorium he or she uses. Call the crematorium and ask questions. If you're unhappy with the answers, you can take your pet to another place. It's your choice. Some crematories even let you stay there while the service is performed.

Pet cemetery

No, it's not anything like Stephen King's portrayal of a pet cemetery. Thank heavens. In fact, pet cemeteries look a lot like our own human cemeteries, except they're much smaller versions. Finding them can be challenging. They aren't all that popular, and many people don't even know this choice exists. Your vet may know which direction to point you in, or a friend may have some experience with one. You can also check out a phone book under "pet cemetery."

The actual burial for your pet can be as simple as picking out the tiny site and delivering the body to the cemetery. Or it can be extravagant (eccentric in the eyes of many). You can have your ferret set up in a special coffin where you can actually view the body in the funeral home before saying goodbye, like at a human wake. Some places allow you to deliver the pet-in-coffin to the burial site and bury the pet yourself. Or you can follow the somber ground crew as they lead you to the site for burial.

A headstone should be purchased so that your fuzzy's gravesite will always be marked with sentiment (see Figure 18-2). This entire burial option can be quite a costly endeavor. Pet cemeteries vary in policies and practices. I'm sure they also differ in prices and available packages in order to suit your needs. One nice thing about pet cemeteries is that you will always have a special place to visit your dearly loved pet.

Together through eternity

I hear that due to popular demand, some human cemeteries are making ground-breaking changes to allow pets to be buried alongside their humans. Well, I love this idea. Except that even after our deaths, my spouse would be complaining that there are too many cats "hogging the bed."

Figure 18-2: Headstones can be simple or custom-made. Ara's will last a lifetime.

The backyard burial

Backyard burials can be personal, private, and inexpensive. They can mean everything in the world to the grieving human. Many families with kids know exactly what I'm talking about. How many of you, as tearful children, made your eye-rolling family members gather around the toilet to bid farewell to the bravest, coolest goldfish that had ever lived? (**Note:** Before you decide to bury your pet in the backyard, be sure to check city ordinances; doing so may actually be illegal in your area.)

Headstones are optional for the backyard burial. My Ara's cost $350 and was custom-designed by me and etched in heavy granite by the stonecutter at the local cemetery. It took forever for it to arrive but was well worth the wait. Of course, after I spent all that money, I started getting dozens of pet catalogs that offered low-cost, simple pet headstones. But none could compete with my personal touch. (Read the sidebar "A personal story" for info about my sweet wolfdog, Ara.)

If your deceased pet was especially close to a child, you may want to encourage that child to celebrate the pet's life by personally making the headstone or grave marker. It's a wonderful way for a child to put a little closure on the huge matter of loss.

A personal story

One of the hardest decisions I ever made was to put my 16½-year-old wolfdog, Ara, to sleep. In the morning, he struggled to rise from his bed. He looked at me with sad, helpless eyes as I lifted his back end up for him. I saw that dignity still glowed dimly in his eyes, and yet the light was fading and I could tell he knew it. We romped slowly in the yard before our vet, Mike, arrived to put him to sleep. I questioned my decision as Ara walked up almost briskly to greet Mike. Maybe it wasn't time. I'd made this decision several times in the few preceding months and selfishly changed my mind just as Mike arrived. But Ara was almost 17 years old and no longer happy. He fought to stay with us much longer than anyone had expected such a large dog to. We moved Ara's bed outside, and he quickly went to it. As he looked up at me, I could tell he trusted me to make the right decision. I held him closely while he left his broken-down body and passed over the Rainbow Bridge.

In my backyard is a beautiful group of six large pine trees set in an imperfect row. And directly below their towering branches are many unmarked graves where dozens of critters that have passed over the Rainbow Bridge rest. Directly north of all these graves lies underground the most handsome, majestic, and loyal dog anyone's ever met. Ara Glen. His headstone reads "Always Faithful, Always Loved." Ara is keeper and protector of my critter graveyard. He watches over the little guys and guides them over the Rainbow Bridge. I visit his grave often when I need to talk, and I know he'd understand. This is why I planted him close to my heart.

This note is actually a Hubby Alert: Just as a matter of clarification, our buried pets will be packed up and moved with us if we ever move from this house. They'll then be reburied in a beautiful place in our new yard. I've warned, you. You think I'm kidding. Here it is in writing.

Getting Help with the Grief

I'll tell you right off the bat that there's nothing worse than grieving a loss that no one seems to understand. People can sometimes make you feel worse. Someone who has never had a pet may even proclaim, "It's only an animal." Well, not exactly. Pets are family members that you've grown extremely attached to. They've been a source of comfort and joy as well as sadness and frustration. Many people view pets as they view human children. But some people out there just don't understand.

I'm surrounded by people who just don't understand how I can cry over the loss of a ferret or any other small critter. A dog or a cat they'd understand — at least a little, so they say. And those who really have no clue rationalize, "It's not like they were humans." Those are the people to avoid. Those are the people who make me like animals more than people.

Surround yourself with people who do understand. And don't think you're strange. I've seen people spend hundreds of dollars to remove tumors from mice, rats, and guinea pigs. It's not the size or cost of the animal that matters. It's how much room they take up in your heart.

Know you're not alone

You may feel crazy for feeling the way you do. Well, let me tell you, many of us out there feel crazy and silly right along with you. Don't let the others kick you when you're down.

Many support groups are out there that deal directly with the loss of a pet. You can do a search on the Internet. If you can, visit the Web site www.tipsforwriters.com/petloss.shtml. It's a neat site that has many wonderful tips and links to other pet-loss sites. If you visit this site or other sites like it, you'll find many hotlines and chat groups and even books dealing with grief issues, all available for you and your family members.

Face the feelings

A variety of different feelings will pop up at any given time. *Feel* them. Don't run from them. Remember that you're not alone. Your feelings are powerful, but they're not unique. Among the emotions that'll creep up are denial, anger, guilt, sadness, and emptiness. We all think we could've been a better pet human after the animal is gone. Hindsight is 20/20. Chances are, you *were* a wonderful parent. Feelings are temporary. While the memories will last forever, the pain slowly fades after a while.

Give yourself time

Many people think that you can run right out and get a new pet as soon as you lose the one you loved so dearly and that doing so will fix everything. Come on. You know better than that. You can never replace a family member.

Give yourself time to grieve your loss. Pets aren't replaceable. You can certainly add to your family when you feel better, but taking on another responsibility when you're grieving isn't fair to you or the new pet. Likewise, don't try to fix someone else's grief by giving a pet as a gift. Grief isn't something to be fixed. It's something that must be worked through over a period of time. And once you're truly ready for a new pet, toss any feelings of guilt or betrayal out the window. Your deceased pet would've wanted you to move on and be happy with a new pet.

Sometimes the loss of one pet will cause another pet to grieve to the point of illness. I've even known a few animals to die from the loss of a playmate. Ferrets are especially prone to severe grief. Take such a matter into consideration when making a decision on whether or not to add a new pet to the household and, if so, how soon you should do it.

Help others deal with their grief

You may have giggled inside when your child dragged you to the toilet for the ultimate farewell to Moby the goldfish. But that child hurt. Recognize that it's very possible that another person will feel the loss of a pet just as, or even more, deeply than you do. Respect those feelings by acknowledging them and providing as much support as you can. Each person is unique. Just because you didn't grieve doesn't mean that others won't or don't have the right to grieve.

Don't forget that animals bond deeply with both humans and other animals. When my wolfdog, Ara, died, my hyper Doberman, Cassie, wanted to do nothing more than sleep. She was lethargic and depressed. Several months later, I introduced two puppies to her, and she hated me for it. I think she still does. But they all play and get along today. She never bonded to them as she did with Ara. The point is, show all your grieving family members extra attention and love during the grieving period.

Part V
Ferret Psychology and Sociology 101

The 5th Wave   By Rich Tennant

@RICHTENNANT

"Mary, go ahead and pet the ferret. Mark, why don't you hold off until we're sure we've got her biting habit under control."

In this part . . .

"**G**ood heavens! You mean I have to know more than just feeding, burping, and changing diapers?" Well, only if you want a truly happy and healthy carpet shark living in your home. This part of the book is as equally important as the other parts. It deals with ferret behaviors, quirks, and training issues. At the very least, this part is designed to show you what is and isn't normal. After all, how can you meet the needs of any pet if you don't understand the needs in the first place?

If, after reading the first two chapters in this part, you still believe your furball is crazy, turn to the third chapter, where I discuss behavior modification tips. I even throw in some for your ferret. I'm here to tell you that you're not alone. Being owned by ferrets can be challenging, but understanding them is the key to making it all work.

Chapter 19

Understanding Your Fuzzball

. . . .

In This Chapter

▶ Understanding ferret sounds

▶ Recognizing your ferret's body language

▶ Other ways your ferret communicates

. . . .

Fuzzbutts are extremely interactive critters. They use many different types of communication, from body language to vocalizations. They're also notorious thieves and affectionate laptops. Watching them can be both amusing and baffling at the same time. Knowing what they're trying to say to us is important. It can mean the difference between a lick on the nose and a nip between the nostrils.

You'll be sure to encounter all sorts of captivating behavior, both good and bad, during your ferret rendezvous. My experience has been that the good encounters are far more plentiful. I spend more time laughing with them even when my furballs are being devilish. Hopefully, this chapter will help you recognize that you're not alone in thinking your ferret might just be a little crazy after all . . . and will put to rest any fears you have that you're crazy for loving every minute of it. Their impish behavior is what makes fuzzies so endearing to us.

Say What? Ferret Language

For the most part, fuzzies are quiet. I mean, jeez, they sleep for hours on end. Occasionally, one of my furkids has a ferret dream and does a little whimpering in his sleep, but that's a rarity. But during playtime, the vocabulary comes out. Seasoned ferret humans (sprinkled with raisins) have their own personal terms for ferret communication that they've come up with over the years. These terms are sort of like understood jokes between ferret and human. However, there are a few terms that most fuzzy humans recognize as universal.

The dook

The most common ferret babble is known as dooking. It's also called clucking and chuckling. It's sort of a low-pitched grumbling gibber. Mine frequently get a case of the verbal "hee hees" while they're dooking. All of these are awesome sounds made out of sheer giddiness or excitement. The stimulation of wrestling with another ferret or rapid counter cruising or even exploring new smells, toys, and hidey-holes cause carpet sharks to make these noises.

People who don't understand the ferret's modes of communication can become frightened or intimidated when encountering them for the first time. Recognizing the difference between a dook of happiness and a screech of anger is important. Not knowing may cause you to react improperly to the messages being given by the fuzzy. Humans often run into this difficulty with their human partners, too.

The screech

The opposite of the dook is the certified sign of terror, the screech. It's often accompanied by or even replaced by a rapid chattering. These noises are high-pitched reactions to extreme pain, fright, or anger. When you hear this unmistakable warning cry, your job as a concerned parent is to jump to your fuzzy's defense. But do so with care. Most animals engrossed in pain, anger, or fright are capable of unpredictable behavior, and ferrets are no exception to this rule. It's a common defense mechanism.

The bark

Sometimes your ferret will surprise you and utter something that resembles a bark. Usually these one or two very loud chirps come from a very excited or frightened furball. A friend of mine has a ferret that will bark if he tries to take away his treasured dried fish or jerky. Some humans make the same barking sound if you prematurely remove their dinner plates, too.

A ferret that's traumatized or excited enough to screech, hiss, or bark can take temporary leave of his senses and nail you good with his chompers — and it won't be his fault. Many situations can cause screeching, barking, hissing, or chattering — from a serious fight between two rival ferrets to having a tail caught in a door to coming face to face with a large, unfamiliar dog. Regardless, go to his rescue immediately but be sure to assess his body language before reaching down with your vulnerable hands.

The hiss

I find the ferret's hissing noise quite amusing. It's sort of a cross between a "hee hee" and chattering. The hissing can be long bursts of sound or short hissy spats, depending on the situation. A hissing fuzzy is a very annoyed or angry fuzzy. Care should be taken when handling this guy.

You Make Me Feel Like Dancin'

If you haven't figured it out by now, ferrets are animated critters with a complex array of behaviors. Often the vocalizations (described in the preceding sections) are accompanied by particular movements and body language, such as open mouth, puffed tail, arched back, and so on. Reading between the lines can sometimes be difficult, if not alarming, to those who don't know how to read music.

The dance of joy

I don't know of a ferret that hasn't mastered the dance of joy (see Figure 19-1). If you run across one, he's probably dead. If he's alive, his ferret human is most certainly doing something terribly wrong. All healthy, happy ferrets partake in this frequent and brilliant performance. This dance is an unadulterated sign of pure happiness and delight. (*Note:* These are professional ferrets. Do not try these movements at home. Doing so may cause irreparable damage to your skeletal structure as well as harm your ego.)

There is no rhyme or reason to this dance. The ferret moves in all directions, sometimes at the same time. Hopping forward and sashaying sideways, with a double twist back. No two dances are the same, and yet all are as amusing as the ones past and yet to come.

The dance of joy is a great way to gauge whether or not your ferret's in shape, also. A very fit and energetic fuzzy will be the last one on the dance floor. Short bursts of dancing thrown in between short ferret naps is also common. If you find he's sleeping more than playing when he gains his daily freedom, try giving the fuzzbutt more exercise. If his energy still seems low over time, take him to the vet for a checkup to make sure that his lack of energy isn't more than just being flabby and out of shape.

Figure 19-1:
Bear
demonstrates
the frizz look
combined
with the
dance of
joy.

The war dance

I like to call this one "dooking it out" even though dooks aren't associated with angry or fearful fuzzies. Sometimes, recognizing the war dance can be difficult because the happy dance covers all the basic body movements, including the notorious arched back. But an angry ferret often hisses or screeches as an additional warning. The war dance can be done with or without another ferret partner. He may choose you as a partner or the family dog. Or it may be an inanimate object that happened to catch him off guard.

The war dance is most often done with an arched back. This is the furball's way of appearing bigger than life. I call it basic trickery. This can also be a slow or a fast dance, depending on the situation. Many angry ferrets back themselves into a corner, arched back and all, and screech or hiss with their mouths wide open. This is usually the time you also find out for sure whether your fuzzy is truly descented. A very angry or frightened ferret lets loose an A-bomb or spray of musk. Although a frizzed-out tail is often appropriate attire for the war dance, it isn't always worn.

A good mom or dad always rushes in without thinking, to save the ferret in distress. This is a good thing. However, keep it filed somewhere in the back of your head that an angry, frightened, or threatened fuzzy is no different from any other animal. Animals, including ferrets, in one of these emotional states are prone to biting, even if they've *never* shown signs of aggression in the past. Rescue the furkid quickly but do so very cautiously. A bite that results from an upset ferret is rarely the fault of the ferret.

More to Behavior than Dancing

Ferrets do a lot more than dance when they're exploring their environment. They appear to always be on mysterious quests, which they sometimes go about with as much grace as a weasel in a lingerie drawer (not that I would know). They appear to feel bored and frustrated at times. Sometimes they seem happy and silly. And other times they just want to cool out in their hidey-holes.

Going for the frizz look

A true sign of excitement, both good and bad, is the frizzed-out tail. I call it the pipe cleaner tail while others call it the bottle brush tail. Nonetheless, if you aren't reading all the other signs that accompany the pipe cleaner tail, you may be in for a surprise.

The situation is similar to when dogs get hackles or when cats do that thing with the fur on their tails. Ferrets often puff out the fur on their tails when they are frightened or angry (and frightened or angry ferrets are more prone to biting). However, the frizz look can also be a sign of surprise or happy excitement. Each one of my furballs has a frizzed tail for several minutes after being bathed. They're simply excited and overstimulated while they search for creative ways to dry off and undo all the cleaning.

The alligator roll

Okay, so he doesn't look like an alligator, but boy, can he flip and roll his partner in seconds flat (see Figure 19-2). Ferrets can appear to be quite aggressive in normal play. This rough play, besides being fun, is often a way of establishing dominance. The skin of the ferret is tough, and what appears to be ruthless biting may in fact just be a bothersome pinch to the recipient. (Ferrets use their paws for grabbing at other ferrets, tackling, and wrestling them to the ground, but their teeth are their main weapons.)

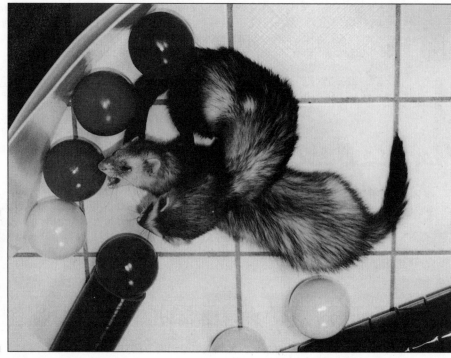

Figure 19-2:
Fidget
screeches
as she
recovers
from an
unexpected
alligator roll.

I've seen all my ferrets perform the alligator roll many times. It's just a form of playing or wrestling. The *alpha* fuzzy, or head cheese, is the master. He quickly grabs another fuzzy by the back of his neck and flips him upside down. Both carpet sharks rapidly roll about.

Trouble is often encountered when a fuzzy chooses a human hand or toe or piece of clothing to perform an alligator roll. Youngsters do this a lot. Overexcited ferrets in play mode may also do this. While it can be amusing and innocent at first, this behavior should not be encouraged. (See Chapter 20 for information on teaching your ferret what is and isn't acceptable behavior.)

The treasure hunt

Next time you get invited to one of those parties where the host sends you and the rest of the guests on a treasure hunt around the neighborhood, grab a fuzzy to help in the search. Ferrets would make excellent detectives.

The job of the fuzzy is to explore every inch, every crack, and every scent of his environment, leaving nothing untouched. A ferret's nose is almost always glued to the ground as he follows scent trails this way and that. He will stop at nothing to get to know everything he can.

Because of this determination and persistence to explore during playtime, proper ferret-proofing is essential to your ferret's safety (see Chapter 7). A ferret can find anything that's not hidden well enough. He then hides the stuff even better. I've even had ferrets present me with cherished things I thought I'd never see again. While I wanted to show my excitement at the discoveries by rewarding the treasure hunters, I also realized that they probably hid them in the first place.

The chase is on

Most animals love to chase each other and even take turns being the pursued, but ferrets are masters at the high-speed chase. This may be the predator coming to the surface, or it may just be the desire to have a good time. Regardless, you don't have to be a fuzzy to partake in this game. I've seen my cats and several furkids cruising around the house at the speed of fuzz. I've even found myself doing the ferret shuffle as quickly as I can to get away from a tailing carpet shark. If enough ferrets join in, I call it a fuzzy reception line.

Overly excited or happy ferrets can appear to be quite nuts. They bounce off of walls, furniture, and body parts, often with mouths gaping wide and teeth showing. This is normal. Many people mistakenly believe this open-mouth gesture is aggression. It is *not*. It's an invitation to play, and it's all part of ferret fun and games.

Many dogs do not like to be chased by ferrets and will snap at them. Kids who don't know how to properly perform the ferret shuffle shouldn't chase ferrets because the poor fuzzies could easily get stepped on. Likewise, if you have kids, they won't understand why you can play the chase game but they can't. The safest way for a person (adult or child) to play chase with a ferret is for all players to be on all fours on the ground. The fuzzy almost always wins this way, and you also reduce the risk of accidentally crushing him.

Wrestle mania

You already know about the alligator roll, but there are several variations of wrestling that almost always come into play when your ferrets are out. Many species of mammals participate in these mock battles to sharpen their survival skills and establish their ranking in the group. Again, you don't have to be a furball to join in this game. Cats have been known to play along, as have humans.

Ferrets appear to be ruthless at times during this type of play. One opponent may scream briefly in protest. Don't interfere unless you truly feel the game has turned into more than a game. Also, if you choose to wrestle with your ferret, use a toy to tackle and wrestle with the ferret instead of your hand. You don't want to encourage the fuzzy to bite your hand, and biting is almost always a part of this game.

Fuzzy stalking

Sometimes a ferret remains very still before pouncing on another ferret or toy. This behavior is also called the ambush. In this way, fuzzies are very similar to cats, although ambushing isn't the preferred method of hunting by the ferret's wild cousins. A more serious variation of stalking is lunging. You'll often encounter the lunge when one ferret is becoming overprotective of a special toy or hidey-hole.

Tail wagging

Some ferrets wag their tails due to sheer excitement or stimulation. I've even heard of some doing it when they're upset. Tail wagging is not as common in fuzzies as it is in cats, but it's hardly cause for alarm when it does happen. Youngsters seem more prone to this funny behavior. Look at it as having a furkid with a tad more character than the rest of the furkids.

Other Ferret Behaviors

Besides understanding vocalizations and reading body language, it's important that you know what other behaviors come with the ferret package. I get calls from people who proclaim excitedly that their ferret hates the litter they've chosen. The ferret tosses or dumps the litter constantly. They ask me what secret litter I use.

Some are relieved when I tell them it's probably not the litter. It's only a natural ferret behavior to dig. Or it could be due to boredom and stress (see Chapter 10 for ideas on enrichment). Some ferret humans want more of a quick fix and seem frustrated with my answers. Ferrets are crazy. That's why we love them so much.

Ferret fixations

Many ferrets become fixated on a certain object and treat it with extra-special care. For some ferrets, that's the understatement of the year. When a ferret claims his love for an object, he often guards it tooth and nail. My Elmo discovered the toy from one of those fast food kids meals before I could even get it out of the plastic. It was a hard plastic lion figure that he ran off with to the hidey-hole. Once he'd familiarized himself with it, he proudly brought it out to show off to his friends. But Elmo never allowed anyone to get too close to it. Like a mother protecting her vulnerable baby, this oversized carpet shark hissed warnings to the other ferrets to keep a safe distance. While Elmo has many toys, this one is never far from his sight. He carries it to the food bowl and drops it in while he eats, and then he carefully buries it in his bedding when he's through. It even accompanies him to the litter box. Now that's true love.

A felon on your hands?

Ferrets would make excellent crooks if they weren't so darned blatant about their thieving ways. It's absolutely normal, although sometimes annoying, for ferrets to steal small objects and carry them off to their secret hidey-holes. Remember, their name appropriately means "thief." (In fact, in several plays written about 2,500 years ago, Aristophanes made fun of political opponents by calling them ferrets, implying they stole public trust and funds in the same way ferrets stole bits of meat and shiny objects.)

Almost anything the fert can grab with his paws or carry in his mouth is fair game. From food to cigarette butts, you'll find the most unusual collections of goodies in the most unusual places. Purses, pockets, and backpacks are frequent targets for ferret raids. If you value anything they may steal, such as car keys, shoes, and jewelry, I suggest that you keep these items up high or out of the ferret's play area altogether.

Hoarding is one of the ferret's most endearing traits, but it can lead to trouble. One fuzzy may favor certain items while another favors completely different items. Some stolen items are big, while others are dangerously small. Remember this characteristic about your ferret when you go about ferret-proofing. Small items can be ingested and cause blockages. (See Chapter 7 for info on ferret-proofing your house.)

Digging to China

Those long claws weren't put there just for looks, you know. Any ferret owner will tell you that digging comes as naturally to a ferret as pooping. If you think about it, though, it all makes sense. First of all, ferrets are burrowing critters. They dig their nests deep into the hard ground. Second, they hunt by sense of smell. When a wild polecat locates food with his sniffer, his claws dig in for the kill. Third, ferrets inherently know that digging drives us humans right up the wall.

Another reason for digging that some people may overlook is boredom or frustration. While you'll never be able to take the urge to dig out of the ferret, you must take into account that ferrets need a lot of stimulation. Digging can, at times, be his way of saying "Pay attention to me!" or "I'll get you for taking away my toy!" Or it may simply indicate that the ferret is attempting to get out of his cage. Normal targets of digging include cage corners, litter boxes, potted plants, and carpeting.

While you won't be able to prevent a ferret from digging, you can do some things to prevent damage done by the excavators:

- Keep your plants up high or cover the soil with wire, large decorative rocks, or tin foil.

- For carpeting, you can try to use plastic carpet runners. Many people find these invaluable to the life of their carpeting. Others simply remove the carpeting where the fuzzies will be playing. Tile is certainly easier to clean, also.

The movers are here

So what happens if the ferret becomes obsessed with something he just can't get his teeth around? Why, he simply tucks it under his belly and secures it there with his front paws (similar to what a dog does with a pillow or human leg but with different motivation). From there, the thief amuses any onlookers with his unique ability to scoot backward with the object in tow. Balls and small, hard objects are often subjected to this tuck-and-scoot method of moving.

So what if the object is too big to tuck and scoot? Well, that pointy honker isn't just for smelling and leaving nose prints on your eyeglasses. And those feet weren't made just for walking. Not only can ferrets drag around heavy things, but they can also push things around (different from bossing us around). If they aren't dragging or scooting objects, they're using their noses and/or their front feet to push items to the desired destination. They'll try for hours to shove an oversized item into an obviously undersized location. They frequently try to drag me under the couch. I never have the heart to point out the flaw in their plan. I'm rather amused at just watching them try to make it work no matter what.

Chapter 20

Basic Training: Easy as 1-2-3

. . . .

In This Chapter

▶ Discouraging biting

▶ Toilet training

▶ Going for walks

. . . .

L ike a dog learning how to sit, come, and heel, a fuzzy must be taught certain things — things like minding his manners, using the litter box, and tolerating a harness and leash. These are the basics every furkid should know.

Fuzzies don't come preprogrammed for ease of use. Some ferrets take to basic training quite quickly, but others need constant reminding of who's the boss. Teaching the basics of good manners means putting on your teaching hat and doing a little home-schooling with your new fuzzy. If your first fuzzy is an adult, chances are that someone else already home-schooled him, and it's now up to you to keep him current on his skills.

As with any animal, including humans, patience and consistency are the keys to success. You've probably noticed that I use the word *patience* a lot in this book. You'll see what I mean when you bring your furball home. But nothing will ever prepare you for the joy a socialized and greatly loved ferret will bring into your household. The patience and effort are well worth it.

Saying NO to Biting

Ferrets are no different from kittens and puppies in that they need to be trained not to bite. While the urge to nip lessens with age, an untrained adult ferret can be dangerously bold and aggressive. It's up to you to let him know while he's young what is and isn't acceptable behavior. (In this section, I talk about baby ferrets, not adults that have been improperly socialized. Getting help for the difficult adult carpet shark is covered in Chapter 21.)

Ferrets are a lot like children. They require patience and consistency. If you allow little Johnny to pick his nose around the immediate family whenever he gets the urge, but you chastise him for doing so in front of guests, you're going to confuse the snot out of him. Likewise, you can't let your ferret bite you during play and expect him to know that nipping your neighbor isn't acceptable. Teach him one thing — not to bite — and stick to your guns.

If you've ever watched a human toddler closely, you were probably amazed at all the stuff that ended up in the kid's mouth. This is how babies, including ferrets and other animals, explore their environment and also ease the pain of teething. Eventually, the toothaches go away, but the nipping lingers on.

If you have a kit, it's important that you pay special attention to the do's and don'ts of nip-training your ferret. If you can begin proper socializing and training when the ferret's young, the chances of him biting as an adult are greatly decreased. The following are suggestions to help with training your fuzzy not to bite:

- ✔ Provide lots of hard chew toys.

- ✔ Use a toy to wrestle with him instead of your hand.

- ✔ Spray Bitter Apple on your hand when playing with him. Once he gets a taste, he usually won't come back for seconds.

    Bitter Apple is a nasty-tasting but harmless substance that is used to deter chewing in all kinds of pets. It's clear, too, and won't harm your furniture, fuzzies, or fingers. Most pet stores carry it.

- ✔ Correct a nip immediately by scruffing the kit and very loudly saying "No" or "No bite." Hissing (not screaming) loudly at the ferret after the "No" is often very effective. Hissing is the way Mother Fert or the other ferrets would discipline the kits. You can also lay your finger gently across his nose after you scruff, say "No bite," and hiss at him.

- ✔ *Do not ever* hit your ferret in your attempt to discipline or train him. Aggression leads to aggression. He may also think you're encouraging him to play harder. Hitting is an ineffective technique and frequently leads to bigger behavior problems.

- ✔ If you're holding the nipping kit, do not reward him by giving him his freedom (in other words, don't put him down). Place him in jail instead (cage him).

Sometimes training a youngster not to nip takes a lot of time and patience. The key to being successful is consistency. It can seem so cute at times to get the little guy all riled up and allow him to play-bite your hand. He won't understand that nipping is okay only when you're in the mood, so don't confuse him. Believe me, the other ferrets will tell the kit just how far he can go with them. It's your job to show him that nipping a human is unacceptable behavior.

This Way to the Bathroom

In this book, I talk rather frequently of the ferret's bodily functions. That's because they seem to poop about every 15 minutes or so while they're awake. And most ferret people spend more time telling animated stories and jokes about their fuzzies' notorious pooping habits than they do cleaning up after their kids. (Okay, I'll admit that's a little weird.)

Mother Fuzzy, if given the chance, often teaches her kits to use the litter box. However, because the kits are delivered to new homes or halfway houses before Mom gets the chance to tell them all they need to know, it's up to the new human mom or dad to do this dirty deed. It's pretty simple to explain to a furkid that the litter box is the designated toilet (see Figure 20-1).

While teaching ferrets what the litter box is for is pretty easy, getting them to use it consistently is a crapshoot. Ferrets don't have the greatest toilet habits. These tips should help:

- ✔ Keep the litter box in the corner of the cage. A corner is a magnet for a fuzzy butt. Ferts prefer to back into the loading zone and unload.

- ✔ If the ferret is tiny (or ill), make sure that the box has a low side or is small enough for him to get in it.

Figure 20-1: Litter training should begin at an early age and comes naturally to most ferrets. Maintaining good toilet habits is not as easy.

✔ When you wake your ferret for playtime, place him immediately in the box until he does his duty. Then let him come out. Don't be fooled by a faux pooh; make sure he's really gone to the bathroom.

✔ Until the kit starts going consistently in the litter box, always keep a little pooh in the box as a reminder that the litter box is a toilet.

✔ Keep a litter box or two or ten in the ferret's play area. Frequently pick him up and place him in the box until he goes. If he refuses, let him be for a few minutes and repeat the process.

✔ If you catch your ferret straying from the plan (usually backing into a corner), pick him up, firmly say "No," and place him in the box until he goes.

✔ *Never, ever* hit your fuzzy for having an accident. Just be thankful he isn't a Great Dane.

✔ *Never* rub a ferret's nose in his poop when he has an accident. This practice is abusive and serves no purpose. (It doesn't work with dogs, either.)

✔ Do not offer food rewards. You'll just teach him how to fake a poopie.

✔ *Always* praise your ferret for a job well done. Use verbal schmoozing as well as petting.

Baby ferrets — or any ferret just learning to use a litter box — should be limited to smaller cages and play areas until the bathroom concept has sunk in. Move him to the larger cage only after he is potty trained, and add litter boxes to higher levels if needed. Also, as you increase the out-of-cage play area, increase the number of litter boxes. If the litter box is close by, he'll be more likely to use it. If you pay attention, your ferret will show you which corners are the best spots for litter boxes. This doesn't mean your fuzzy will "go" for it, but it does increase the odds of a hit.

I have some ferrets that back up to the outside of the litter box and poop on the tile. Which just goes to prove that, sometimes, even when you do everything right, things can still go wrong. Go figure.

Being Taken for a Walk

Fuzzies are explorers and can cover a lot of ground in only a few seconds. Often, it's nice for both the ferret and the human to explore the outside world. Unfortunately, it won't take long for your fuzzy to get beyond your safe reach and get into trouble. I advise anyone who takes a ferret outside to play to always keep him leashed (see Figure 20-2). Just as an extra precaution, consider fastening an identification tag to your fuzzy's collar or harness in case he does escape. (The next section explains how to get him used to a harness.)

Figure 20-2:
Most ferrets tolerate leashes and harnesses after getting used to them.

Choose an H-shaped harness designed specifically for ferrets (see Chapter 6). A tight collar (not too tight) works as long as you keep a close eye on the traveling ferret and he can't get out of it. I personally don't like using collars. I like harnesses better because ferrets need less time adjusting to the new article of clothing. A tug on a collar, on the other hand, sometimes sends the startled ferret into a frantic roll to get away from you. Also, a struggling fuzzy can often slip right out of the collar and book for freedom.

Most ferrets struggle when you put the harness or collar on, but once it's on, most go about their business of exploring. Once in a while, I come across a rebellious carpet shark who takes more time getting used to the new constraint; see the next section, "Getting him used to a harness," for suggestions.

Getting him used to a harness

Before you take your ferret out, get him accustomed to a harness and leash. Start off slowly. First get him used to wearing the harness in the house — supervised but without a leash attached. As he forgets about his new piece of clothing, add a leash and walk him around the house. Once he accepts his limited freedom, he's ready for the outside world.

The harness should be just tight enough to prevent him from slipping out should a struggle ensue, but I like to have my ferrets get all their struggling out inside the house, just in case. There's nothing like the panic that races through you as you're trying to catch a loose ferret outside. Some people even attach bells to the harness to keep track of the fuzzy's whereabouts.

A lot of people keep harnesses or tightly fitted collars on their ferrets all the time. I think this is a dangerous practice. Ferrets get into everything and squeeze into small places. For the same reason I never leave a halter on my horse in her stall, I advise you to never leave a collar or harness on your ferret while he's unsupervised. It's very easy for a ferret to get caught up on something and either get stuck or strangle himself. I have a friend whose ferret managed to strangle himself in his own cage.

Don't leave a harness or collar on due to frustration or anxiety about having to put it back on later. If it's a battle getting the harness on, practice more often.

Basic rules when you're out and about

Here are some basic rules for safety and sanity when you're out and about with your fuzzy:

- ✔ Never tie your tethered ferret to something and leave him unsupervised. Besides being an easy target for predators, he'll get bored and frustrated and do everything he can to escape. Many succeed.

- ✔ Never let your leashed ferret wander into shrubbery. He can become entangled in branches, making it difficult for you to rescue him. At worst, he can get stuck and wiggle his way out of his harness or collar.

- ✔ Never use stretchy collars. They're easy to pull off.

- ✔ Never use plastic collars or harnesses. They're too tempting to chew on and swallow. Although the ferret wearing the collar might not chew it, a visiting playmate might.

- ✔ Never leave a collar or harness on an unsupervised ferret. He can get caught up on something and possibly get strangled.

- ✔ Be sensitive to the temperature. Just as you'd never walk your fuzzy across hot coals, don't walk him on hot pavement. Likewise, those of us who've hopped frantically across the beach know how brutally hot sand can get. They don't make sandals for carpet sharks. Snow is okay as long as your ferret isn't in it for too long. The fuzzy's paw-paws are very sensitive, you know.

Wah-lah. There's little more to training than just harnessing the little guy. Some ferts may need some time getting used to having dead weight holding them back, but I've never seen a fert revolt the way a puppy sometimes does. Ferts don't heel or walk peacefully by your side like a mutt. A harness is merely a convenient way to tow you behind them as they go on their merry little ways doing what ferts do best, only in a safe manner.

Definitions *not* found in Merriam Webster's

Even if you're a new ferret parent, you'll soon discover a plethora of defintions that amusingly — and accurately — describe the universal quirks of carpet sharks. Here are just a few for your enjoyment:

- **Back peddle:** The animated backward dance a ferret often does. Sometimes done while also scooting an object grasped between the front paws.
- **Beast master:** The alpha male ferret.
- **Black hole:** Any darkened opening that irresistibly draws ferrets inside.
- **Bulldozing:** When a ferret uses its head to push stuff off desks and shelves.
- **Cat scan:** A ferret looking for felines to torment and nip.
- **Cruise control:** A ferret leash and harness.
- **Delayed gratification:** When a ferret waits patiently for you to return the freshly cleaned litter box so he can christen it.
- **Edging:** When a ferret poopie lands half on and half off the newspaper.

- **Electric slide:** The dance of the angry, frizzed out fuzzy!
- **Ferret juggling:** The insane human act of trying to single handedly manage multiple ferrets at one time.
- **Hostile takeover:** When a ferret claims another ferret's hidey-hole or treasures.
- **Mopping the floor:** When one ferret drags another around by the neck.
- **Much ado:** Most corners when ferrets are in residence.
- **Ne'er doo well:** A ferret that never hits the litter box.
- **Nip and yip:** The warning bark and bite of a cranky ferret.
- **Procrastinate:** What ferret owners do instead of picking up poopie.
- **Stop sign:** A tap on the nose to stop biting.
- **Target practice:** What ferrets are really doing when they "accidentally" miss the litter box.

Chapter 21

Dealing with the Behaviorally Challenged Ferret

- -

In This Chapter

▶ Meeting behavioral challenges head on

▶ Handling and taming the biting fuzzbutt

▶ Understanding "accidents" and retraining your ferret to use the litter box

- -

Sometimes, even after reading books and magazines on ferrets, you're still not prepared for the endless possibilities until you've actually walked several miles with them attached to your shoes. Many experienced fuzzy owners encounter unexpected problems after years of perfect fuzzdom. It's not just the newcomers who get all the surprises. And who knows? It may be *you* who's the problem and not the poor fuzzy at all.

This chapter is mostly about problem-solving. It deals with some of the reasons people give up their ferrets in the first place: The behaviorally challenged carpet sharks know who I'm talking about. They're the biters, the misunderstood ferts of the world. The exceptions to the rule. I'm speaking also of the litter box deviates, who aren't very exceptional at all.

Dracula in Fuzzy Clothing

Once in a blue moon, you'll find a ferret that is just plain mean, and not much can be done. Most ferrets, though, are loving and playful family members. Out of all the ferrets that have passed through my shelter or have remained permanent residents, I've only encountered four severe biters. So problem biters do exist, but they're the exception, not the rule. My experience has been that the lovable pooch is still far more dangerous than the typical fuzzy.

The good news is that there is hope for the biting ferret. Most biting ferrets can be turned into gentle critters if you're willing to work on your relationship. If you're serious about being a fuzzy human, you'll do your best not to dump the problem carpet shark off at the nearest shelter. This section is for the ferret lover who is willing to work to keep the ferret a part of the family.

Ferrets can bite for many reasons. While you may not have all the colorful information about your fuzzy's personal history, you may be able to put all the pieces together just from being a good observer. It may mean learning how to deactivate the bomb before it goes off. Or it may mean taking the precious time to convince your fuzzy that not all humans are evil. Usually, it's the latter case. Once you identify why biting is occurring (you usually discover that a human is the root of the evil), you can address the situation appropriately. The following sections take a look at the most common reasons ferrets bite. The section "Handling the Beast" tells what you can do to correct the problem.

You should recognize the difference between playful biting and aggressive biting, even though both should be corrected. An aggressive biter may bite you and hold on. Or they may bite so hard they draw blood. The pain caused by an aggressive ferret bite is unmistakable. Playful, non-aggressive bites include mouthing, light nips, and even "nip and runs." While playful bites cause little to no discomfort, it should be discouraged to prevent future bigger problems.

Growing pains

Baby ferrets are natural nippers. If your biting furball is a youngster, I tend to think the situation really doesn't fall into the classification of problem — yet. Kits will be kits. Like all mammals, they explore the world with their mouths. They have teething pains that can be severe at times, and gnawing on the closest available thing — your arm or a chew toy — helps to alleviate the pain.

Baby animals (humans, too) live to test their limits. They need to be taught at an early age what is and isn't acceptable behavior. So, if your "problem" fuzzy is still a baby, head to Chapter 20 for info on nip-training youngsters. If you don't stop the nipping when your ferret is young, you'll be back reading this chapter in the near future — only you'll truly have a problem on your hands (literally).

Not all ferret bites should be considered attacks. In fact, most aren't. There's usually a good reason for the bite, and biting is sometimes the only way that a ferret can communicate his needs or wishes. For example, a fuzzy can't reach up and smack you on the back of the head to say, "Tag, you're it," but a nip on the ankle may be just as effective. Tag, by the way, is a favorite ferret game.

TIP

Blind Bernie

I was once bitten by one of my newer lovable ferrets, Bernie. His seemingly unprovoked attack surprised me. Once I got over the initial shock and hurt, I observed him closely as he interacted with the other fuzzies. My Bernie was completely blind, and I hadn't noticed until then. I startled him and he bit me, as I would've done in his place. Now I call his name loudly before I pick him up. He hasn't bitten again. Blind and deaf ferrets can make wonderful pets. But, if you scare them, they may understandably bite you. Most won't. Take extra care when interacting with these little guys. Get the blind ferret's attention by using his hearing or sense of smell. Get the deaf ferret's attention by allowing him to see or smell you first. It's only fair. Deafness and blindness in ferrets, known or unknown, should always be considered when trying to identify the cause of aggression.

Nobody told me not to bite

Many people fail to nip-train their ferrets at an early age when training is so crucial. Your fuzzy may never have had the limits set for him. It may be your fault, the fault of a previous caretaker, or even a pet shop that failed to handle the cute babies on display.

Often, people dump their ferrets at this stage because they just don't know how to set the limits and be the human boss. The reason is due purely to frustration and lack of education. Unfortunately, innocent kit nips turn into bold bites if you don't stop the nipping early.

I'm in pain, darn it!

Because your ferret has limited ability to say "Hey, my belly aches" or "I got these nasty bugs in my gosh darn ears," he may bite instead. Your biting furball may be suffering from something treatable, such as a severe ear mite infestation, or something more chronic, like a systemic disease.

Take your biter to the vet (warn the vet in advance about aggression) for a complete physical. Rule out illness or injury that may be causing the ferret to lash out in pain. Be a good human and be mindful of sudden changes in behavior. Many times he just isn't feeling well and needs your help.

The manly or bully ferret

Unneutered male ferrets can frequently be more aggressive than their altered counterparts. As with some teenage boys, it's their hormonal duty to dominate whoever they can. Usually, the unneutered ferret chooses other male ferrets to bully. Female ferrets are also targets of this type of male aggression. Sometimes, he bullies the human who unknowingly tests his ferthood. Neuter that boy.

Some ferrets suffer from "little fert syndrome" (the ferret equivalent of the Napoleon complex), and biting is the ferret's way of saying, "I'm big and bad and capable of kicking butt if necessary, so watch out!"

Facing change

Change, whether good or bad, is scary. Imagine this: Some giant rips the roof off *your* house, picks you up, and plops you down in the middle of who knows where. Strangers may be poking at you. Everything smells and looks funny. There may be some big, wet nose sniffing at you and blowing snot on you. The new noises are enough to make your head explode. If you had a tail, it would be puffed out like a bottle brush. You don't know whether to poop or run away or bite. Heck, for all you know, you're in for the nightmare of your life.

A ferret in a strange situation can be scared and confused. Whether he's with the human he's loved and trusted for years or he's in the care of a brand new human, he doesn't know what to expect. When he's under this much stress, he may bite. Keep in mind, though, that not all ferrets in new or strange situations bite. Most don't.

It always worked before

If your ferret had a previous human (or perhaps you were the culprit), it's possible that the fuzzy may have inadvertently been trained to bite. I don't mean "Caution: Guard Fert on Premises!" I'm talking about the weenie human who gave the ferret his way every time he nipped. The fuzzy was picked up, he nipped, and he was put down and allowed his freedom. Or the ferret bit, the human thought that he must be hungry, and so he was rewarded with food. The human was trained by the ferret.

Never positively reinforce a biting ferret. Biting should not be viewed as the cute way he's trying to tell you something.

Fighting back

Most often, the cause of a biting ferret is mistrust of humans. Humans can be pretty nasty animals. Some humans react violently or impulsively to stuff they don't understand. Other humans are just jerks who thrive on being cruel. Fuzzies are frequent victims of human abuse. In these cases, what else could you possibly expect? These fuzzies learn several things during their abuse: 1) Attack or be attacked. 2) Hands equal hitting, feet equal kicking, and humans equal pain. 3) Every ferret for himself.

Working with an abused ferret takes extra time and patience. If you've ever been badly hurt by someone, physically or emotionally, you know how long it can take to trust once again.

Other reasons for biting

Some ferrets react to particular noises, smells, or objects. My ferret Sybil (appropriately named), for example, was dropped off with two other nut cases, Buster and Fidget. Sybil reacts aggressively when the dogs start barking, no matter where they are or why they're barking. She runs up and bites me when they bark. I've heard of other ferrets that react similarly to other things, such as new smells (especially on the hands or clothes), the ruffling of newspapers, vacuum cleaners, brooms, loud music, and so on.

Some carpet sharks get extra freaky around freaky people. This type of carpet shark may chase a timid person around the room and nip at the ankles. Most of these quirky ferts are otherwise lovable and sweet, as most fuzzies are. If you're smart enough to identify the trigger, then you should be smart enough not to trigger the fuzzy when he's out of his cage. (Oh, and by the way, most ferrets do have foot fetishes.)

Handling the Beast

It's unusual to come across a fuzzy that's just determined to be aggressive no matter what you do. A hopeless fuzzy case is a rarity. If you think you've got the eccentric head case, I suggest that you just haven't found the right approach or haven't been consistent with your technique. Your fuzzbutt may even be suffering from a combination of fuzzy neuroses. Every ferret is a unique individual and will respond differently to methods of resocializing. Your job as the fuzzy human is to find the best combination of love and gentle discipline.

Norm and his way with ferrets

Norm Stilson of the Greater Chicago Ferret Association uses the same method for all biting ferrets and has a tremendous success rate. He admits that this reconditioning process can take anywhere from a few weeks to a couple years. It depends largely on the severity of the ferret's mistrust of humans (how big of a jerk the previous human was) and how much time he has to work with the biter. Still, I've seen him in action and watched him transform the seemingly most hopeless biters into snuggly, happy fuzzbutts. Norm uses the upper body grip, described in the "Getting a grip" section, and spends a lot of time talking gently to the ferret. He uses the other hand to stroke the fur on top of the fuzzy's head and neck at the same time. He cuddles the fuzzy up against him (keeping control of the ferret's head) and even kisses the top of the fuzzy's head. Norm's method, in my opinion, is the best.

Getting a grip

Some people think thick gloves (leather) are great for working to tame the aggressive ferret. They can help protect your hands from the serious ouchies an aggressive biter can inflict. Using gloves also allows you to handle the fuzzy confidently and without fear if you're serious about taming him down. If you're skittish around ferrets to begin with, this option may be the way for you to go.

While many people advocate using gloves with the biter, doing so may actually defeat the purpose. There's something a little more soothing to the feel of a gentle but firm human paw as opposed to a stiff, groping glove (see Figure 21-1). Being held with a leather glove may feel a bit more like being manhandled, which may be why the furball's so ticked off in the first place. Try to do without them. I've never used gloves. They're too bulky on my tiny hands, and I can't seem to hold the fuzzy comfortably. Also, I never want to give the ferret the impression that my skin is tough and can withstand such torture.

I find that the best way to handle an aggressive carpet shark is to firmly hold the upper part of his body from underneath but with more control over his head. You may have to distract him a little to seize him this way. Simply grab him by the scruff of the neck. Take your other hand and hold the ferret from underneath just above the chest. Wrap your fingers around the fuzzy's neck. A paw may also go in between your fingers. Once you're confident that you've got the ferret safely but firmly in your grip, release the scruff. Now you can use your free hand to smother him with gentle petting. In this secure position, the meanie usually can't twist his head around and latch on to some vital part of your body. This is a great handling method and preferable over gloves. And it usually works, too (see Figure 21-2).

Figure 21-1:
Norm demonstrates a safe and proper way to hold a biting ferret.

Figure 21-2:
Believe it or not, this nasty little girl was transformed into an angel.

Try distracting an angry ferret with Ferretone or Linatone. Use one hand to tilt the bottle for him to lick; use the other hand to pick up the ferret or hold him. I have one ferret who usually only bites after I release her from a scruff — and she comes attacking, teeth bared! If I allow her to lick Linatone while I scruff and continue to allow her to lick Linatone when I put her down, she generally forgets to attack me.

Getting unstuck

If a ferret should bite you and not let go (an uncommon behavior), there are some things to remember. Unless you're an experienced ferret handler, though, you'll probably be too busy panicking and overreacting to think about these things logically, as you try to fling the ferret from whichever body part he's latched onto. Just in case you do keep your wits about you, some of the following tips may come in handy:

✔ Place a tiny amount of Bitter Apple or Bitter Lime into the corner of the ferret's mouth (use a cotton swab or small controlled spray). While he's ptooeying out the taste, your flesh will be ptooeyed along with it.

Don't spray Bitter Apple or Bitter Lime directly into the ferret's face. *Ever.* Doing so is painful and cruel, and his next bite will really be justified.

✔ Find a helping hand to gently squeeze the carpet shark's jaws open and aid you in prying him off you, one tooth at a time.

✔ Push your finger, hand, or whichever part of the body is being bitten farther into the ferret's mouth to make him gag. (I've needed help this way with many snakes that found my hand irresistible. At least the ferret's teeth don't curve backward.)

✔ Don't try to release the ferret by pulling him or jerking away. In other words, don't send him for a flying lesson. Doing so only causes you more damage. And you feel really stupid.

✔ Drip some Ferretone or olive oil over the tip of the ferret's nose. The ferret will automatically start licking the treat and release you in the process. Although I stress the importance of not rewarding biting with treats, this is a justified exception for an extreme, prolonged bite. Here the object is to get unhooked without causing further trauma to you or the frightened ferret.

✔ Find a cold body of water, such as a toilet, bathtub, or sink, and submerge him until his desire to breathe overtakes his desire to mangle you. You can also use cold running water from a faucet. This is a last-resort solution.

Don't flush him down the toilet or drown him in the process of trying to release him. Bite wounds heal. Death is irreversible. Guilt haunts for a long time.

Things not to do, or "I will probably bite you even harder if you . . ."

- Spray Bitter Apple or another deterrent in my face.
- Bite me back on the ear or head (some people actually do this).
- Flick me on the nose or head when I bite.

- Hit me or throw me across the room.
- Isolate me from the world for long periods of time.

These things usually only make the problem worse.

The main thing to remember when being bitten by any animal is don't panic. Panicking or overreacting usually makes the situation worse. If you know you're dealing with a biting ferret, don't handle him unless someone else is around to come to your rescue. Eventually, you won't need anyone around. Your ferret will probably be as sweet as raisins if you follow the right path.

Taming the critter

In my opinion, aggression only leads to aggression whether you're dealing with a human or a fuzzbutt. Chances are, what got you to this stage had something to do with some human who was being a jerk. So throw away all the tough love stuff and put on your compassionate hat. Don't get me wrong: There will be times when you'll need to throw a helmet over the hat for extra protection. But for the most part, gentleness and patience will get you through the trying times.

Depending on your ferret's personality and his past life experiences, he may or may not respond to certain methods of reconditioning. Some fuzzies learn quickly that humans can be trustworthy and that humans can also make great playmates. Others need quite a bit more time to come to this conclusion. Following are some ideas that may or may not work for your biting ferret.

Here are some obvious solutions. Give these a try first:

- If your companion biter is an unaltered male, neuter him.
- Get veterinary care for any illnesses or injuries.
- If you know the biting trigger, such as barking dogs, don't subject your ferret to it.
- For the visually and hearing impaired fuzzies, take extra care not to startle them when handling them.

- Make sure that your ferret is well fed and given a proper diet.
- Spend more quality time with your ferret instead of keeping him cooped up in jail for days on end.

Here are some creative ideas. Use these in whatever combination you need to:

- Put Bitter Apple (the spray works but cream is better) on your hands so the bite doesn't taste as good. I've heard of some people using something more distasteful, such as Tabasco sauce. While it may work for some, I find this approach to be borderline abusive.

- Screech, growl, hiss, or yell "Ouch!" or "No!" loudly when the ferret bites (simple words, not sentences). Some people scruff and do a quick, firm shake while verbally reprimanding the biter and find this to be a successful combination. Many ferrets see this as a sign that biting is definitely not a good thing to do. *Note:* Some ferrets may bite harder if the verbal reprimand is accompanied by a scruff and shake. This is a definite individual thing.

- Sentence the ferret to short-term jail time by placing him back in the cage for biting. A fuzzy should always get a time-out shortly — but not immediately — after biting.

Time-outs are important but should be used with care. Some people believe that an immediate time-out after biting is viewed as a reward to the ferret that wants to be left alone anyway. So if you can, try to physically hold the fuzzy for several minutes after the bite occurs before putting him away for a time-out. Obviously, you should put him away immediately if you're too angry to be rational or too busy cleaning up your wounds. If immediate time-outs don't seem to work for your biter, try the "I'm gonna hold you anyway" method to see if this form of dominance works better. And get your tetanus shot updated.

- If he currently has no playmate, try introducing a fuzzy friend so that he'll have someone to rough and tumble with. He may be bored to frustration.

- Immediately substitute a toy for a human body part and allow him to only bite that.

- Tell him "I'm in charge, darn it!" and place the ferret submissively on his back and hold him there. Hold him high up on his body and firmly to keep control of his head. After a few minutes, give him a time-out.

- Wrap the fuzzy securely in a towel and carry him around like a bundled baby. Talk to him and stroke the top of his head gently.

Not all of these methods work for each ferret. Unfortunately, some may even make matters worse, but it may only be temporary. Don't give up on the tactic right away just because it doesn't work the first time. Winning over the biter takes patience and consistency. If, however, the biting gets more severe and more frequent after much patience and consistency, you probably should try a new tactic.

Aggression is not a training or conditioning tool. It is only a way to put the ferret on the defense and trigger his attack mode. The biting ferret only reacts positively to a firm but consistent nonviolent approach. Don't forget to always reward the ferret for acceptable behavior. Ferrets are extremely intelligent and learn according to how you teach them.

Keeping your cool

It goes without saying that dealing with a biting fuzzy is extremely draining on you, both physically and emotionally. You'll probably need some cool down periods during the resocializing process. Don't beat yourself up for occasionally slipping into reaction mode versus action mode. You're only human. Learn from your mistakes and vow not to repeat them. While you need to work with the ferret consistently, avoid doing so when you're angry or stressed out. Otherwise, you'll only be looking to pick a fight, and no one will come out a winner.

If you feel you absolutely can't properly care for a biting ferret, find someone who has experience. Seek help from a ferret shelter or another ferret fanatic. Sometimes a change of home *is* the best thing for everyone.

Litter Box Woes

You know, there's a reason why the words *poop* and *poopie* are mentioned an abundance of times throughout this entire book. Ferrets go to the bathroom a lot. While they're pretty clean animals, they're not particularly anal about where they choose to go. I mention a few helpful litter box retraining hints in this short section, but keep in mind that most ferrets have accidents. Some do it out of spite, others digress due to laziness, and some have their own mysterious reasons. Just know that you're not alone.

Every corner of every shelf in every ferret cage in my house has been christened (or crusted, I should say) with fuzzy poop. For that matter, every corner in almost every room of my house has also been fertified. It's the nature of the beasties. When ferrets have to go, they have to go *now*. They have speedy metabolisms and short digestive tracts. They can't hold it like dogs and cats — or people, for that matter. If a litter box isn't in sight or the one available is either occupied or too dirty for his liking, he'll back into the nearest loading zone (usually a corner) and drop his load. Following are some helpful tips for both you and the forever-pooping fuzzy.

Try the following for problems in the cage:

- ✔ Read (or review) the section on litter box training (see Chapter 20).
- ✔ Make sure that the litter box is in the corner of the cage.

✔ Add more litter boxes to the cage.

✔ If the fert is tiny, sick, or old, make sure that the box has a low side or is small enough for him to easily get in and out.

✔ Scoop the litter box more often.

✔ Try a different kind of litter.

✔ Thoroughly and frequently clean the crusty corners with a safe odor neutralizer so the fuzzy won't follow his nose back to the crime scene. That doesn't mean his butt won't become magnetized to it again, however.

For problems outside of the cage, try these suggestions:

✔ When you wake your ferret for playtime, place him immediately in the box until he poops. Ferrets have to go as soon as they wake up. It's a ferret rule.

✔ Reduce the size of his play area so that the litter box is more convenient to your fuzzy. You can increase his play area as his toilet habits get better.

✔ Keep a litter box or two or ten in the fert's play area, particularly in corners.

✔ Frequently pick him up and place him in the box until he goes. If he refuses to unload, let him be for a few minutes and repeat the process a few minutes later.

✔ Place newspapers in corners and under litter boxes (since they often go just outside of the box).

✔ If you catch your ferret straying from the plan (usually backing into a corner), pick him up, firmly say "No!" and place him in the box until he goes.

✔ Treat the poopy corners with a safe odor neutralizer so your furball won't be tempted to go back.

✔ Place food or bedding in favorite off-limits pooping areas. Most ferrets won't poop near their food or bedding.

✔ Give extra praise for a poop well done.

Most of the ferrets I've known have been problem poopers. If they weren't, we ferret fanatics would have much less to talk about and laugh about. I do have one blind ferret, Bernie, who seeks out a litter box no matter what, even if it's the cat's tall box (bless his bottom). Many of the others go whenever or wherever they feel. Thank God for newspaper and Nature's Miracle.

Part VI
If You're Thinking about Breeding

The 5th Wave   By Rich Tennant

SLOTH/FERRET PROJECT

"We figure if they mate it will either result in a sloth that's interesting to watch or a ferret that's easy to catch."

In this part . . .

1f you need to read a book about breeding, then I must say that you probably aren't qualified to breed your ferrets at this point in time. It takes many books, years of owning ferrets, and a great deal of research before anyone should even think about breeding carpet sharks. However, while I certainly don't advocate the indiscriminate breeding of ferrets, I include this part about the basics, and I do my best to talk you out of bringing more ferrets into this world. As the director of a small shelter and Mom to 23 previously unwanted fuzzbutts, I don't see the sense in random ferret breeding. Take a good long look at the ferret shelters listed in the appendix of this book. Between all of them, thousands of ferrets are waiting for good homes.

Breeding ferrets should be left to the few people who know exactly what they're doing and why they're doing it. Breeding should only be done with genetically superior ferrets — ferrets whose offspring are going to better the species as a whole. While most of us think our ferrets are superior and capable of passing on only the best, the truth is, only a small percentage of ferrets possess the high standards required for responsible breeding. The rest should be neutered and allowed to do what they do best: drive us crazy with their fuzzy antics. Please read this part carefully and consider all the ramifications of bringing more ferrets into the world before you actually do. (And even if you don't want to breed, this part helps you know a little more about your lovable fuzzbutt.)

Chapter 22

Should You Breed Your Ferret? Looking at the Big Picture

In This Chapter
▶ The costs of breeding: the emotional, financial, and time commitments
▶ The ramifications of careless breeding
▶ Why you might not want to breed your ferret

*B*eing able to breed ferrets responsibly and successfully requires years of owning ferts and a great deal of research. In fact, I strongly urge you to have your ferret neutered or spayed and leave breeding ferrets to the few people who know exactly what they're doing, why they're doing it, and what they're getting into.

This chapter discusses things that many beginner breeders don't think about. Before you decide to breed ferrets, see whether you have what it takes. And, even if you decide that you do, you need to ask yourself whether you *should*.

What It Takes to Be a Responsible Breeder

Way more is involved in breeding ferrets than just throwing two amorous fuzzies in a cage and hanging up the Do Not Disturb sign. Responsible breeders carefully choose their breeding pairs and breed for good temperament, as well as good looks and conformation. They're prepared for emergency medical situations and spend most of their free time caring for moms and kits.

Responsible breeders don't just sell their kits to anyone. Money should be the last thing on the responsible breeder's mind. The honest truth is that unless you're mass-producing hundreds of kits a year and selling them wholesale to pet shops, you probably won't make much money. If you're lucky, you may break even. A responsible breeder breeds because he or she simply loves the ferret and wants to put the best ferrets in the best homes.

There's a lot more that responsible breeders need to have and do. The following sections outline these things.

Deep pockets

I mean forking over money for the cost of caring for the pregnant jills (unspayed females) and kits (babies). There are always expenses involved in breeding, but have you thought about emergencies or unplanned situations? Responsible breeders must take into consideration

- Proper cages and setups for jills and kits
- Routine vet care for moms and kits, including supplements and any medication needed
- A first vaccination for each kit before they go to their new homes
- Vet care for other complications such as uterine infections and *mastitis* (infected and hardened mammary glands)
- Emergency C-section for the jill in trouble
- Humane euthanizing of kits with severe deformities or providing lifelong care for these babies
- Spaying bad moms (see the following section for what a bad mom is) or retirees — and providing lifelong care for them if good homes aren't found
- Providing lifelong care for any kits that aren't sold

The emotional stake

Breeding isn't always smooth sailing; often, a lot of heartache is involved, and so are many decisions that you'd probably rather not have to face. Ferret moms, for example, are often not good moms at all. Many kits die from being cannibalized (eaten by Mom) or neglected. It can be heartbreaking. Hand-rearing a newborn kit is also next to impossible. Most breeders arrange to have two ferrets giving birth within a few days of each other so they can also serve as foster moms if necessary. That plan doesn't always work, though, especially if the litters are large.

Ask yourself how you would feel about the following, because if you're a breeder, you'll face these situations at one time or another:

- Kits dying suddenly
- Moms cannibalizing or killing the kits

- ✔ Losing kits because Mom fails to nurse or is incapable of nursing
- ✔ Losing Mom during a difficult pregnancy or labor
- ✔ Getting your hopes dashed when you find out it was a false pregnancy (common in ferrets)
- ✔ Worrying about all the kits you helped into the world and stressing over how they're doing in someone else's care
- ✔ Needing to euthanize kits with severe birth defects
- ✔ Having fuzzies returned to you for one reason or another

Time to care

Breeding ferrets, providing support during and after pregnancy for moms and kits, and finding the perfect homes for your precious babies can be extremely time-consuming. Consider the fact that you'll probably have to forgo your karate classes to do the following:

- ✔ Keep diligent records (financial and pedigree).
- ✔ Talk to and learn from other responsible breeders. (Responsible breeding is *not* a competition; it's a shared interest.)
- ✔ Check weights on kits regularly to make sure that they're gaining weight and take the necessary steps to correct problems when discovered.
- ✔ Chauffeur ferrets to and from the vet.
- ✔ Spend time socializing kits and begin training before they go to their new homes. Good breeders hang onto kits until they're at least 8 weeks old.
- ✔ Spend an enormous amount of time on the phone talking to potential buyers and new fuzzy parents. Good breeders are choosy about whom they sell their babies to. They also provide ongoing before and after sales support.

Ferreting out some pros

Kits are simply adorable and there's little more satisfying than raising a beautiful, healthy fuzzy (except for possibly giving a good home to the old fuzzy abandoned in a shelter). Responsible private breeders offer an alternative for fuzzy people who want kits, but don't want to go to pet shops for farm-raised ferts. Responsible breeders are more interested in the kit's well being than money, thus are more concerned about weeding out the less-than-desirable fuzzy homes and placing them in the best possible homes. Private breeders get to spend oodles of time sharing their wealth of information with the people who seek them out.

Retiring a myth

Breeding animals is *not* the way to teach a child about the miracle of life (and death, in many cases). If you feel your child is missing out in this area of growing up, rent a video, buy some books, or tune in to the Discovery Channel or Animal Planet. These are great alternative ways to spend quality time with your kids and still teach them the value and beauty of life. Of course, also explain to your kids the devastating effects of overpopulation so they'll understand why a video may be far more responsible than the real thing.

Time to find out what you don't know

Responsible breeding means knowing a lot about ferret biology and genetics. For example, did you know that ferrets are similar to chinchillas in that breeding certain color variations together may cause lethal genes? This situation results in most, if not all, of the kits from that litter dying. Additionally, the new exotic ferret colors being produced may be the result of mutant or recessive genes. No one knows for sure yet whether these funky-colored ferrets will have more health problems down the road. How can you know whether you're creating one of these tragic situations?

You also need to know rules governing the sale of ferrets. For example, when it comes to selling your kits, did you know that breeders who wholesale their ferrets (those who sell to pet shops, for example) are required to be USDA licensed? This means even more emphasis on keeping good records and maintaining good husbandry practices. Inspectors can pop in at any reasonable time — unannounced — to inspect your facility, animals, and records. Also, ferret breeders may be required to have additional permits or licenses depending on where they live.

If you still think you've got what it takes to be a responsible fuzzy breeder, put the thought on the back burner for a little longer.

✔ Research the subject a little more. Call your local ferret shelter and put in a few hours of volunteer work each week. If you don't have time to do that now, you certainly won't have the time to breed ferrets responsibly.

✔ Locate and talk with a few reputable ferret breeders to get the inside poop. They're bound to be able to share more pros and cons with you than I can. Just be sure to get all the facts before taking on this fuzzy endeavor.

✔ Finally, read the following section. If you love ferrets (and presumably you do if you want to breed them), you don't want to bolster the need for shelters.

The Big Picture: Are You Creating a Need for Shelters?

Most people have heard at one time or another the statistics on how many dogs and cats are killed each year in shelters. The senseless deaths of these once-loved pets number in the millions. As ferrets gain popularity as companion pets in households, the number of furballs winding up in shelters also increases. And so does the number of deaths of these homeless fuzzies (see Figure 22-1).

It's no surprise that careless breeding by humans is the cause for overpopulation. The population of fuzzbutts at the Greater Chicago Ferret Association fluctuates between 60 and 100 ferrets at a time. That's a lot of displaced furkids. Many are geriatric fuzzies that no longer fit into that perfect pet mold their humans illogically created. They get dumped for younger or different pets.

Figure 22-1: Every one of these shelter orphans was once somebody's baby.

No ferret breeder can guarantee that every one of the kits he or she is responsible for producing will remain in permanent, loving homes. Too many people treat animals as property. These people put little thought into getting pets and end up abusing them, neglecting them, selling them to the highest bidder, or just giving them away to whoever shows up first. Sometimes fuzzies are dumped into the wild to futilely fend for themselves or are abandoned at shelters where their future is unknown. This revolving door syndrome is also passed on by example to children. It's morally and ethically wrong to treat any life with such disregard. It's a cycle that needs to be stopped.

Small children should always be supervised around any pet, including your ferret.

Ferrets are clean critters. When they're not playing or sleeping, they're usually content just grooming themselves.

Although some ferrets enjoy swimming in a shallow tub, they can tire easily and should never be left unattended around or in water.

Bathing should be part of your ferrets grooming routine. But be careful not to get soap in your ferret's eyes, ears, and mouth.

© Eric Ilasenko Photography

Most ferrets stop for frequent rests during play.

This ferret is a perfect example of a hooded sable.

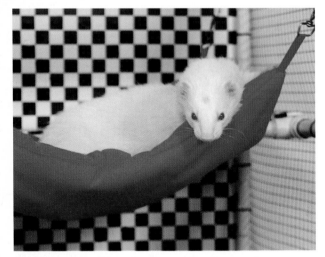

As this pretty albino shows, no cage is complete without a comfy hammock to lounge in.

Being burrowing creatures, ferrets easily make they're way into the strangest places.

Routine physicals for your ferret are a must. Early discovery of a problem can help save or prolong a life.

Ferrets are natural diggers and enjoy opportunities to put their skills to the test.

Ferret cages should be multi-level and provide enough room for hammocks and toys. This one holds a custom ferret wheel.

Ferret beds come in many shapes and sizes, but avoid ones containing exposed foam rubber, which the ferret may be tempted to eat.

This handsome silver mitt wold surely take a blue ribbon in the popular costume class at the local ferret show.

Ferrets like to chew. Make sure your ferret's toys are made of material that can't be easily chewed up and ingested.

Ferrets will find a way to have fun with any toy their provided with. Make sure the toys you provide are safe.

Ferrets are highly intelligent animals and should be provided with as much new stimulation as possible.

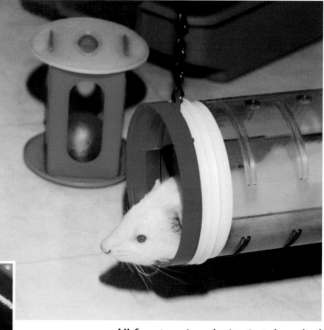

All ferrets enjoy playing in tubes. And when they're done, you may find one or two curled up inside a tube, sleeping.

Treats are a great way to bond with your ferret and reward him for good behavior, but treats should be given sparingly.

Although shades of sable seem to be the most common ferret colors, dark-eyed white (DEW) ferrets like this one are becoming increasingly popular.

© Eric Ilasenko Photography

Ferrets are expert climbers and will look for any opportunity to climb out of an open-top cage.

This gorgeous hob shows just how tasty some supplements are. Like treats, supplements should be used sparingly. *(Photo courtesy of Jen Taylor)*

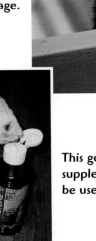

This ferret is emerging from a nap under the bedspread. You should know where your ferret is before plopping onto a bed or couch.

Ferrets have many vocalizations and body languages. An open mouth accompanied with a dance is usually an invitation to play.

© Eric Ilasenko Photography

When lined with mom's fur, hay makes a suitable nesting material.

Bouka, a pretty sable, has many physical characteristics similar to her distant relative, the endangered black-footed ferret.

Ferrets can run fast and should be kept on a leash and harness when outdoors. A stray ferret won't last long in the wild. Fortunately, a human scooped this little gal up.

This hedgehog is smart to be overly cautious. Ferrets can easily harm small animals, and any interaction should be closely supervised, if allowed at all.

Ferrets should always be provided with lots of soft, clean bedding in their cages to snooze on and burrow under.

Ferrets are extremely playful and mischievous, as these two sables demonstrate. Most ferrets enjoy the company of other ferrets.

Chapter 23

Mustelid Love Unmasked

- -

In This Chapter

▶ Understanding the signs of the season

▶ Courtship and mating

▶ What you need to know about your ferret's pregnancy

- -

*O*nce you've identified the perfect pair of fuzzies to breed, getting them to cooperate may be difficult. While we humans tend to think that guys have one thing in mind and are always in the mood, the male ferret, or hob, has his equally long bouts of "Not now, dear — I have a headache."

Headache aside, courtship and mating can often be primitively brutal and unromantic. Once the deed is done and the male scoots off to put another notch in his chew toy, the female, or jill, needs some extra-special attention. Being the good humans we are, our job is to see that her needs are adequately met. This means more than just running out for a late-night pickle purchase. It means providing a whole lot of tender, loving care, supplying a good place for her to hunker down, and filling her belly with extra-good stuff.

This chapter gives you an overview of the ferret's reproductive system, as well as mating habits. A lot of emphasis is given to the do's and don'ts of breeding your ferrets. This is a particularly important chapter to pay attention to if you're even considering bringing more fuzzbutts into the world.

Fine-Tuning the Organs

Hormones and sexual maturity can cause wondrous changes in the appearance, behavior, and habits of animals, including our lovable ferrets. These changes occur over time, as the body develops and, as is the case with ferrets, peak during the mating seasons, or *ruts,* once sexual maturity has been reached.

It's important to know how ferrets develop and what changes you can expect to encounter in your unaltered ferrets, especially if you're still considering breeding them. This brief section gives you an overview of the ferret's reproductive system, as well as mating habits.

The boy

If you haven't already figured it out yet, unneutered male ferrets are quite the smelly boys. They can be extremely aggressive toward other male ferrets and even their humans — especially when they're out to capture a female's heart. Unaltered boys do not usually make good pets when they're in rut because they have other things on their minds.

The male ferret's testicles begin to mature approximately six months after birth. Full maturity takes close to three months. You can tell when the boys are beginning that confusing time of puberty when their testicles begin to increase in size, mainly due to the increase in the male hormone testosterone. This increase in testosterone also causes them to notice the girls a little more. Boys ready to breed wear a discolored, yellowish undercoat, which is caused from an increase in oil production in the skin glands.

They may tease the girls (only because they like them) and grab the backs of girls' necks to show them how much they care. Of course, like with the overactive male dog, pelvic thrusting and mounting various objects (both inanimate and animate) occur frequently. They may also begin to stash ferty magazines under their snooze sacks and spend way too much time on the phone. This interest in the girls and increased aggression, however, normally only lasts between the months of December and July. Then they return to being just one of the stinky guys.

Some people don't want to keep unaltered males due to the smell and aggression that comes with the territory. Hooking up with another ferret breeder may enable you to use the services of a stud fuzzy. Payment for services rendered may be a small fee or pick of the litter for the owner of the stud.

The girl

The unaltered girls become sexually mature at about 6 months of age under normal lighting conditions. The onset of *estrus* (heat period) is closely associated with the increase in daylight during the normal seasonal change. Females exposed to shorter light days are late bloomers, reaching sexual maturity as late as 12 months of age.

Romantic lighting?

You can mess around with the fuzzy's reproductive cycle just by increasing or decreasing the amount of light the ferret is subjected to daily (photoperiods). Ferrets residing in the southern hemisphere have slightly different breeding seasons for this very reason. Under normal conditions, females are ready for breeding between March and August. Males are in the mood from December to July. This need to breed during the longer days indicates the excellent survival tactics passed on to ferrets by their wild cousins. Longer days usually bring warmer days and plenty of food and water. In the wild, this environment would help ensure that the babies were well fed, thus increasing the survival rate and continuation of the species.

A female in estrus is easy to identify. Her pink *vulva* (genitals) swell due to an increase in the female hormone estrogen. There may be a clear or slightly discolored discharge. She may get crabby and sleep less (I refer to it as PMS, or Pre-Mustelid Syndrome). But unlike female humans, the ferret in estrus usually cuts back on her food intake.

Inside her body, some other stuff is going on, too. The mucousy lining of the uterus begins to swell, and follicles containing eggs develop in the ovaries. Then she just sits back and waits for her dream ferret to come by and sweep her off her fuzzy feet.

Getting them together: Enter Neanderthal ferret

A female should be bred about two weeks after the swelling of the vulva becomes noticeable. Typically, she should be brought to the male's condo for the rendezvous. It would be wise to stay close to chaperone the first date to be sure the chemistry isn't overly explosive. Expect a lot of noise and commotion. The female may even adamantly reject the hob's advances. If he persists, the female usually wins after a horrific fight ensues.

Romance and schmoozing are the last things on a male fuzzy's mind when he meets up with his dream girl. No courtship is involved — unless you call clubbing her over the head and dragging her off by the fur to the nearest cave romantic. Typical mustelid love averages an hour or so, with ten minutes being noted for some unimpressive fellows and an awesome three hours being noted for some marathon guys. Okay, okay. Some males are gentle, and their mates actually seem to enjoy themselves. But, for the most part, unaltered boys are no Don Juans.

The male ferret practically tackles the female when he grabs her by the nape of the neck to mount her. He uses her to mop every corner of his condo, even though she may be screaming and biting in protest. Once she's in submission, he has his way with her. It's not uncommon for him to return for second or third helpings if they're left together.

Following are a couple of things you should know:

- ✔ The mating ritual of ferrets, specifically neck biting and prolonged intercourse, causes the release of hormones, which stimulates ovulation. Without it, the female will not release her eggs and will remain in heat.

- ✔ Females often receive puncture wounds on the neck during the mating ritual. Blood is not uncommon. Violently shaking the female and/or causing wounds serious enough for profuse bleeding is *not* normal. Separate the pair immediately.

- ✔ The male's penis has a bony hook at the tip that causes it to become latched inside the female once penetration is made. And the male remains hooked until he decides he's had enough and no sooner. *Do not* try to separate ferrets in the middle of the act. Besides ruining the mood, forcing the matter may injure one or both fuzzies.

Many breeders recommend keeping the breeding pair together for two to three days. Any longer than that and the male quickly gets on the female's nerves, causing arguments (and an occasional throwing of dishes). This lack of tolerance on the female's part often indicates that she's got little buns in the oven.

Breeding the female two days in a row may cause her to produce a bigger litter. If the fuzzy has fewer than five kits to nurse, she may go back into heat two to three weeks after the kits are born. This occurrence is called *lactational estrus.*

Pregnancy Basics

Female carpet sharks are *induced ovulators,* which means that their eggs aren't released until mating actually takes place. Pressure on the cervix, caused from the act of mating, and neck biting stimulates the eggs to be released (ovulation) 30 to 40 hours after the deed is done. Sperm can survive in the female for 36 to 48 hours. As many as 18 (typically 5 to 13) eggs are fertilized. The vulva begins to dry and shrink after a week and returns to normal size in 3 to 4 weeks — longer if breeding took place long after estrus began. If this shrinkage doesn't begin after a week or so, your fuzzy has not established pregnancy, and a new date should be set with the Neanderthal fert.

About two weeks into the pregnancy, you should be able to gently palpate the female's belly and feel the small walnut-sized babies. However, she may not show the typical bulging signs of pregnancy until one month into the pregnancy. The kits should arrive in about 41 to 43 days (usually 42 days), barring any unforeseen circumstances. Depending on the time of year, the new mom goes back into heat either two or three weeks after the kits are weaned or when the next breeding season arrives. A healthy ferret can have up to three successful litters a year, although most reputable breeders stick with one or two litters a year per fert.

If you're serious about breeding your female, find another breeder (if you don't have another female to breed yourself) who will have a ferret whelping around the same time as your little girl. Make prior arrangements to place your kits with the other nursing female if your mom proves to be an unfit mother for one reason or another. (Ferret moms aren't always good moms; sometimes they eat their kits, neglect them, or become physically unable to nurse them.) Hand-rearing kits is next to impossible.

What Happens If Your Unaltered Ferret Isn't Bred

A female fuzzbutt should be bred about two weeks after going into season. However, what if you decide not to breed your fuzzy once she's in estrus? Because ferrets are induced ovulators, they remain in heat indefinitely until they're bred. The result of such a prolonged estrus can be deadly.

When a ferret is in estrus, the level of estrogen rises dramatically. This raised level of hormone suppresses the production of blood cells in the bone marrow, resulting in a condition called *aplastic anemia*. This condition is almost always fatal if not treated because the ferret's red blood cells are simply not replaced as needed and/or she succumbs to bacterial infections from the lack of warrior white blood cells. Other signs may include pale gums, hind end weakness, patches of fur loss, and small areas of bleeding under the skin.

There are several ways to bring the female ferret out of estrus:

✔ Breed her to an unaltered male.

✔ Breed her to a vasectomized male. (The hormones are still going strong, but the road is blocked.)

✔ Have a ferret-knowledgeable vet give her a hormone injection to fake her out of heat.

✔ Spay her.

A hormone injection or breeding to a vasectomized male is a short-term solution that causes a false pregnancy in your female. She'll eventually come back into heat and be presented with the same problem. If you've decided that breeding your female is not for you, you should have her spayed.

Chapter 24

Preparing for the Bundles of Joy

- -

In This Chapter

▶ Pampering the mom-to-be and preparing for the arrivals

▶ Serving as midwife

▶ Recognizing and taking care of problems

▶ The hard facts about (and hardship of) rearing the kits yourself

- -

*I*f you're still thinking that breeding your ferret is a path you'd like to travel, you have quite a long way to go. You may be glowing with anticipation and excitement, but there are still many hurdles to overcome if you and your ferret get this far. Special care and attention for your female during, as well as after, the pregnancy is vital.

In addition to addressing the needs of a pregnant ferret, this chapter also discusses the actual birth of the kits. The mortality rate in newborn fuzzy kits is high. I tell you the basic things that can go wrong and what you might be able to do to help. This section is also great for people, especially shelter workers, who unexpectedly find themselves with a pregnant ferret.

This chapter isn't meant to be a step-by-step guide to breeding fuzzies. That takes years to learn. Consider this an overview of typical things encountered when breeding ferrets. If anything, it's meant to further convince you to leave the breeding to the experienced and responsible experts.

Mothering the Mom-to-Be

Get ready to pamper and schmooze the pregnant ferret even more than you already do for at least a couple of months. If you're a true ferret lover (and you'd better be), this part of the job shouldn't be too difficult. Just triple your current efforts. Your care may very well be rewarded with a healthy litter of adorable kits. On the other hand, complications are common no matter how well you care for Mom.

If she isn't already, your pregnant fuzzy should be handled gently and very frequently to get her as comfortable with you as possible. This positive interaction between you and the mom is critical, especially if you need to physically intervene during or shortly after birth. An unfamiliar hand poked into the nest may cause Mom to reject and/or cannibalize her kits.

Strange cravings?

Pickles and ice cream are not likely to be on the list of things your pregnant fuzzy craves. However, a pregnant ferret needs some extra nutrition to help her keep up her strength and maintain good health and body condition before the kits arrive. The extra nutrition is necessary during the nursing period, as well.

Experts recommend that the pregnant ferret's diet contain 35 to 40 percent protein and 10 to 20 percent fat, with the fat being increased to 30 percent once the fuzzy begins to *lactate*, or produce milk. Most nursing moms are extra thin, so keep up on the extra nutrition.

- ✔ Keep extra tubes of Linatone and Nutri-Cal on hand for frequent treats during playtime and cuddling. She should also have her basic food (kibble, if you choose) available at all times, as well as plenty of fresh water.

- ✔ Many breeders supplement the pregnant and nursing ferret's basic diet with cooked meat and eggs. You can use a thicker Duck Soup (see Chapter 14) or Bob's Chicken Gravy (see Chapter 29) or come up with your own creative recipes.

Pregnant and nursing ferrets are prone to some ailments that can be life threatening to both Mom and kits. Some of these ailments include mastitis, eclampsia, and nursing sickness. It's important that you monitor your female's health and behavior closely. For information on nursing sickness and mastitis, see the sidebar "Conditions your female may encounter" and the later section "The fuzzy mom on medical leave."

The maternity ward

Pregnant fuzzies can be kept with other pregnant fuzzies, but they *must* be separated and given private rooms at least two weeks before the kits are due. Private rooms should be secure enclosures with extra bedding and a snuggly nest box. Your nest box can be a large parrot nest box, a plastic kitty litter box, or something similar. The nest box itself should be clean and smooth to prevent injuries to the mom and kits and contain appropriate bedding.

Providing a nest box is imperative. It helps to keep the babies closer together and warmer. A baby that gets separated from the nest quickly chills and dies. The box also provides much-needed privacy for the new family.

- ✔ The cage itself should contain no openings greater than ¾ by ¾ inches because newborns are about the size of the average pinky finger. If necessary, you can kit-proof the nursery by safely attaching cardboard or sheet metal "guards" inside the cage around the entire perimeter and extending 5–6 inches high.

- ✔ Be careful about what type of bedding you choose. Avoid terry cloth or other materials that can snag little claws or unravel and strangle tiny heads and limbs. Shredded paper can work well, as can soft, durable cloth or clean straw.

As her due date draws close, Mom will begin to arrange the baby room just perfectly. She'll almost always pluck some fluffy wads of fur off her body to line the nest with (see Figure 24-1). Do not remove it. The soft fur will be an extra comfort to the helpless kits.

Figure 24-1:
Mom will begin pulling out her own fur to line her cozy nest before the birth of her kits.

Conditions your female may encounter

Your ferret may develop the following conditions. Here's a quick rundown of what to look for. All these conditions need immediate veterinary attention:

✔ **Eclampsia:** Occurs late in pregnancy, but before kits are born. Can kill both the mom and unborn kits. *Signs:* Loss of appetite, lethargy, dehydration, black, tarry poop, severe coat shedding. Cause unknown. Possibly related to diet and stress.

✔ **Mastitis:** Bacterial infection that occurs during early stages of lactation. *Signs:* Swelling, hardening, discoloration and tenderness of mammary glands; anorexia; lethargy; inability to nurse kits in severe cases.

✔ **Nursing sickness:** Occurs shortly before or shortly after kits are weaned. *Signs:* Loss of appetite, weakness, weight loss, incoordination, dehydration, possible death. Cause unknown. Possibly related to diet and stress.

✔ **Vaginitis:** From general irritation to the vulva and secondary bacterial infection, often from bedding material such as hay, straw and wood chips. *Signs:* Yellow discharge from vaginal area.

✔ **Pyometra:** Bacterial infection of the uterus that occurs in unspayed, *not* pregnant females. *Signs:* Pus discharge from vaginal area, distended abdomen from pus-filled uterus, lethargy, depressed appetite, increase in water consumption, fever.

Another option some breeders choose is to add an element of heat because kits can't maintain body heat without help from Mom or another source:

✔ You can hang a heat lamp (talk to a reptile person) several inches over one corner of the cage. The danger here is the possibility of making the nesting area too warm.

✔ You can place a heating pad under the cage (out of reach of the ferrets of course). Never put the entire nest box over the heating pad. Leaving the nest box half on and half off the heating pad gives the fuzzy the option to move toward or away from the warmth as needed. Again, be sure the heating pad doesn't turn the bottom of the nest box into a frying pan. Likewise, check it regularly to make sure it's still working and doing the job.

Finally, be quiet and limit your activity around the maternity ward as delivery approaches. That means no playing your bongos or allowing the dogs to romp and shake the cage. Such disturbances may cause Mom to panic and eat her kits when they finally do arrive. Also, the person who handled Mom most often during pregnancy should be the only person to invade the nest if invasion becomes absolutely necessary. Why? Again, cannibalism.

Off to the Delivery Room

Marking off the days on your calendar is a great idea. Ferrets in labor usually show very little signs of the imminent moment. She won't scream and holler and call the dad every terrible name in the book. She won't repeatedly threaten you if you fail to provide the proper pain relief.

The typical delivery

A normal delivery can happen quite quickly, with two to three hours being typical for average-sized litters. In larger litters, it may take a little longer, with several kits arriving each hour. Mom should be quietly observed for arising problems during this time but not disturbed unless absolutely necessary.

✔ Watch for kits still stuck in the placental sack. You'll have to help them out if Mom fails to do so. She'll lick them clean and stimulate their breathing once they're out. A kit stuck in the sack for too long will suffocate.

✔ Most kits die inside Mom if they aren't delivered by the 44th day. Kits that are overdue also continue to grow and will present problems, if delivery ensues, by blocking the birth canal (see the section "The difficult delivery").

Allow Mom to chew the umbilical cords in half instead of you cutting them. The crushing force of the chomp keeps the loose ends from bleeding. Also, make sure that Mom eats all the placental material. As disgusting as this practice seems to us, the placenta provides much needed nourishment for the fatigued mom. The placenta contains hormones that help the uterus to shrink and is also rich in iron to promote milk production.

The primary caretaker should clean up all the leftover mess over a period of a few days but beginning no sooner than 24 hours after the kits' arrival. Leaving the mess helps the kits to imprint through smell recognition and bond with Mom.

The new fuzzy mom usually curls up around her new kits, and they in turn immediately begin to suckle (see Figure 24-2). Many ferret breeders agree that the first three days of the kit's life are the most crucial. If the kit survives these difficult days, the chances of long-term survival are greatly heightened.

The difficult delivery

Many deliveries are far from typical. Many things can go wrong with a delivery that can lead to death in the kit, death of your fuzzy mom, and/or emergency cesarean section. The following are common occurrences:

Figure 24-2:
This new
mom nestles
up with her
day-old kits.

Photo courtesy of Jean Caputo-Lee

✔ Kits born too quickly for Mom may be a mass of entangled umbilical cords, resembling a small pile of spaghetti and pinky meatballs. Entangled kits can't nurse. They get cold quickly and die. Also, limbs and lives may be lost to the constriction of the drying cords and placentas around body parts. Watch carefully and shorten the umbilical cords as the kits are born, if necessary.

✔ A kit in an unusual birthing position (such as head tucked into chest) almost always blocks the birth canal, where it then dies and prevents the other kits from making their grand entrance. Then these poor kits also die. And then Mom cries, neglects the kits already delivered, and acts restless.

✔ Kits with congenital defects often become stuck in the birth canal and die.

✔ Small litters or overdue litters produce dangerously large kits. Large kits also cause a holdup in the birth canal.

Make sure that you have a very knowledgeable ferret vet close by and ready in case of delivery emergencies. In the case of kits stuck in the birth canal, it may be necessary to remind your vet *not* to administer *oxytocin*, a drug that causes intense contractions to eliminate the rest of the gunk inside of Mom. Doing so can cause a ruptured uterus and separation of the placentas, both leading to the death of any unborn kits.

Depending on the cause for the difficult delivery, your vet may inject your fuzzy mom with a labor-inducing drug. A cesarean section is a common procedure that many fuzzy moms face. If the healthy mom is well cared for after the surgery, she almost always is physically capable of nursing and caring for her kits properly.

Never assume that the delivery is complete. Making sure that no kits are left behind is essential to the life of your fuzzy mom. Make sure that you (if you're qualified) or your vet feels the jill's belly to rule out the possibility that another kit (dead or alive) is still inside her. Failing to check may lead to the death of your new mom and any unborn kits.

Some Problems You May Face

Maybe you'll got get lucky, and all the kits will arrive safely and soundly. You'll be happy as a clam and looking forward to helping raise the fuzzy family. What could possibly go wrong now? You name it. You still have a long way to go before the babies are out of the woods.

Some ferrets just aren't cut out to be moms. And even if you have the perfect mother fuzzy, situations often arise that prevent her from nursing her babies. In these situations, described in the following sections, a foster mom is vital in keeping the kits alive — unless the kits have already been cannibalized. Also, don't forget the role of a foster mom in the event that your fuzzy mom dies during pregnancy or delivery. As sad as it seems, the idea is not that far-fetched.

The difficult mother

Nervous or new moms often make poor mothers. Some ferrets just weren't meant to be moms and reject or cannibalize their babies for no apparent reason.

- Fuzzy moms like their kits warm. Cold babies almost always are rejected. If Mom is away for a period of time (surgery), keeping the babies warm while she's away is essential. Or, if kits wander away and get chilled, warm them up before returning them to the nest. Heating pads, lamps, and warm water bottles are good for this type of thing. Watch that you don't overheat them.

- Some moms require a meal before cozying up to their new babies. If your ferret seems uninterested after delivering all those kits, offer her some warm canned food or her kibble moistened with warm water.

- Fluctuations in cage temperature, noise, and/or activity surrounding the nest can make a mom cannibalize or reject her youngsters, so keep the area calm (now's not the time to let the kids come in to see the new arrivals).

The fuzzy mom on medical leave

Some fuzzy moms simply don't produce enough milk, or any milk at all, for the kits to nurse on. You should monitor the activity level and growth of all kits at all times while they're nursing. Kits should gain weight daily, tripling it by day 10. A kit that doesn't get enough nourishment slowly starves. He loses the desire to suckle, chills, and eventually dies. Weigh your babies daily. A newborn fuzzy can live three long days without eating before he dies.

If some milk is being produced, it's okay to leave the kits with Mom as long as you supplement the feedings with puppy or kitten milk replacer. The best solution, however, is a foster mom (see the section "Calling on the Foster Mom").

Mastitis, or bacterial infection of the mammary (milk) glands, is also very common in jills. Symptoms include hardening of the affected glands, tenderness, swelling, and discoloration. Moms with mastitis stop nursing. Kits must be removed until the jill has been successfully treated with antibiotics and is infection-free. Failure to treat the mom may result in her death.

Calling on the Foster Mom

A responsible breeder always has a foster fuzzy mom waiting in the wings in case an emergency arises. Most foster ferrets readily take new kits into their nest. The foster fuzzy is probably already nursing kits close in age to the ones being introduced. If she's a good milk producer, foster-nursing shouldn't be a problem since ferrets can nurse more kits than there are available nipples.

The best way to introduce the "orphans" into the nest is to first remove the foster mom. Allow the new kits to intermingle with the existing kits so that the new kits' scent becomes less distinct from the others' scent. If everyone smells the same, then no one can complain.

In the rare instance that the foster mom rejects the kits (monitor them closely), you need to find an immediate replacement foster mom. If one can't be located, hand-rearing the kits is an option, but a very difficult one. If the kits are less than ten days old, they will most likely die. The success rate increases with older kits.

Most of us have heard of animals taking on foster babies of their own species, but did you know that some individual animals would readily accept an orphaned baby of a completely different species? At our sanctuary, we've had nursing domestic cats raise raccoons and squirrels. We've also had nursing domestic rats raise hedgehogs (although the rats chewed off the quills). We know of dogs that have raised kittens and raccoons. Not all nursing moms will be up for the task of taking on orphans, especially ones of a different species. While it may be a risky venture, and I don't know personally of any ferrets being raised by another species, this might be an avenue I would consider if the odds of hand-rearing the ferret kits were highly unfavorable.

Hand-Rearing Kits

Hand-rearing a young kit is an emotionally and physically exhausting endeavor that rarely pays off. The mortality rate, even with experienced fuzzy humans, is high. Kits need Mom's milk for at least ten days in the beginning. Successful hand-rearing might be accomplished if you start with healthy kits that are 2 weeks old. In any case, you should give it your best shot if hand-rearing is your only option.

Give puppy or kitten milk replacer every four to six hours via a plastic eyedropper or bottle. Tube feeding is difficult, even for the experienced, and may lead to aspiration pneumonia in the kits.

If you make it to week 3, introduce the babies daily to a soft diet, such as canned cat or ferret food. They still need supplemental feedings until they're 4–5 weeks old.

Chapter 25

From Birth to Bundle of Energy

*I*f you make it through the pregnancy and birthing ordeal, you may just be fortunate enough to watch a kit or two grow up. Healthy kits grow rapidly, both physically and emotionally. It won't be long before you wipe away the tears in your eyes as you proclaim, "It seems like only yesterday Scooter was covered with newborn fuzz."

This chapter takes you step by step through the developmental stages of carpet sharks. Some stages aren't too pleasant, but they're only temporary if you do your part as a good fuzzy human. From physical changes to behavioral changes, I tell you what to expect almost every step of the way. However, when it comes to fuzzbutts, nothing is set in stone.

Fuzzy Infancy: Birth–3 Weeks

Kits are born into the fuzzy world completely helpless and dependent on Mom for survival (see Figure 25-1). Their eyes and ears are sealed shut, rendering them blind and deaf. A small layer of fuzz covers their tiny bodies, which are smaller than a normal tube of lipstick. Newborns typically weigh in at a whopping 6–12 grams at birth. Most kits are born without any teeth, although baby incisors usually appear by day 10.

Figure 25-1: The mortality rate in young kits can be high. These 2-day-old babies still have a long way to go.

Photo courtesy of Jean Caputo-Lee

Emotionally, healthy newborn kits have only two goals: food and warmth. If allowed, immediately after birth, they latch onto one of Mom's nipples and remain there for long periods of time, gorging themselves on rich milk. Adequately fed newborns should gain between 2 ½–3 grams per day during the first week of life, doubling their birth weight by day 5. Despite having just been squeezed through the birth canal and dropped into the cold world, newborns are active and mobile, although they have nowhere to go just yet.

Except for eating and sleeping, kits do very little in the first couple weeks of life. They explore their nest a tiny bit and start to develop the little muscles in their legs. They're also able to recognize Mom and siblings through smell. During these first few weeks, the young kits also need to be stimulated by mama fuzzy to go to the bathroom (see Figure 25-2).

Figure 25-2:
At 1½ weeks, these ferrets still depend 100 percent on Mom.

Photo courtesy of Jean Caputo-Lee

During the second week of life, well-fed kits should gain about 4 grams per day. By 10 days old, they should have tripled their birth weight and average about 30 grams. During the third week, the daily weight gain should be 6 grams. And by 3 weeks old, your fuzzy kits should be at least ten times heavier than when they were born. At this age, the males and females are easier to tell apart just by looking at them (without cheating and turning them over). Females are daintier and have narrower heads. The boys are butterballs with their wide heads and stockier builds.

Even though fuzzies are born with their eyes closed, you can tell whether they're albinos because the color of the eyes shows through the thin skin. If you can't see dark color behind the semitransparent eyelids, you know you have a bouncing baby albino.

Fuzzy Toddlerhood: 3–6 Weeks

Three-week-old kits are rapidly developing their nest legs as they boldly explore their environment with more tenacity (see Figure 25-3). Mom is still keeping a close eye on kits that may wander too far away. Although the kits still rely on Mom for the majority of their nourishment, natural weaning should begin at this age. Kits should be offered a soft mush or canned food a few times a day. The baby canine teeth and some baby premolars begin to erupt. Also during this period, permanent incisor teeth are breaking through and already pushing baby incisors out.

Weaning doesn't involve taking Mom away for good and plopping down a crock of odd-smelling mush in front of your confused kits. It's a gradual process that should begin at age 3 weeks and be complete at around 6 weeks of age. Kits need time to adapt to the nutritional change. During these three weeks, kits will rely less and less on Mom and begin to prefer the replacement diet.

Figure 25-3:
Three-week-old ferrets aren't much bigger than a tube of lipstick.

Photo courtesy of Jean Caputo-Lee

Week 4 is somewhat of a turning point in a kit's new life. Eyes and ears begin to show signs of opening up to the exciting world outside. The soft white fuzz should now be taking on some color and pattern, giving you a glimpse into the future. More baby premolars are erupting around this time. Healthy kits at this age should also be eager to dive into the bowl of soft mush and stuff themselves, while still taking advantage of Mom's milk supply. While Mom may still want to help with reminding the kits to go to the bathroom, the kits are showing signs of being the self-proficient poopers that their parents are.

By week 5, eyes and ears have opened and kits are ready to get into trouble. They are extremely active and are starting to rough and tumble with their siblings. By week 6, the kits should start eating more soft food and start relying less and less on Mom for nutritional support. Some breeders introduce the dreaded first distemper vaccination at this age. Chapter 13 has all the necessary details on types of vaccines and the vaccine schedule.

The Terrible Fuzzy Twos: 6–10 Weeks

Emotionally, at 6 to 7 weeks old, kits should be spending a lot of awake time playing mock-combat with their siblings. This play is important in developing hierarchy among the youngsters and preparing them for their futures as possible top furball in their new homes.

Also at around 7 weeks, they should quit hanging on Mom so much and start relying almost completely on soft food. Permanent canines are usually pushing through the sensitive gums, sometimes erupting just beside the baby canines. This is a pretty painful ordeal to the small fuzzbutt, who may now be in the throws of teething behavior. It's not unusual to have kits with canine teeth side by side for several days until the baby canines finally fall out.

Kits in the 6- to 10-week age range are extremely active and testing their humans to the limits. This is the critical training period, which many ferret humans fail to recognize. The furkids need to be handled frequently and gently. They need consistency and someone who'll teach them what is and isn't acceptable behavior. Because many kits arrive at pet shops at this age, they frequently don't receive the proper human guidance. Many of these toddlers will inevitably become troubled teenagers for their unsuspecting humans. Therefore, it's imperative that training begin as early as possible. For information on training, head to Part V.

At 8 weeks old, kits should now have four permanent canine teeth and be capable of eating the hard kibble that most other ferts are kept on. If you want to maintain your babies on a more natural diet (see Chapter 9 for details), now is the time to start introducing them to new tastes and smells. Babies are so impressionable.

Many private breeders begin to let their kits go to their new humans at around this age (see Figure 25-4). Some breeders wait as long as 12 weeks.

Figure 25-4:
These 8-
week-old
sable kits
are just
about ready
for their
new homes.

Photo courtesy of Jean Caputo-Lee

For those kits that received their first distemper shot at 6 weeks old, 9 weeks of age is the perfect time for the second attack on the heinie. For complete information on vaccine schedules, head to Chapter 13.

Adolescence Already? 10–15 Weeks

Your kits have almost all of their permanent teeth by 10 weeks of age. The little indentations on your fingers and arms are proof enough. Kidding aside, if your kits received the proper fuzzy guidance during their Terrible Twos stage, adolescence shouldn't be too bad.

By 3 months old (12 weeks), well-adjusted kits are learning that humans can be fun companions. While the activity level of kits this age still far surpasses the average human's (even with a double espresso), kits do begin to mellow a little bit. Emphasis on *a little bit*. Personalities are becoming well formed and defined during adolescence. Even though kits of this age range are still highly influenced by the humans who interact with them, it's relatively easy to pick out the alpha males and females (top furballs) by watching them interact with siblings and humans.

Teenagers and Puberty

Chances are, if you've been reading this whole Part VI deal on breeding, then you probably already know a little about puberty. In a nutshell, boys and girls typically arrive at this confusing emotional and hormonal state of disarray at the same time, or 6–12 months old, depending on the situation.

While mass producers of fuzzies (ferret farms) neuter their kits long before this age, many private breeders recommend that it be done at around 5 or 6 months old, or even older. This is when ferrets may start to show signs of the dreaded hormonal surge. Boys get stinkier and start bulging in places that didn't bulge before. Girls get a little more hyper, and their vulvas swell. If you can stand the smell and possible aggression, waiting to neuter the boys closer to 7 or 8 months of age usually results in larger fuzzy boys. At this age, both males and females are considered adults, or fully grown, though they don't act like it.

Part VII
Ferrets: Past and Future

The 5th Wave   By Rich Tennant

"Give it up. You're never going to train that thing to lie on your neck and act like a collar."

In this part . . .

This part guides you through a brief history of the relationship between humans and ferrets. Ferrets weren't always pets. They played many important roles throughout history. This part is important if you're interested in who boosted the image of ferrets. It also gives you information on the black-footed ferret. While man was a positive influence in terms of bringing the domestic ferret into our homes, the domestic ferret's endangered relative was not as fortunate at the hands of man. See just how related our ferret really is to this beautiful rare creature. If you're serious about your love of weasels and the environment, this part points you in the direction of helping not only the black-footed ferret, but also the land and animals they need to survive.

Chapter 26

The Historical and Hunting Ferret

• •

In This Chapter

▶ The historical timeline of the ferret

▶ How the ferret's skills were used in history

▶ A look at the sport of ferreting

▶ Famous ferret keepers and ferret references

• •

*H*ere's the bottom line up front: We don't know who's responsible for domesticating the ferret. Although it's clear that throughout documented history the ferret has been treasured for being the champion hunter it is, no one knows exactly *when* people began utilizing the ferret's skills. Sure, scientific theories exist and ancient hieroglyphic writings show *something* on the wall, but the history of the domestication of the ferret still remains wrapped in mystery. Physical evidence is lacking and inconclusive.

This chapter bores through the past, taking note of historical ferret sightings — some of which are more like hallucinations. You find out why the beloved ferret was so prized in the first place and that not only common folk enjoyed the company of weasels. You also get a brief lesson on the art of ferreting, as well as a stern lecture on why your pet ferret should only be hunting within the safety of your home.

Ferret Sightings in History

Tracking the ferret timeline is both factually difficult and headache causing. Many sources cite Egypt as the domesticator of ferrets, but there's no proof that this theory is true. Actually, more evidence points *away* from this theory than points to it. Egyptian hieroglyphics regularly portrayed images of weasel-like creatures, but several animals can fit the description — the mongoose being one of them. Prior to the domestication of the cat, the mongoose held the high esteem of snake catcher and keeper of the house in Egypt — and does so still today. So we can logically conclude that these hieroglyphics weren't showing ferrets at all but, rather, another animal native to the land. After all, there have been no reports of ferret mummies ever discovered in Egypt, and the Egyptians seemingly mummified everything.

Additionally, these hieroglyphics date back almost 500 years prior to the domestication of the cat, which happened about 4,000 years ago. Domestic ferrets bounced into the lives of humans only 2,500 years ago.

The first known written reference to an animal likely to be our domesticated ferret was around 400 BC by the Greek satirical writer Aristophanes (448–385 BC) in a series of at least four plays. Later, in 350 BC, there was another written reference by the Greek naturalist and philosopher Aristotle (384–322 BC). A reference was supposedly even made in the Bible, but it turned out to be a mistake in translation. The word in question, translated correctly, really means "small crawling things," or in modern day translations means "gecko."

Experts estimate that the ferret was introduced to North America a little more than 300 years ago. But only in more recent years (about the past 30 years) have we discovered the ferret's "fetching" personality.

No one really knows without doubt who's responsible for domesticating the ferret, but *thank you* to whoever it was.

A Knack for Meeting Man's Needs

Earlier civilizations must have found the ferret to be quite the efficient exterminator because Caesar Augustus received a request at around 60 BC to sail several ferrets via first class to the Balearic Islands to control a rabbit population explosion. And ferrets are no strangers to the seas; during the American Revolutionary War, it was quite common to keep several ferrets on board ships to patrol for rodents. In fact, a ship was even named after a ferret. In an 1823 newspaper article, the U.S. schooner, *The Ferret,* was reported to be chasing (capturing) pirates, giving strong evidence that the little animal was well known and respected. Being the small, flexible critters they are, ferrets were also used to navigate wire, cable, and tools through small openings and tunnels. People just tethered the wire or rope to the ferret and sent the ferret on through.

There are many more documented reports on the use of ferrets to control pests. Two of the greatest ferret keepers were said to be the German Emperor Frederick II (1194–1250) and Genghis Khan (1167–1227), ruler of the Mongol empire who kept ferrets strictly to hunt small game. This sport was called *ferreting* — a word still used today, both literally and figuratively.

Britain was graced with its first ferrets at around the 11th or 12th century. Curiously, to control the hunting of rabbits (a highly valued meat in Europe during the Middle Ages), ownership of ferrets was restricted to only those who could earn more than 40 shillings ($300) a year. This practice kept legal ferret ownership restricted to the middle and upper classes. It is also rumored that more bootlegged ferrets existed in the homes of peasants than all the legal ferrets in the middle and upper classes combined.

This Sport of Ferreting

The sport of ferreting (hunting with ferrets) probably developed hand in hand with the domestication of the ferret. The keeper, or ferretmeister (similar to a wisenheimer), would release a couple of ferrets near rabbit burrows and send the ferrets in to find the game. Like today's pointers and other gun dogs, working ferrets were kept track of by bells that were placed on their collars. Or sometimes a string was tied to the ferret. The purpose of the ferret was not to hunt but rather to simply chase the rabbit or other game out of its burrow. Often, the fleeing animal became entangled in nets that were used to prevent escape. The hunter then killed the prey animal with a club or gun. Sometimes, instead of using nets, the hunter used dogs or hawks to catch the game.

Sometimes a ferret would stay in the hole, eat its share of the catch, and go to sleep. The aggravated keeper would then have to send in another ferret tethered to a line to locate and awaken the stuffed, sleepy ferret. The keeper could then follow the line and dig out the ferrets and what was left of the carcass. Another option was to cover up all the exit holes except for one, set a mink trap, and hope the thieving ferret would be caught by morning. Because ferrets sometimes fell down on the job, working ferrets sometimes had their jaws physically wired or roped shut to prevent them from killing and eating the game. Although this jaw wiring practice was strongly discouraged, it was common to use muzzles on ferrets or even break off their canines.

Ferret keepers were sometimes poachers. The ferrets were hidden in the poacher's pants and taken out at night to hunt. Poachers were possibly the first large scale pet ferret owners. This would make sense if you consider that a poacher would typically spend more time bonding with and socializing the ferret, so as to reduce the risk of getting caught. Poaching with ferrets that were handled infrequently and only with gloves would be pretty risky since the lack of schmoozing would make ferrets particularly cranky. (This makes me wonder why anyone would put a cranky ferret in his or her pants . . . for whatever reason.)

As ferreting became more popular and the ferret gained respect, highly educated people took up the sport of ferreting, most keeping their ferrets in conditions far superior to what most people at that time would ever experience.

The sport of ferreting is still enjoyed by many people in Australia and Europe (see Figure 26-1). However, it's illegal in the United States and Canada. Although traditional ferreting is illegal in the United States today, our fuzzies remain quite the charmers, as well as beloved snatchers of our small worldly possessions.

Figure 26-1:
Working
ferrets are
teamed up
with their
hunting
humans.

I don't advise trying your hand at the sport of ferreting for many reasons:

✔ It's illegal.

✔ Your ferret could get lost, maybe even for good.

✔ Exposing your ferret to disease is quite possible.

✔ It's cold and dark and scary in those rabbit burrows (to me, anyway).

✔ Your ferret would prefer to be cuddled up with you in a safe, warm house.

✔ Your ferret could drown in water-filled burrows.

✔ What did that rabbit ever do to you?

Ferrets Catching On

Ferrets have tunneled their way into the lives of historical figures in many different capacities — from Caesar Augustus, who was asked for the working ferrets' services to rid an island of rabbits, to Queen Elizabeth I, who had a portrait done with one of her royal fuzzies. Ferrets were frequent subjects of famous artists, such as Leonardo da Vinci. Other famous ferret humans include comedian Dick Smothers and actor Dave Foley. Ferrets have weaseled into the theater in such movies as *Kindergarten Cop, Starship Troopers, Star Trek: The Next Generation* and *Beastmaster,* to mention just a few. The list goes on.

Ferrets have also made brief appearances on some television shows. Even Dr. Wendy Winsted and her ferrets Melinda and McGuinn made a guest appearance on what was then called *Late Night with David Letterman*. They (the ferrets, that is) performed the roll-over trick for a lap of milk and a bite of a stagehand's leftover roast beef sandwich.

Ferrets also are the source of punch lines and jokes. Take, for example, the television series *M*A*S*H*. Major Frank Burns was often referred to as "ferret face." I'm not sure where the insult lies, however. And David Letterman has frequently used the ferret in his Top Ten lists. I suppose that I can see some humor in it. After all, I have some very weaselly friends. They know who they are.

Chapter 27

A Note on the Black-Footed Ferret

• •

In This Chapter

▶ Meet the world's most endangered species

▶ The domestic ferret and black-footed ferret side by side

▶ Who's responsible for this mess?

▶ Past and present efforts to save the species

• •

A classic example of man's arrogance run amok, the black-footed ferret is considered by most to be one of the rarest mammals in the United States and perhaps the entire world. What could cause such a skilled hunter and cousin to our domestic ferret to earn such a title? It's no doubt that the plight of the black-footed ferret was caused both directly and indirectly by the human race. Sadly, his future remains uncertain as man continues to walk with heavy feet and little comprehension.

This chapter describes the physical traits of the black-footed ferret and how our domestic ferret stands up in comparison. In this chapter, you also find an overview on how the black-footed ferret compares to our domestic ferret, where the black-footed ferret came from, where he's been, and where he's heading. For those of you who are owned by your domestic ferrets, this chapter can make you a little more grateful for having your ferret so close in your safe home.

A Little Background Info

The black-footed ferret, known as *Mustela nigripes,* is a small, carnivorous predator that weighs between 1.5 and 2.5 pounds (0.7–1.1 kg) — approximately the same size as the mink and our domesticated fuzzy, or slightly larger than the weasel. In captivity, he may live as long as nine years, two to three times longer than expected in the wild.

It's easy to mistake the black-footed ferret as the great-grandparent of our lovable fuzzy ferrets because they share very similar features, and share the same ancestors: the steppe and the European polecat. Both the domesticated ferret and the black-footed ferret are European derived, but the black-footed ferret adapted in North America long before the ferret was even domesticated.

A close relative of the Siberian polecat, the ancestral black-footed ferret is thought to have come from northeast Asia, crossing at the point now known as the Bering Strait. The actual time period he scampered into North America remains uncertain. The estimates date as far back as 1 million years ago to as recent as 100,000 years ago.

The black-footed ferret arrived in North America as an efficient predator, but it was in North America that it evolved into the specialized predator of prairie dogs. It's known to be the only native North American ferret and is the smallest of the polecats.

Are Black-Footed Ferrets That Different?

Black-footed ferrets and our domesticated fuzzies share many similar physical features, body size, and behaviors. Skeletally speaking, they are almost identical. Small differences appear in the skull. The domestic ferret has a shorter and more rounded head and a slightly smaller nose. Its smaller ears give it an appearance of having a more pointed snout than the black-footed ferret. Both have strong front paws for digging and burrowing. The black-footed ferret has a more tubular tail unlike the tapered tail of the domestic ferret. It also has noticeably larger nocturnal eyes and broader ears needed for extra keen senses, along with a noticeably longer neck.

The black-footed ferret's nose is almost always solid black. It also always has the distinctive dark brown feet, legs and tip of tail. While our domestic ferrets can vary a great deal in color, shade and pattern, only limited variations in shade of body color exist in the black-footed ferret. Always present is a white, cream or buff full bib and a saddle of brown on its back. The saddle area is filled in with dark-tipped guard hairs that are lighter towards the roots of the hairs. Fur generally becomes lighter in shade towards and on the belly. All areas of brown can vary from light medium to dark depending on season and individual animal. Also very prominent on the black-footed ferret and almost all polecats is a white spot just above the top inner corner of each eye.

The Black-Footed Ferret's Territory

The black-footed ferret's range was once thought to be as vast as the prairie dog's. It thrived only where prairie dogs thrived, covering over 700 million acres. From southern Canada to northern Mexico, the prairie dog colonies were the life source for the black-footed ferret. Making up 90 percent of the black-footed ferret's diet, the prairie dog also furnished essential burrows, which were vital in providing shelter to the black-footed ferret. These burrows were safe havens that kept out the extreme weather and protected the black-footed ferret from predators. The burrows were also convenient places to whelp and rear offspring safely.

So with the essential presence of millions of prairie dogs inhabiting the territories, what could possibly push the black-footed ferret to the edge of extinction?

Enter Intolerant Man

The most devastating human actions leading to the demise of the black-footed ferret were not against the ferret at all but, rather, its food source — the prairie dog. Prairie dog colonies were viewed by local residents with extreme abomination for many reasons. Ranchers complained that the colonies competed with the local livestock for vital food. Agriculturists argued that they destroyed the land. As frequent carriers of sylvatic plague bacteria, introduced to North America by none other than the human animal, prairie dogs were also considered extreme health risks to nearby humans.

Prairie dogs knew as well as people where the best living environment was. Unfortunately, the locals didn't want their peaceful neighbors. With the help of the U.S. government, the lack of tolerance and understanding lead to rapid decimation of prairie dog populations.

How many were there?

Some biologists believe that the black-footed ferret was never an abundant animal to begin with. Others believe them to have numbered in the millions before human interference only 100 years ago. The latter argument could be supported by the fact that black-footed ferrets are generally secretive and elusive evening predators and would not generally be witnessed by the average human observer.

The most reckless attack on the prairie dog came in the form of mass poisoning; cans of cyanide gas were tossed into the burrows, or strychnine pellets were left disguised as treats. Contaminated carcasses were often eaten, which killed the unaware diner, including the black-footed ferret. And other animals inhabiting the burrows fell victim to these cruel assaults. The prairie dogs that survived the various strikes lost their habitat to land-clearing machines such as the bulldozer.

Experts estimate that 99 percent of the once vast prairie dog range remains cleared of these peaceful critters, leaving only 1.8 million acres with surviving colonies. In fact, legal poisoning and shooting of prairie dogs continues to this day.

Fighting for Survival

With the black-footed ferret's food source practically decimated, its demise rapidly grew closer. In 1960 people realized that the black-footed ferret population might be in danger, but by then it was too late. By the mid-1960s, the first in-depth studies began to indicate how grim the future looked for the black-footed ferret. In 1967 the black-footed ferret became legally protected — only 116 years after being given its official scientific name. And in 1973, the black-footed ferret was one of the first animals to be placed on the current Endangered Species List.

The last wild black-footed ferret was initially thought to have been seen in 1974, but a small group was discovered in Wyoming in 1981 after a dog presented an unusual and unfortunately dead animal to its bewildered human. The discovered colony flourished and reached almost 130 animals. However, the population was destroyed by 1985. Turns out that 50 percent of the prairie dog population feeding this hopeful Wyoming ferret colony tested positive for the rodent-decimating sylvatic plague bacteria, known to humans as the bubonic plague. Ferrets themselves are generally immune to the plague (see the sidebar "Natural immunity"), but prairie dogs aren't. The Wyoming prairie dogs died, taking away the black-footed ferrets' food source.

Natural immunity

All polecats, including the domestic ferret, are generally immune to the plague, although there may be some less resistant to the disease. The reason is probably because polecats and the plague originated in Europe. Polecats eat a variety of small mammals that include plague-infested rodents. Polecats probably developed an immunity to the disease over time.

Even more tragic was the fact that canine distemper, 100 percent fatal to black-footed ferrets, swept through the fragile group. This was as big a factor in wiping out the black-footed ferret as was killing off its food supply. The race was then on to capture the remaining wild black-footed ferrets. Between 1985 and 1987, the last 18 black-footed ferrets were rescued. The last-known wild ferret was taken alive in February 1987 in Wyoming — that is, before the reintroduction of the critters began taking place.

The Black-Footed Ferret Recovery Plan

The monumental goal of the Black-Footed Ferret Recovery Plan, developed and approved by the U.S. Fish and Wildlife Service in 1998, is to establish not less than ten geographically separate populations of wild, self-sustaining black-footed ferrets by the year 2010. Originally, this idealized plan called for the establishment of 1,500 sexually mature adults. In order to do this successfully, 500 or more individual black-footed ferrets were needed to maintain genetic diversity. While this task seemed like a positive step in the right direction, experts concluded that no prairie dog population currently exists in the United States that is large enough to sustain this huge number of black-footed ferrets. So the goal was downsized. As for the genetic diversity, the current population is known to be from a rather small gene pool.

Only since 1991 have attempts been made to reintroduce this species into the wild through captive-breeding efforts. These efforts have met with sobering obstacles, from the limited gene pool to the inability to successfully rehabilitate captive-reared juveniles into the wild to the lack of cooperation and care given by some of those in charge of protecting this beautiful, rare species. In addition, funding appears to be a major roadblock in the desperate attempt to save the black-footed ferret.

The first release of 49 black-footed ferrets yielded only 4 confirmed survivors 6–9 months later. A second release in 1992 of 90 youngsters proved just as disappointing. Within 30 days, only 14 remained. The largest contributor to the failure was predation by coyotes, though these predators were greatly reduced through culling prior to releasing the ferrets. Through the present, many other releases have been attempted in Wyoming, South Dakota, and Montana — with disheartening results. The survival rate is less than 10 percent. The precious small number of black-footed ferret survivors are located only in those three states, although Nebraska claims to have sightings but with no confirmed proof.

Although successfully killing prairie dogs is an innate behavior for the black-footed ferret, the ability to recognize and avoid predators has been severely impaired in captive-born and preconditioned ferrets. This fact proves to be their second biggest hurdle. Although preconditioning routines and procedures continue to be developed and modified, it's unclear what really needs to be done for the black-footed ferret in order to ensure its survival. Sadly, what is known is that the governmental policies that led to this tragedy remain largely unchanged and that the world is on the brink of losing one of its most fascinating creatures.

What You Can Do

Although the government recognizes that the survival of the black-footed ferret depends directly on the survival of prairie dog colonies, the government continues to support the mass killing of prairie dogs. It's possible that because the black-footed ferret is a specialized hunter and has not adapted to an alternate diet, we'll soon lose these beautiful critters forever.

Write to or call your local conservation office to find out how you can become directly involved in saving your local prairies. And if you're in a state where prairie dogs reside, step forward and take action. Find out what you can do to help protect the prairie dog's future.

To learn more about preserving our prairies and how you can help save the black-footed ferret, write to The Black-Footed Ferret Fund, National Fish and Wildlife Foundation, 1120 Connecticut Avenue, N.W., Suite 900, Washington, DC 20036. Or visit the group's Web site at www.blackfootedferret.org.

Part VIII
The Part of Tens

The 5th Wave   By Rich Tennant

"What I don't understand is how you could put the entire costume on without knowing the ferret was inside."

In this part . . .

If I could keep on writing about ferrets, I would do just that. But there's just too much information out there to put into one book. This part gives you a head start on new and exciting ferret recipes to keep your fuzzy from getting bored in the kitchen. It also lists many other resources available to you so that you can get all your fuzzy needs met — from the latest ferret information to the coolest novelties — and where you can go to meet other people who are as ferret fanatical as you are.

Chapter 28

Ten Common Myths and Misconceptions

• •

*W*hat kind of ferret book would this be if I didn't dedicate at least one small chapter to beating the tar out of the common myths and misconceptions? There are always at least one or two poor groups of animals out there getting a bad rap. All pets have their ups and downs, their pros and cons — just like people. But to stereotype an entire group based on a few misconceptions is just plain irresponsible. While some ferret misconceptions are way out in left field, one or two have a *little* merit. (I emphasize *little* because they're usually little things that are blown way out of proportion and attached to the entire business of ferrets.)

Following are 10 (well, almost) misconceptions associated with ferrets and reasons why they aren't true.

Ferrets Are Rodents

Get out of here. Ferrets are much cuter. Contrary to popular belief, not all small furry animals are rodents. Ferrets are relatives of polecats. Ferrets are carnivores. Most carnivores like to eat rodents. Most ferrets, however, are too busy sleeping or playing to care.

Ferrets Are Wild, Dangerous Animals

Sure. And pigs can fly. Occasionally, ferrets get wild with excitement during playtime. And the most dangerous thing about them is that you may die of laughter just watching them be ferrets. Except in California (boo hiss), ferrets legally meet the definition of *domestic:* They're fond of home life and household affairs. (I like that one — too bad they don't cook.) They're tame and made fit for domestic life. They've adapted or been bred to live with and be of use to man.

In fact, ferrets have been domesticated for thousands of years. They can't survive on their own and require human assistance. Like dogs and cats (which have more bite incidents than ferrets ever will), all domesticates have their moments. They can have bad days and need time-outs. In most cases, however, a well-treated ferret is a very, very loving and trusting ferret.

Feral Ferrets Will Take Over

The fear that escapees will form feral colonies and destroy native wildlife is basically unfounded and virtually impossible for several reasons. First of all, the majority of would-be escapees are already neutered and spayed. Second, unless some little old lady is leaving piles of ferret food under the bush and ferts actually get a chance to snarf it down before another animal steals it, escapees frequently die of starvation. Another reason they won't take over is because there's not a natural niche for them to fill in the wild. Most environments already have efficient predators filling all the possible niches. The domestic ferret let loose in North America's wild would be low on the food chain and would be eaten and pooped out the other end before you could even dook three times. (To see how difficult it is to reintroduce even *wild* ferrets — black-footed ferrets — into the wild and have them establish viable colonies, read Chapter 27.)

New Zealand has the only established feral colony of ferrets and these ferrets were purposely conditioned and introduced to control the rabbit population (another of many introduced species). New Zealand had no other predators when the ferret was introduced, and the colony successfully maintained itself on other prey animals (which they'd been conditioned to eat). New Zealand brought in several other species of predators at the same time as the ferret and also later to fill newly developed niches. These niches were made possible when more non-native land mammals were introduced to New Zealand's ecosystem.

Ferrets Are Vicious Biters

I won't kid you by saying that ferrets never bite. They can bite for many reasons (see Chapter 21). As with kittens, biting and nipping in young ferrets is a normal part of playing. They can be quickly taught not to bite their human. Some ferrets are more temperamental than others, and these guys may need more patience. Like most domestic animals, in most instances, the more love you give, the more you receive. Ferrets need daily handling and loving care. This daily attention reduces the possibility of biting due to fear or overstimulation when they finally are handled. Even the toughest ferrets can be turned around with proper handling, time, and patience.

Ferrets Pose a Serious Rabies Risk

Believe it or not, ferrets are extremely resistant to the rabies virus. There has never been a documented case of a human contracting rabies from a ferret. New studies indicate that ferrets may not even pass the virus through their saliva via a bite. There have been less than a handful of reported rabies cases in domestic ferrets in the 20th century. Still, all ferrets can and should receive their annual FDA-approved rabies vaccination formulated especially for ferrets.

Ferrets contract dumb rabies if infected (see Chapter 16 for a discussion of *dumb* versus *furious* rabies). And recent scientific studies note that the amount of rabies virus found in the saliva of an infected ferret is negligible. This data suggests that ferrets probably don't pass rabies via a bite at all. While many states still get paranoid and automatically impose the "off with its head" sentence to a misunderstood biting or scratching ferret, some states have come out of the fog and issue quarantine sentences instead. Hooray for the smart states.

The Stink Will Never Go Away

All ferrets have scent glands next to their heinies, from which they can emit a foul odor. Unneutered, non-descented males are the worst offenders. Many ferrets are descented and neutered at a young age.

Descented ferrets can stay odorless for quite some time, but skin glands produce a similar smell over time. Your ferret should be bathed as he approaches the borderline of tolerable stink (but no more than once every month or so). Because a poor diet can cause your ferret to smell a little more musky than a ferret on a high-protein, low-ash diet, make sure that you feed him a high-quality diet. Also, bad teeth and dirty ears are two more causes for stinky ferrets, so take care of his grooming and get him regular veterinary checkups. Basically, the stink of a ferret depends on your attentiveness as a ferret mom or dad.

Although I always push neutering, descenting is not necessary in order for you to live with your ferret. The odor is usually let loose when the animal is scared, overstimulated, or aggressive. Unlike with the skunk, the smell dissipates rapidly. Believe it or not, some people actually enjoy the smell of ferret and skunk spray. Manufacturers have even bottled the skunk smell and marketed it with good results. Go figure.

Chapter 29

Ten Recipes Your Ferret Will Love

OK, will you settle for seven delicious recipes instead of 10? Whether you're looking to add some variety into your ferret's diet or needing that perfect homemade "soup" for the sick or recovering ferret, we've got the right recipe for you! This section has some great recipes, compliments of my friend Bob Church, for you to try with your ferret.

With a few exceptions (Bob's Chicken Gravy has sent dozens of blenders to the great garbage dump beyond and is splattered on the kitchen walls of many seasoned ferret owners), most recipes are easy to make. You may even get one or two recipe ideas of your own. Remember, I believe the key to good health for any animal, including our ferrets, is a well-balanced and varied diet.

All of these recipes have been taste tested and fuzzy approved by ferrets all over the world! However, you may have noticed that the exact ingredient measurements are missing from most of the recipes. Bob's left this part mostly up to you. This may lead to some trial and error on your part. It's likely that no two recipes will ever be made the same unless you write down exactly how much you chose to use of this, that, and the other thing.

Bob's Chicken Gravy

This easy-to-digest and gentle-on-the-stomach recipe is great for ferrets who aren't feeling too well or those coming off a liquid diet and moving back onto solid foods. This recipe is about 70 percent chicken and roughly 30 percent animal fat, so you'll need a heavy-duty blender (or hand-cranked meat grinder) and probably some goggles. If you need to, cut the recipe in half.

Ingredients
1 whole roasting chicken, cut into small pieces (do not remove the skin, fat, bones, or giblets)

1 tablespoon olive oil

1 tablespoon vitamin supplement, such as Ferretone or Linatone

1 cup ferret, mink, or high-grade cat kibble

2 tablespoons fine bran, whole oats, or Metamucil

1 tube Nutri-Cal (use half or quarter tube for insulinoma ferrets)

3 or 4 eggshells

4 tablespoons honey

1 cup fat trimmings (uncooked)

Directions

Put on your goggles. Puree the chicken with the fat, kibble, and eggshells. Add water until you make a thin gravy. Remove your goggles. Pour the mix into a pot and cook for 30 minutes or until it has the consistency of cream or thick gravy. Add the rest of the ingredients and mix well. Let the mixture cool before serving.

Dip small pieces of bread in this mixture if your ferret doesn't readily accept the gravy on its own. He should begin to get used to it this way. You can also use a feeding syringe to introduce the gravy to the fuzzy. Take what's left over and pour the stuff into zipper bags or ice cube trays. Store it in the freezer.

When serving the gravy thawed, add water or Pedialyte to get the desired consistency and microwave it until it's warm. (**Note:** You can blend to desired consistencies for special needs.)

Bob's Chicken Ferretisee

Ingredients
Chicken (cut-up)

Lard or olive oil

Vitamin supplement, such as Ferretone or Linatone

½ cup kibble, ground up (a coffee grinder works well)

Directions

Cut pieces of chicken (including the bone) into ½-1 inch cubes. Melt some lard (or heat olive oil) in a wok until it is about ⅛-inch deep. Quick-fry the chicken cubes in the lard until they're golden brown. (The goal is to kill off any possible bacteria but leave the inside as raw as possible.) Set the chicken cubes aside to drain and cool. Place the chicken cubes in a bowl and lightly spray them with Ferretone or Linatone (use an atomizer). Add the ground-up kibble. Toss like a salad.

Freeze the unused portions and thaw as needed.

Foster's Tuna Shake

Ingredients
1 can tuna packed in spring water

⅛ cup heavy cream

1 teaspoon smooth peanut butter

4 chicken bones

Pedialyte (optional)

Directions
Dump the tuna (including the spring water) into a blender. Add the heavy cream, the peanut butter, and the four chicken bones. Blend to a milkshake-like consistency. You can also add a little Pedialyte if you'd like.

For any recipe that includes heavy cream or another dairy product, you can blend in a Lactaid tablet if you know beforehand your ferret is a little lactose intolerant or he shows signs (gets diarrhea) after eating it. Most ferrets tolerate the lactose in heavy cream, while some don't.

Bear's Jerky

Ingredients
Brisket (cheap cut)

Vitamin supplement, such as Ferretone or Linatone

High-quality bone meal

Directions
Cut the fat off the brisket. Slice the meat into ¼-inch thick strips. Place the strips onto a dehydrator screen and spray the surface of the meat with Ferretone or Linatone. Then sprinkle the bone meal on the top. Let it dehydrate before serving.

Stella's Super Soup

Ingredients

Water

Leftovers from your last turkey or chicken dinner

1 teaspoon chicken soup stock

Ground kibble or heavy cream

Directions

Bring about a half gallon of water to a boil. Add all the leftover bones from your last turkey or chicken dinner. Cut up the discarded skin, giblets, chicken fat, and meat into small pieces. Add the pieces to the boiling water. Boil until the bones begin to get soft (about 20 minutes). Add the chicken soup stock. Use ground up kibble or heavy cream to thicken the stock. Let the mixture cool before serving.

Tui's Chewie

Ingredients

Water

Non-flavored gelatin

Chicken or beef, finely chopped

Beef or chicken bouillon

Directions

Dissolve nonflavored gelatin in boiling water. (Make a supersaturated solution by adding only enough water to where no more gelatin will dissolve; you'll still see some bits floating around.) Toss in the finely chopped chicken or beef. Add flavor with chicken or beef bouillon. Pour the mixture onto a cookie tray sheet (or cookie molds). Cut it into rectangular shapes when it's dry. Place it in a cool dehydrator until it's rubbery and hardened. You can also store the small rectangular yummies uncovered in the freezer to freeze dry them a bit.

Carnivore Stew

Ingredients

Trimmings from a meat-based meal (skin, bones, giblets, fat, and meat waste)

Whole bits of kibble

Lard or fish oil (optional)

Directions

Boil the trimmings until they're cooked completely. Add kibble so that the kibble makes up ⅙ of the stew. If the mixture is low on fat, add a little lard or fish oil.

Chapter 30

Ten Ferret Resources

*F*inding good information on our beloved ferrets isn't nearly as difficult as it used to be. Once we had to drag ourselves to the library and bury our heads in books, if we could even find any good ones on the subject. While libraries are still wonderful sources of information, and several good ferret books have been published over the years, this chapter deals with more than just ferret books. In addition to mentioning some great books, I also tell you about some good magazines, Web sites, ferret forums, and ferret specialty stores. (And because there are so many good resources, I just *had* to include more than ten.)

Reading List

Books and magazines are the good 'ol fashioned way of learning things. They're not subject to power outages or Internet spam. They don't make you feel stupid in public. They just sit right there on your shelf or are piled neatly away for future reference right at your fingertips if necessary. My reading list consists of some ferret great books every ferret owner should consider adding to his or her library. It also contains a couple magazines specifically created to keep you updated on current ferret information.

- ✔ *Working Ferrets,* **by Jackie Drakeford (Swan Hill Press, 1996).** This book gives pet ferret owners a sneak peak at the sport of ferreting. Not only does it show you how they use and train ferrets to chase rabbits out of their burrows, but it also goes into great detail on the equipment and training aids used.

- ✔ *Biology and Diseases of the Ferret,* **by J.G. Fox (Williams & Wilkins, 1998).** This is an excellent advanced clinical book designed for use by veterinarians, but suitable for ambitious ferret owners who want to learn more about the ins and outs of their ferrets.

- ✔ *Ferrets, Rabbits and Rodents: Clinical Medicine and Surgery,* **by E.V. Hillyer and K.E. Quesenberry (W.B. Saunders Company, 1997).** This is an advanced clinical book, which you'll find on most veterinarians' shelves. It's great for the resourceful ferret owner who also happens to own rabbits or rodents, too.

✔ *Essentials of Ferrets: A Guide for Practitioners,* **by Karen Purcell, DVM, with Susan Brown, DVM (American Animal Hospital Assocation, 1999).** *Essentials of Ferrets* is perhaps one of the best books on the market today. It covers all areas of the latest ferret medicine for the ferret veterinarian, yet it is written in a manner that most pet owners can understand. In addition, this book provides an extended list of resources invaluable for both pet owners and veterinarians. It is available through the American Animal Hospital Association. To order, call (800) 883-6301.

✔ *A Practical Guide to Ferret Care,* **by Deborah Jeans. (Ferrets Inc., 1994).** This cute paperback is a must-have for all ferret owners. Written in an easy to understand format, this book covers all important areas of ferret care in an enjoyable manner.

✔ *The Ferret: An Owners Guide to a Healthy, Happy Pet,* **by Mary R. Shefferman (Howell Book House, 1996).** This is one of the best "quick reference" ferret books on the market. This compact hardcover packs all the basics into a comprehendible guide for new ferret owners.

✔ *The Wit and Wisdom of the Modern Ferrets: A Ferret's Perspective on Ferret Care,* **by Mary R. Shefferman (self published, 2000).** This is a unique look into ferret care and ferret fun from the eyes of the ferrets themselves. This is an all around enjoyable book that all ferret lovers should own.

✔ *Modern Ferret.* This wonderful magazine is published by ferret lovers for ferret lovers. It is a bimonthly publication every ferret owner should subscribe to. For information, contact:

Crunchy Concepts, Inc.
P.O. Box 1007
Smithtown, NY 11787
Web site: www.modernferret.com
E-mail: ModFerret@aol.com

✔ *Ferrets.* This bimonthly publication offers great up-to-date information on general ferret care and medicine. Another resource not to be forgotten! For information, contact:

Fancy Publications, Inc.
P.O. Box 55983
Boulder, CO 80322
800-365-4421
E-mail: Ferrets@fancypubs.com

Web Sites

Web sites are great places to find current information regarding our fuzzy ferrets, from disaster relief to novelties to shelters and more. Chances are, if you don't find what you're looking for on a particular Web site, the Web site you do find will have a link to get you where you need to go.

- ✔ **Ferret Friends Disaster Response International (FFDRI),** www.geocities.com/ffdri/index.html. A must-see Web site catering to the needs of all ferrets and ferret owners in distress. Check in regularly to see which projects they're working on currently and be sure to send them your support!

- ✔ **Animals for Awareness,** www.animalsforawareness.org. OK, so I'm plugging my own Web site! But this site has some awesome exotic animal care sheets, as well as ferrets available for adoption. It's an all-around cool site. In addition, I added a page on the site that lists a few other neat things that, if space had permitted, I would have put in this book — things like "Definitions only a Ferret Owner Can Appreciate" and the poems "Rainbow Bridge" and "The Meaning of Rescue." Enjoy them and don't forget to sign my guest book!

- ✔ **FerretWare,** www.ferretware.com. Novelties and supplies for ferrets and their humans. You can also contact FerretWare via Hildy Langewis, P.O. Box 1249, Magalia, CA 95954. Phone inquiries: 530-873-4720. Orders: 800-337-7389. E-mail address: hildy@ferretware.com.

- ✔ **Ferret Central on the WWW,** www.ferretcentral.org. This is the *best* ferret site on the entire Internet — a must for your Favorite Places folder. All the best ferret resources, nationally and internationally, can be reached from Ferret Central. You can also contact Ferret Central via Pamela Greene at pamg@alumni.rice.edu.

- ✔ **Ain't No Creek Ranch,** www.aintnocreek.com. Supplier of small animal supplies (including the custom ferret wheel), gift items, and other cool novelties. You can also contact Ain't No Creek Ranch via Dawn Wrobel, 1655 Union Ave., Chicago Heights, IL 60411. Phone inquiries: 708-754-5680.

- ✔ **The Ferret Company,** www.ferretcompany.com. This company is run by Jeanne Carley, talented photographer and creator of the fabulous Ferret Calendar. She also supplies other wonderful ferret items.

- ✔ **Corner Creek Acres,** www.cornercreek.com. Builder of custom homes for your precious pets. These cages are gorgeous, practical, and affordable! You can also contact Corner Creek Acres via Greg at 1603 S. Milner, Ottumwa, IA, 52501. Phone inquiries: 641-684-7122.

- ✔ **Ferret Information Bank,** www.acmeferret.com/info_toc.htm. This Web site maintains a database of articles, information and updates relating to all facets of ferret ownership, from bite statistics to current medical treatments.

✔ **The Ferret Store,** www.ferretstore.com. This is by far the very best internet source for ferret supplies and accessories. The site is well run, easy to navigate, and has fantastic customer service! You'll be pleasantly surprised by their large inventory for both ferrets and other pets. You must visit The Ferret Store!

✔ **International Ferret Congress.** www.ferretcongress.org. An outgrowth of the International Ferret Symposium Committee, this organization coordinates educational events, so check in regularly to see what's new!

Ferret Discussion Groups

True ferret lovers enjoy nothing more than talking about their ferrets! Not only are mailing lists and forums great places to share what you know, they're also wonderful places to get information quickly and meet people who have something very much in common with you.

✔ **Addictedtoferrets,** http://groups.yahoo.com/group/addictedtoferrets. This is a large group of fuzzy owners discussing all aspects of ferret care!

✔ **Ferret-Health-List,** http://groups.yahoo.com/group/Ferret-Health-List. This group is a must-join for anyone serious about learning more on ferret health. This forum has many experienced ferret owners and ferret vets on board, so don't miss this one!

✔ **Ferret Mailing List (FML),** ferret-request@cunyvm.cuny.edu. This is my all time favorite Internet group! An excellent mailing list for serious ferret owners. I encourage everyone to join. Send an e-mail to the above address, leave the subject line blank, and in the body of the e-mail type **Subscribe Ferret <Your first name> <Your last name>.** You'll then receive a daily digest of the latest posts and have access to the extensive archives. You can also contact Ferret Mailing List via Bill Gruber, P.O. Box 6179, New York, NY, 10150 or phone 800-9FERRET.

✔ **ferretlovers,** http://groups.yahoo.com/group/ferretlovers. A small, but growing group of ferret enthusiasts share stories, questions and concerns. This is a nice group!

✔ **Ferret-Talk,** http://groups.yahoo.com/group/Ferret-Talk. This is one of the bigger ferret mailing lists on e-groups dedicated to ferret owners and their concerns.

Appendix

Ferret Shelters, Organizations, and Clubs

· ·

Most of the shelters and contacts listed in this appendix are from the Internet and are for your reference only. Except for the Greater Chicago Ferret Association, which is top-notch, I can't testify to the quality or reputation of any of the other organizations listed. (***Note:*** Because shelters close or move and phone numbers are reassigned, I did not include phone numbers. Sorry if that dooks anyone off.)

This information is current as of July 1, 2000. For an up-to-date listing of shelters and resources in your state, send a SASE (self-addressed, stamped envelope) to STAR*Ferrets: Shelters That Adopt & Rescue Ferrets, P.O. Box 1832, Springfield, VA 22151-0832 or visit their Web site at www.thepetproject. com/starferrets.html.

U. S.

Following are shelters in the United States, arranged alphabetically by state.

Alabama

Cloud Nine Ferrets, Inc., Mark Zmyewski, Huntsville, AL 35801. cloud9ferrets@yahoo.com.

Gulf Coast Ferret Rescue, Mrs. Marty Loeffler, 522 Highway 43, Chicksaw, AL 36611.

Heaven Scent Ferret Rescue/Shelter, Sandi Robinson, #20 Mathews Tr. Pk, Midland City, AL 36350. fuzzyslave@aol.com, www.hometown.aol.com. fuzzyslave/.

Alaska

Rascal's Ferret Pals Shelter and Resort, Pete and Lisa Summers, P.O. Box 771229, Eagle River, AK 99577. ferretak@aol.com.

The Ferret Farm, Diana Ashton, 131 Dunbar Ave., Fairbanks, AK 99701.

Arizona

Central Arizona Ferret Club, Chere Gruver, 454 No. 95th Pl., Mesa, AZ 85207.

Ferret Corner Rescue and Adoption, Sharon Tucker, PO Box 64274, Tucson, AZ 85728. grey7399@aol.com, www.geocities.com/ferretcorneraz.

Heartbeat Ferrets, Helen White, 3415 N. 88th Ln., Phoenix, AZ 85037.

Huachaca Wuzzles Halfway House, Joanne Ruffner and Shawn McBride, 289 Patton St., Huachaca City, AZ, 85616. samls@theirver.com, www.geocities.com/huachacawuzzles/.

Arkansas

Fuzzy Kisses Ferret Shelter, Marta Towne, PO Box 457, 1199 CR 935, Green Forest, AR 72638.

Thieves Haven Ferret Rescue, Vikki L. Mick, 2926 E. State Hwy 150, Blytheville, AR 72315-7108. vmick@missconet.com.

California

Bay Area Legion of Superferrets, Lee Donehower, P.O. Box 5608, Berkeley, CA 94705. BayFerret@aol.com and LOSSF@aol.com.

CA SunFerret Shelter & Rescue/CA LOS, Suni Parker, P.O. Box 443, Ferndale, CA 95536-0443. SunFerret@aol.com and CALOS@aol.com.

California Domestic Ferret Association, CDFA, P.O. Box 1249, Magalia, CA 95954. Hildy@ferretware.com and www.cdfa.com.

Californians for Ferret Legalization & The Ferret Education Foundation, Jeanne Carley, 410 Mt. Home Rd., Woodside, CA 94062. ferretnews@aol.com and www.ferretnews.org.

Ferrets Anonymous, Claudia T., P.O. Box 6497, Torrance, CA 90504. FAMail@ferretsanonymous.com and www.ferretsanonymous.com.

Ferrets Anonymous, San Diego Chapter, Pat Wright, PO Box 6497, Torrance, CA 90504. DSRJ@cox.net, www.ferretsanon.com.

Golden State Ferret Society, M. Wilton, P.O. Box 2856, Fremont, CA 94536-0856.

Colorado

Colorado Ferret Rescue, Scottie Lewis, 8284 S. Cody St., Littleton, CO 80123. scotti@ix.netcom.com.

Especially Ferrets, Inc., Randy and Gloria Horton, 718 Uvalda St., Aurora, CO 80011. especiallyferrets@earthlink.net, www.especiallyferrets.org.

Ferret Rescue of the Western States / BFF Society, Carolyn R. Kinsey, 140 W. 29th St., Suite 191, Pueblo, CO 81008-1016, or P.O. Box 15194, Colorado Springs, CO, 80935, kinseyc@pcisys.net, www.ferretgates.com.

Ferrets Etc., Stephanie and Rick Sheme, 15775 Greenstone Circle, Parker, CO 80134. FerretsEtc@aol.com and www.geocities.com/Petsburgh/2786/.

The Crafty Ferret Rescue, Vickey Bishop, 1903 Lodestone Dr., Leadville, CO 80461. Ferrets@chaffee.net.

Connecticut

Ferret Association of CT, Inc., Ann and L. Vanessa Gruden, 16 Sherbrooke Ave., Hartford, CT 06106-3838. agruden@ferret-fact.org and www.ferret-fact.org.

Delaware

Delaware Valley Ferret Shelter, Steve Krouse/Cindy Sooy, 5 Cedar Ct., Newark, DE 19702.

The Ferret Zone, Patty Records, 86 Three Rivers Dr., Newark, DE 19702.

Florida

Broward Ferret and Rescue Referral, Carin Riley.
fuzzbutt@mindspring.com.

Central Florida Ferret Friends / LOS FL, Debbie Coburn, 1947 Bonneville
Dr., Orlando, FL 32826-4805. losfl@bellsouth.net.

Dookie's House Ferret Rescue & Shelter, Pat Elmore, 1312 Emerald Ave.,
Sebring, FL 33870. ferrets@dookieshouse.org and
www.dookieshouse.org.

Ferreteyes4ever, Dale and Kathy Hood, 515 Sandy Ln., Laguna Beach, FL
32413. ferreteyes20@aol.com.

Ferret Advocates of Florida, P.O. Box 431, Lacrosse, FL 32658-0431.
kitquest@hotmail.com.

Ferret Friends of Indian River Co., Chere McCoy, 8775 20th St., Lot 614,
Vero Beach, FL 32966. AgeDog1@aol.com.

Ferret Rescue at Mutt Management, Jeanine Brawn, 3635 Webber St.,
Sarasota, FL 34232. www.bigfoot.com/~muttmanagement.

Ferrets in the Sun Club & Rescue, Megan Scott, P.O. Box 4456,
Boynton Beach, FL 33424. fermom@attglobal.net, www.isabellascott.
com/ferret.

Ferrets on the Go (FOG), Deena Canals, 506 Miller Ln., Niceville, FL 32578.
DCanals@aol.com, www.webabout.com/fog.

Gainesville Ferret Meisters Club, Debbie Kemmerer DVM, Newberry, FL.
www.atlantic.net/~weah.

Loki's House Ferret Rescue & Shelter, Lorie Cotes, 92 W. North Shore Ave.,
N. Ft. Myers, FL 33903. ferrets@lokishouse.org and
www.ferrets@lokishouse.org.

NW Florida Ferret Rescue FL, Beth Crimmins, 1655 Bennetts End, Ft. Walton
Beach, FL 32547. BCKIWI@aol.com.

South Florida Ferret Hotline (info only), Mike Janke.
info@miamiferret.org and www.miamiferret.org.

The Dook Nook, Jackie Hawley, PO Box 441535, Jacksonville, FL 32222. ferrets@dooknook.com, and www.dooknook.com.

The Ferret Center, Pam Williams, 8940 S.E. Hobe Ridge Ave., Hobe Sound, FL 33455.

The Weasel Watch, Stephanie Mazzeo, 1605 S. Central Ave., Flagler Beach, FL 32136-3805.

Woodland Retreat Ferret Rescue (NE FL Branch of the former S FL Ferret Club & Rescue), Barbara Ludt, P.O. Box 984, Penney Farms, FL 32079-0984. tsunami9@bellsouth.net.

Widget's Halfway House, James Higgins, Winterhaven, FL 33884. stillkcn@gate.net and www.widgetshh.org.

Yoda's FAIRS (Ferret Adoption, Information, Rescue and Shelter), Pennie Paulik, Tampa, FL. PPaulik@Tampabay.rr.com.

Georgia

Ferret Business of Georgia, Juliana Quadrozzi, 1403 Old Virginia Ct., Marietta, GA 30067. ferretdiva@mindspring.com or ferrets@playful.com.

Idaho

Ferret Haven Shelter / Rescue, Gay Maulden, 2712 North 28th St., Boise, ID 83703. GMaulden@aol.com.

Linda's Ferret Haven, Linda Frandsen, 6243 South 3100 West, Rexburg, ID 83440. lindaf@ida.net.

North Idaho Ferret Rescue, Toni Sumerlin and Greg Snapp, 2680 Grand Tour Drive, Hayden Lake, ID 83835. ferretrescue@nidlink.com.

The Ferret Pad, David and Stacey Hieb, 125 Wilson Dr., Mountain Home, ID 83647.

Illinois

Animals for Awareness, Kim Schilling, P.O. Box 56, Palos Park, IL 60464. CrittersOnTheWeb@aol.com and www.animalsforawareness.org.

Greater Chicago Ferret Association, GCFA, P.O. Box 7093, Westchester, IL 60154-7093. www.GCFA.com.

Samson's Ferret Stopover Rescue of SW IL, Marge Szelmeczka, Lot 56, Rock Springs Mobile Estates, Shiloh, IL 62269-4819. anelderlyfert@moosemail. com and www.angelfire.com/journal/AnElderlyFerret/index.html.

Indiana

Circle City Ferret Club, Sally Childs-Helton, P.O. Box 2272, Indianapolis, IN 46206-9813. ferrets@circlecityferretclub.org, and www. circlecityferretclub.org.

Ferret Rescue & Halfway House, Mason Lowrey, 7150 St. Rd. 44, Martinsville, IN 46151.

Iowa

Dooks & Crooks Ferret Shelter, Candi Gerritson, 2812 Arbor St., Ames, IA 50014. feiveferretmommy@aol.com or DooksandCrooks@aol.com.

Eastern Iowa Ferret Association and Shelter, Suzanne Hoofnagle, 1422 Plato Rd., West Branch, IA 52358. suzanne-hoofnagle@uiowa.edu.

JaCY's Desert Rose Shelter, Apryl Lucius, PO Box 211, Cleghorn, IA 51014. calucius@netins.net or www.jdrferretry.com/adopt.html.

QCA Ferret Association, a.k.a. The Bandit Brigade, Cathy Humphreys, 1851Tanglefoot Ln., Bettendorf, IA 52722. Suds53@aol.com.

Kansas

Ferret Family Services, Troy Lynn Eckart, P.O. Box 186, Manhattan, KS 66505-0186. sprite@ksu.edu.

KS Ferret Association, Julie Thornton, 121 East 19th St., Lawrence, KS 66046.

Louisiana

Frisky Ferrets Info & Rescue, Tricia and Joe Conley, P.O. Box 4177, Shreveport, LA 71134. FFerrets@aol.com and members.aol.com/ fferrets/index.html.

JC's Ferret Shelter & Rescue, Cathy Wilkinson, 221-A Madison St., W. Monroe, LA 71291.

Poo's Little River Hideaway, Annette Leckie, 128 Hilderbrand Rd., Pollock, LA 71467. AnnetteL51@aol.com.

Maine

Ferret Club of Maine, 429 Parker Farm Rd., Buxton, ME 04093. www.ferretclubofmaine.org.

Ferret Rescue of Maine, Jim and Crystal Kennedy, 429 Parker Farm Rd., Buxton, ME 04093. jkdlivr@yahoo.com and www.geocities.com/fert_resq.

Mainely Ferrets Association, Adrienne Goldsmith, RR 4 Box 7300, Skowhegan, ME 04976.

Maryland

All About Bandit, Carol and Jim Scott, 252 Long Point Rd., Crownsville, MD 21032. AABferrets@aol.com or baferret5@aol.com.

American Ferret Association, AFA, P.O. Box 255, Crownsville, MD 21032-0255. afa@ferret.org and www.ferret.org.

Baltimore Ferret Club & Shelter, Diane Rogers, 2306 Pickwick Rd., Gwynn Oak, MD 21207. baferret2@aol.com or www.baltoferret.com.

Rocky's Ferret Rescue and Shelter, Barbara Clay, 832C Falls Rd., Parkton, MD 21120. bdoclay@msn.com and www.gfme.com/ferretrescue.

Treasured Ferrets, Pat Musick (formerly Ball), 4811 Rockford Dr., Hyattsville, MD 20784.

Massachusetts

Falmouth Friends of Ferrets Shelter, Laura Bancroft, 17 Mello St., E. Falmouth, MA 02536.

Frisky Ferret Shelter, Lorraine Denicourt, 8 Pluff Ave., N. Reading, MA 01864. FurCritter@aol.com.

Gimme Shelter Ferret Rescue, Jan DeJesus, 152 Great Nick Rd., Wareham, MA 02571. Gimmeeshelter@mediaone.net.

Massachusetts Ferret Friends Inc., MaFF, P.O. Box 3123, Wakefield, MA 01880. Info@maferrets.org and www.maferrets.org/.

New England Ferret Foster, Education, and Rescue, Inc. (NEFFER), Dianne Wood, PO Box 1165, Westfield, MA 01085. www.neferrets.org.

The Educated Ferret Association, Donna Spirito, 43 North Main St., Apt. 1, S. Hadley, MA 01075. educatedferret@aol.com or www.theeducatedferret.org.

Michigan

Enchanted Castles Kings & Queens, Carolyn Distel, 9393 Rattlee Lake Road, Clarkston, MI 48348. enchantedcastle9393@yahoo.com

Fascinating Ferrets, Debbie Miller, 11702 Ziegler, Taylor, MI 48180. FasFerr-GLFA@glblnet.com.

Midwest Ferret Connection, Dee Gage, 1370 Dewberry Place NE #16, Grand Rapids, MI 49503. trofeo@sol.com.

Midwest Ferret Fellowship, 510 W. Howe Ave., Lansing MI, 48906. furdragonsden@yahoo.com and www.midwestferretfellowship.org.

MKARESQ, Mary Mewton, 13840 Couwlier Rd., Warren, MI 48089. sirk6@msn.com or www.MKARESQ.com.

Ferret Locator Services & Rescue, Bill Kettler, P.O. Box 90471, Burton, MI 48509.

FuzzButt Hut, Melanie Swider, 45 Avonlea SW, Wyoming, MI 49548. Frrt2@aol.com.

Mid-Michigan Heart Bandits, Marie Schatz, 327 Northfield Dr., Battle Creek, MI 49015.

My Last Home, Diamond Louks, 38028 Main St., New Baltimore, MI 48047.

Sunshine Ferretry and Shelter, Victoria Sims, 1104 W. Bissonette Rd., Oscoda, MI 48750-9226.

Suzy's Second Chance Ferret Shelter, Bruce Plaisier, 1250 Emerald NE, Grand Rapids, MI 49505.

Minnesota

F.R.O.L.I.C., Liz Tveite, P.O. Box 854, Stillwater, MN 55082. frolicclub@aol.com and 65.103.27.60/itcoferrets/club/index.html and www.freehomepages.com/frolic.

...in the Company of Ferrets Inc., Laura Palmer, Stillwater, MN 55082. luvfuzzies@aol.com and www.freehomepages.com/itcoferrets.

Mississippi

Ferret Rescue/Referral Organization, John W. Pummill, 1436 Whitworth Cove, Southaven, MS 38671-2213. pummill@bellsouth.net.

Loving Arms No-Kill Shelter, 102 Jasmine Dr., Picayune, MS 39466.

Mississippi Ferret Friends, Bobby and Julie Reed, P.O. Box 5508, Pearl, MS 39288.

Missouri

FURRY, Kurt and Sara Petersen, 7301 Watson Rd., Suite 303, St. Louis, MO 63119. furry@furryshelters.com and www.furryferrets.org.

Kansas City Ferret Hotline Association, Bobbi McCanse, 904 E. 28th St., Kansas City, MO 64109.

Montana

Guardian Angel Ferret Rescue, George Edison, P.O. Box 85, Shepherd, MT 59079. gedison@imt.net.

Nebraska

Carwin's Ferret Rescue, Pat Butcher, 7010 Edna St., LaVista, NE 68128-4302.

Cherokee Ferret Rescue/Shelter, Omaha, NE 68105. Nbr1ferret@aol.com.

LOS of NE Shelter, Chris and Shelly Knudsen, P.O. Box 762, Hastings, NE 68902-0762. ferrets@tcgcs.com and www.tcqcs.com/~ferrets.

Nevada

24 Carat Ferret Rescue & Shelter, CJ Jones. weaselwom@aol.com and www.geocities.com/a_24k_ferret/.

Angel Ferret Shelter Inc., Donna Carlsen, 1448 Daybreak Rd., Las Vegas, NV 89108. AngelFeret@aol.com.

Club Ferret Las Vegas, Samantha Rosier, 6170 West Lake Mead Blvd. #164, Las Vegas, NV 89108. ClubFerret@aol.com and www.freeyellow.com/ members4/ ClubFerret.

New Hampshire

4 Li'l Paws Ferret Shelter, Joan and Dick Bossart, 1 Blair Rd., Merrimack, NH 03054-2511. Rbossart@aol.com and www4lilpaws.org.

Ferret Services of Freedom, Stephanie Mudgett, RR 1, Box 1592, Freedom, NH 03836. ferret.svcs@rscs.net.

Ferret Wise Rescue & Education Center, P.O. Box 561, Marlborough, NH 03455. ferretwise@ferretwise.org.

Luv of Ferrets Shelter & Rescue, Jo and Ed Fowler, New London, NH 03257. weldj@aol.com and www.luvferrets.com.

White Mountain Ferret Fanciers, S. Mudgett, 61 VFW St., Conway, NH 03818.

New Jersey

Ferret Hollow, Denise Jackson, 129 W. Westside Ave., Red Bank, NJ 07701. www.ferrethollow.org and deniseoj@home.com.

Ferret Lifeline Rescue / Adoption, Ellen Demchak, 2 Red Oak Rd., Wantage, NJ 07461.

Fuzztech, Jim Kauczka and Anne Ryan, 127 Aspen Dr., North Brunswick, NJ 08902. ducklite@aol.com.

NW Jersey Ferret Association, John Williamson, 40 Regency At Sussex, Sussex, NJ 07461.

NW Jersey Ferret Haven, Jane Casale, P.O. Box 136, Ogdensburg, NJ 07439-0136.

Support Our Shelters, Ela Heyn, 304 Hillside Ave., B11, Nutley, NJ 07110. ferret@instantlink.com.

New Mexico

Ferrets "R" Fun, Mini Tafoya, 8706 Second St. NW, Albuquerque, NM 87114. TannerMini@aol.com.

New Mexico Ferret Rescue, Ramona Keenan, 4600 Sunset Canyon Pine, Albuquerque, NM 87111. rkeenan@unm.edu.

New Mexico Ferret Shelter & Rescue, Amanda Christmas, 2730 Morningside NE, Albuquerque, NM 87110. AChristm@cph.unm.edu.

New York

A Ferret Club (AFC), Nina Trischitta, P.O. Box 6248, N. Babylon, NY 11703. ferretsafc@aol.com.

Ferrets & Friends of Upstate NY, Jeanne Stadtmiller, 226 Lawton Rd., Hilton, NY 14468-9773. FfUNYgirl@juno.com.

Home Again Rescue, Gale and Jay Putt, 123 Lower Sheep Pasture Rd., Setauket, NY 11733. GPutt@sescva.esc.edu.

NY Ferret's Rights Advocacy, David Guthartz, 94 Jeffery Ln., Oceanside, NY 11572-5936. NYFRAPRES@aol.com.

Obadiah's Ferret Rescue & Shelter, Patricia Nothnagle, 147 Shumway Rd., Brockport, NY 14420.

Southern Tier United Ferret Friends (STUFF), John Gordon Sr., 159 Lewis St., Endicott, NY 13760. jhgordo@aol.com.

W NY & Finger Lakes Ferret Association, WNYFLFA, P.O. Box 10085, Rochester, NY 14610-0085. WNYFLFA@aol.com.

WNYFLFA Shelter, Sandy DeBout, 356 Holt Rd., Webster, NY 14580-9138. sandy_debout@xn.xerox.com.

North Carolina

Exclusively Ferrets, Margaret Lehman, Rt. 1, Box 64A, Gilliam Mtn Rd., Hendersonville, NC 28792. cyberjoc@worldnet.att.net.

Ferret Guardian Rescue Haven, Diane Campbell, 111 Bay Berry Ct., Statesville, NC 28677. DianCamp@BellSouth.net and www. ferretguardian. org.

Triangle Ferret Lovers, Shari Gunter, P.O. Drawer 249, Efland, NC 27243. ShariDiane@aol.com and www.trifl.org.

Western North Carolina Ferret Association, Judy and Gary Skinner, 3219 Oran Yount Ln., Granite Falls, NC 28630. ferrethut@twave.net and users. twave.net/ferrethut/default.html.

Ohio

Ferrets Unlimited Ferret Shelter, Jean Caputo-Lee, 4116 Bucyrus Ave., Cleveland, OH 44109. ferret@en.com and www.ferretsunlimited.org.

Heart of Ohio Ferret Association & Rescue, HOFA, Scarlett Gray-Saling, 1762 Norma Rd., Columbus, OH 43229. ScarlettG@aol.com and www. HOFA-RESCUE.org.

International Ferret Congress, Linda Iroff, 46180 Butternut Ridge Rd., Oberlin, OH 44074. Linda.Iroff@oberlin.edu and www. ferretcongress.org.

Little Orphan Ferret Shelter & Rescue, Michelle Abner, 3655 St. Paris Park, Springfield, OH 45504. www.homestead.com/littleorphansferrets/ index.html.

Lori Sies, 3973 Elljay Dr., Cincinnati, OH 45241-2815. w3.one.net/~ferret.

Mystyx Critters & Rescue, Kim Wolf, Galloway, OH 43119. rescue@mystyxcritters.com and www.mystyxrescue.petfinder.com or www.mystyxcritters.com/rescue.html.

Northern Ohio Ferret Association, Jeff and Lana Bogusz, PO Box 110574, Cleveland, OH 44111. ohioferret@aol.com and www.ohioferret.org.

Robbie Christ, P.O. Box 62258, Cincinnati, OH 45262-0258. w3.one.net/ ~tsfc.

The Raisin Retreat, Laurie Long, 664 Bell Ave., Elyria, OH 44035.

West Central OH Ferret Shelter, Julie Fossa, 4525 Ottawa Rd., Lima, OH. 45801. julie_fossa@yahoo.com.

Oregon

Cascade Ferret Network, Elayne Barclay, P.O. Box 14884, Portland, OR 97293-0884. elayne@teleport.com and www.cascade-ferret.org.

Lane Area Ferret Lovers, Lucy or Marsha, P.O. Box 21854, Eugene OR 97402. www.michelsv.com/LAFL.

Oregon Ferret Association, OFA, P.O. Box 90682, Portland, OR 97290. www.oregon-ferret.org.

Oregon Ferret Shelter, 17560 S. Holly Ln., Oregon City, OR 97045. Slinky@teleport.com.

Pacific Ferret Shelter Network, Lin Miller, P.O. Box 5007, Oregon City, OR 97045. pfsn@ferretnet.org.

Pennsylvania

Dale F. Nupp, 107 Eldon Ave., Lansdowne, PA 19050. Dale_Nupp@icdc.com.

Ferret Frenzy Rescue, Kasey Mack, 2861 N. Charlotte St., Apt. C, Gilbertsville, PA 19525. dweasle@bellatlantic.net.

Ferret's Friends of Pittsburgh, Chris Sayne, 229 Paul Street, Pittsburgh, PA 15211. ferretfriendsofpgh@att.net and http://home.att.net/~ferretfriendsofpgh

Fran's Ferret Rescue, Fran Wiles, 870 Barlow-Greenmount Rd., Gettysburg, PA 17325-8711. fwiles@mail.cvn.net.

Furry O's Ferrets, Mike and Denise Orlowski, 439 Gruber Rd., Harleysville, PA 19438. feretrus@worlnet.att.net.

Last Chance Ferret Rescue, Diane Bodofsky, 389 Clair Rd., Southampton, PA 18966-3263. lcfertr@erols.com and www.newrainbowbridge.com.

Legion of Superferrets National, LOS Headquarters, P.O. Box 866, Levittown, PA 19058-0866. LOSPA@aol.com.

Oxford Ferret Rescue, Samantha Vulliet, 118 S. 6th St., Oxford, PA 19363.

PA Ferret Rescue & Club, Kymberlie Barone, P.O. Box 45, Gilbertsville, PA 19525. kym@ferretrescue.com and CLUB@ferretrescue.com and www.ferretrescue.com.

PA Ferret Rescue Association, Centre Co. Branch, Mary McCarty-Houser, P.O. Box 1206, State College, PA 16804-1206. mary@ferretrescue.com and www.ferretrescue.com.

PA Ferret Rescue Association, Westmoreland Co. Branch, Chris and Tara Palaski, P.O. Box 724, Greensburg, PA 15601. In2Ferrets@aol.com and ChrisAndTara@ferretrescue.com and www.ferretrescue.com.

Philly Pherrets, Michelle and Mike Tonkinson, 1626 S. Bailey St., Philadelphia, PA 19145. paferret@netreach.net and www.netreach.net/~paferret/phillyferrets.htm.

Sage Ferrets, Regina Hart, 3011 Pine Grove Rd., Industry, PA 15052. ferret@usaor.net and www.geocities.com/Petsburgh/1122.

Second Chance Ferret Referral Service, Ann Styer, 1136 Butter Ln., Reading, PA 19606. secondchanceferrets@juno.com.

Starfire's Ferret Shelter, Jodi and Steve Schroth, 3807 Over Dr., Harrisburg, PA 17109-1230. Starfire19@aol.com.

Support Our Shelters, Judith White, 1236 Belfield Ave., Drewel Hill, PA 19026-4211. ferreton@unidial.com.

The Ferret Lady, Betty Jones, P.O. Box 217, Fountainville, PA 18923.

Three Rivers Ferret Club, TRFC, P.O. Box 7412, Pittsburgh, PA 15213-0412. Contact Dolly Archey, 6600 Brighton Rd., Pittsburgh, PA 15202. trfc@trfn.clpgh.org and trfn.clpgh.org/trfc.

Three Rivers Ferret Council, Inc., PO Box 7412, Pittsburgh, PA 15213. trferretcouncil@att.net and http://home.att.net/~trferretcouncil.

WarmFuzzy Rescue, Harnesses, C. and Shirley Hertzog, RD 2, Box 2118, Maidencreek Rd., Fleetwood, PA 19522. warmfuzzy@aol.com.

Rhode Island

Ferret Association of Rhode Island (FARI), Holly and Moe Cyr, 181 Stony Ln., N. Kingstown, RI 02852-3823.

South Carolina

Legion of Superferrets — SC, Mary Wells, 4801 Sunset Blvd., #53, Lexington, SC 29072.

Tennessee

F.A.C.Tn., Mary Geiger, 403 Knob Hill Dr., Bristol, TN 37620.

Ferret Education & Rescue of TN, Teresa Glasgow, 745 Donna Dr., Lenoir City, TN 37771. glasgoww@usit.net.

Fuzzy Friends Safe Haven, Cheryl Chambers, 3416 Erin Rd., McEwen, TN 37101.

Ferret Rescue/Ref Org of Memphis Area, Lorie Frezza, 6320 Valleydale Dr., Memphis, TN 38141.

Texas

Ferret Haven, Kevin and Lori Goats, P.O. Box 442, Port Neches, TX 77651. ILuvNursin@aol.com and www.fortunecity.com/greenfield/vine/311.

Ferret Lover's Club of Texas, Debra Thomason, P.O. Box 286, Bedford, TX 76095-0286. flc@texasferret.org and www.texasferret.org.

Ferrets First Rescue & Shelter, serving east and north central Texas. Contact Patricia Curtis, P.O. Box 2368, Weatherford, TX 76086. Ferrets1st@aol.com and www.ferretsfirst.com.

For the Love of Ferrets, Jimena and Gail Hummel, 2304 Kingsway Dr., League City, TX 77573. ferret@hal-pc.org.

Fuzz Busters Ferret Lovers Club, Nancy C. Judd, 102 Indian Oaks Dr., Harker Heights, TX 76548. the_judds@N-Link.com.

Houston Area Ferret Association, Noni and Dave Clark, 18615 Twigsworth Ln., Atascouta, TX 77346. Nonette@aol.com.

Kozy Kingdom Ferret Rescue, Matthew Stevens, P.O. Box 201013, Arlington, TX 76006. ferretrescue@kozykingdom.com and www.kozykingdom.com/ferretrescue.

Michael's Ferret Rescue, Michael Pardue, 2804 South Bandera Dr., Wichita Falls, TX 76302-1319.

Raven's Ferret Retreat, Peggy Clow, 1206 Independence St., Plainview, TX 79072. `stormy@texasonline.net` and `www.geocities.com/Area51/Rampart/2390`.

Rio Grande Domestic Ferret Club, G. Shaw, P.O. Box 26928, El Paso, TX 79926. `RGDFC@yahoo.com`.

S. A. Ferret Enthusiasts, The Ferret Safe House — the Whites, P.O. Box 190042, San Antonio, TX 78280-0042. `SAFERick@aol.com`.

Schermerhorn's Ferret Shelter, Sharon Schermerhorn, 1713 Aggie Ln., Austin, TX 78757. `the_ferrets@hotmail.com`.

The Ferret Boarding House Inc., Cynthia Hill, 722 Wilken, Houston, TX 77008. `iluvferrets@juno.com`.

WhyNot? Ferrets Rescue/Assistance, Carla Smith, 14798 Bombay Ct., El Paso, TX 79927.

Utah

Ferret Shelter of St. George, Sherry or Arnie Unruh, 1614 W. 1470 N., St. George, UT 84770. `sunruh@infowest.com`.

United Ferret Organization, Rick Roller, 668 Union Square, Ste. 234, Sandy, UT 84070. `uferreto@SRYNET.com`.

Virginia

Chaotic Ferrets, Meg Carpenter, 8230 W. Boulevard Dr., Alexandria, VA 22308. `ChaoticFer@aol.com`.

Ferret Rescue of Tidewater, Joe Vautrinot III, 2800 Mayon Dr., Chesapeake, VA 23325. `billnpam@exis.net`.

Ferrets R#1 Shelter & Rescue, Faith Hood, 5906 Boston Dr., Falls Church, VA 22041. `FerretsR1@aol.com`.

Just A Business of Ferrets (JBF), Vickie L. McKimmey, P.O. Box 2371, Leesburg, VA 20177. `jbferret@mindspring.com` and `www.mindspring.com/~jbferret`.

Lisa's Friendly Fuzzies, Lisa A. Profitt, 8389 Woodline Ct., Manassas, VA 20110. `lv@lynchval.com`.

McCraig's Menagerie, Carole McCraig, 201 N. Lynnhaven Rd., Virginia Beach, VA 23452. ferrets@vabch.com.

Richmond Ferret Rescue League, Marlene Blackburn, 2940 Dundas Rd., Richmond, VA 23237. PrePet@erols.com.

Shelters That Adopt & Rescue Ferrets, STAR* Ferrets, P.O. Box 1832, Springfield, VA 22151-0832. STARFerret@AOL.com and www.netfopets. com/starferrets.html.

The Ferret Haven "By-the-Sea," Lisa Leidig. ferret@ferrethaven.org and www.ferrethaven.org.

Washington

Best Little Rabbit, Rodent & Ferret House, Sandi Ackerman, 14325 Lake City Way NE, Seattle, WA 98125. sandi@houserabbit.org.

Ferret Haven of Spokane, Paula Johnson, 2411 W. Rowan, Spokane, WA 99205.

Ferret Rescue of Spokane, Tracy Kilmer, N. 5408 Ash, Spokane, WA 99205. FerritLady@aol.com.

Ferrets NorthWest, Ed Lipinski, 4321 86th Ave. SE, Carol Ln., Mercer Island, WA 98030.

The Critterpen by Chemayn, C. Nordgulen and V. Riedinger, 1223 NE Central St., Olympia, WA 98506-4413. critterpen@earthlink.net and home.earthlink.net/~critterpen/index.html.

Tri City Ferret Club/Shelter, Glenda Mitchell, 325 Sanford, Richland, WA 99352. sychfert@gte.net.

Washington State Ferret Association/Shelter, Liane Beckwith and Charleen Schuster, Bellevue, WA 98029. liane@ferretlovers.com and Cferrettails@aol.com or www.washingtonferret.org.

West Virginia

Little Critters Association, Monty and Deborah White, HC 81 Box 29-C, Foster, WV 25081. Whitebuffalo@petlover.com.

Wisconsin

Ferret Fanciers of Greater Milwaukee (FFGM), P.O. Box 11625, Milwaukee, WI 53211-0625.

Kettle Moraine Ferret Lovers, Diane Lemberger, 2402 Park Ave. #3, West Bend, WI 53090.

The Ferret Den, S. Van der Linden, 1530 South 54th St., Milwaukee, WI 53214.

The Ferret Nook, Kathy Fritz, P.O. Box 3, Cambridge, WI 53523-0003. FerretNook@aol.com and www.ferretnook.com.

Wyoming

Frazzled Ferret Rescue, Tonya Reimers /Ann Clark, 257 West 7th St., Sheridan, WY 82801.

Canada

Ferret Rescue and Education Society (FRES), Marcy Kimura, 164 Manora Hill NE, Calgary, Alberta T2A4R9. fres@ferrets.ca or fres@shaw.ca and www.ferret.ca.

The Alberta Ferret Society, Barbara Gustafson, Site 1 Box 85, RR2, Tofield, Alberta T0B4J0. www.ferrets.edmontonab.com and ferts@telusplanet.net.

The Ferret Aid Society, Randy Belair, P.O. Box 1305B, Mississauga, Ontario L4Y4B6. magick@echo-on.net and home.echo-on.net/~magick.

The Ottawa Ferret Association, Pegge Clarke and Marlene Humphreys, PH10-900 Dynes Rd., Ottawa, Ontario K2C3L6. pegge@boondocks.ca and www.ottawaferretassociation.com.

New Zealand

New Zealand Ferret Protection & Welfare Society, Inc., John Chessum, Private Bag 25128 St. Heliers, Auckland. FerretPaws@clear.net.nz and www.geocities.com/heartland/village/9074.

Index

● E ●

Notes

Notes

FOR DUMMIES®

The easy way to get more done and have more fun

PERSONAL FINANCE

0-7645-5231-7

0-7645-2431-3

0-7645-5331-3

Also available:

Estate Planning For Dummies
(0-7645-5501-4)

401(k)s For Dummies
(0-7645-5468-9)

Frugal Living For Dummies
(0-7645-5403-4)

Microsoft Money "X" For
Dummies
(0-7645-1689-2)

Mutual Funds For Dummies
(0-7645-5329-1)

Personal Bankruptcy For
Dummies
(0-7645-5498-0)

Quicken "X" For Dummies
(0-7645-1666-3)

Stock Investing For Dummies
(0-7645-5411-5)

Taxes For Dummies 2003
(0-7645-5475-1)

BUSINESS & CAREERS

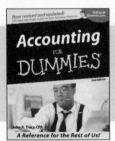

0-7645-5314-3

0-7645-5307-0

0-7645-5471-9

Also available:

Business Plans Kit For
Dummies
(0-7645-5365-8)

Consulting For Dummies
(0-7645-5034-9)

Cool Careers For Dummies
(0-7645-5345-3)

Human Resources Kit For
Dummies
(0-7645-5131-0)

Managing For Dummies
(1-5688-4858-7)

QuickBooks All-in-One Desk
Reference For Dummies
(0-7645-1963-8)

Selling For Dummies
(0-7645-5363-1)

Small Business Kit For
Dummies
(0-7645-5093-4)

Starting an eBay Business For
Dummies
(0-7645-1547-0)

HEALTH, SPORTS & FITNESS

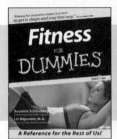

0-7645-5167-1

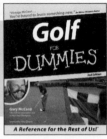

0-7645-5146-9

0-7645-5154-X

Also available:

Controlling Cholesterol For
Dummies
(0-7645-5440-9)

Dieting For Dummies
(0-7645-5126-4)

High Blood Pressure For
Dummies
(0-7645-5424-7)

Martial Arts For Dummies
(0-7645-5358-5)

Menopause For Dummies
(0-7645-5458-1)

Nutrition For Dummies
(0-7645-5180-9)

Power Yoga For Dummies
(0-7645-5342-9)

Thyroid For Dummies
(0-7645-5385-2)

Weight Training For Dummies
(0-7645-5168-X)

Yoga For Dummies
(0-7645-5117-5)

Available wherever books are sold.
Go to www.dummies.com or call 1-877-762-2974 to order direct.

FOR DUMMIES®

A world of resources to help you grow

HOME, GARDEN & HOBBIES

Feng Shui

0-7645-5295-3

Gardening

0-7645-5130-2

Guitar

0-7645-5106-X

FOOD & WINE

Cooking

0-7645-5250-3

Cookies

0-7645-5390-9

Wine

0-7645-5114-0

TRAVEL

Italy

0-7645-5453-0

Hawaii

0-7645-5438-7

Las Vegas

0-7645-5448-4

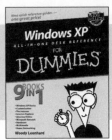

FOR DUMMIES®

Helping you expand your horizons and realize your potential

INTERNET

The Internet FOR DUMMIES

0-7645-0894-6

The Internet ALL-IN-ONE DESK REFERENCE FOR DUMMIES

0-7645-1659-0

eBay FOR DUMMIES

0-7645-1642-6

Also available:

America Online 7.0 For Dummies
(0-7645-1624-8)

Genealogy Online For Dummies
(0-7645-0807-5)

The Internet All-in-One Desk Reference For Dummies
(0-7645-1659-0)

Internet Explorer 6 For Dummies
(0-7645-1344-3)

The Internet For Dummies Quick Reference
(0-7645-1645-0)

Internet Privacy For Dummies
(0-7645-0846-6)

Researching Online For Dummies
(0-7645-0546-7)

Starting an Online Business For Dummies
(0-7645-1655-8)

DIGITAL MEDIA

Digital Photography FOR DUMMIES

0-7645-1664-7

Photoshop Elements 2 FOR DUMMIES

0-7645-1675-2

Digital Video FOR DUMMIES

0-7645-0806-7

Also available:

CD and DVD Recording For Dummies
(0-7645-1627-2)

Digital Photography All-in-One Desk Reference For Dummies
(0-7645-1800-3)

Digital Photography For Dummies Quick Reference
(0-7645-0750-8)

Home Recording for Musicians For Dummies
(0-7645-1634-5)

MP3 For Dummies
(0-7645-0858-X)

Paint Shop Pro "X" For Dummies
(0-7645-2440-2)

Photo Retouching & Restoration For Dummies
(0-7645-1662-0)

Scanners For Dummies
(0-7645-0783-4)

GRAPHICS

PowerPoint 2002 FOR DUMMIES

0-7645-0817-2

Photoshop 7 FOR DUMMIES

0-7645-1651-5

Macromedia Flash MX FOR DUMMIES

0-7645-0895-4

Also available:

Adobe Acrobat 5 PDF For Dummies
(0-7645-1652-3)

Fireworks 4 For Dummies
(0-7645-0804-0)

Illustrator 10 For Dummies
(0-7645-3636-2)

QuarkXPress 5 For Dummies
(0-7645-0643-9)

Visio 2000 For Dummies
(0-7645-0635-8)

Available wherever books are sold. Go to www.dummies.com or call 1-877-762-2974 to order direct.

FOR DUMMIES®

The advice and explanations you need to succeed

SELF-HELP, SPIRITUALITY & RELIGION

0-7645-5302-X

0-7645-5418-2

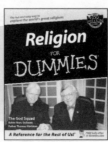
0-7645-5264-3

Also available:

The Bible For Dummies
(0-7645-5296-1)

Buddhism For Dummies
(0-7645-5359-3)

Christian Prayer For Dummies
(0-7645-5500-6)

Dating For Dummies
(0-7645-5072-1)

Judaism For Dummies
(0-7645-5299-6)

Potty Training For Dummies
(0-7645-5417-4)

Pregnancy For Dummies
(0-7645-5074-8)

Rekindling Romance For Dummies
(0-7645-5303-8)

Spirituality For Dummies
(0-7645-5298-8)

Weddings For Dummies
(0-7645-5055-1)

PETS

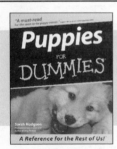
0-7645-5255-4

0-7645-5286-4

0-7645-5275-9

Also available:

Labrador Retrievers For Dummies
(0-7645-5281-3)

Aquariums For Dummies
(0-7645-5156-6)

Birds For Dummies
(0-7645-5139-6)

Dogs For Dummies
(0-7645-5274-0)

Ferrets For Dummies
(0-7645-5259-7)

German Shepherds For Dummies
(0-7645-5280-5)

Golden Retrievers For Dummies
(0-7645-5267-8)

Horses For Dummies
(0-7645-5138-8)

Jack Russell Terriers For Dummies
(0-7645-5268-6)

Puppies Raising & Training Diary For Dummies
(0-7645-0876-8)

EDUCATION & TEST PREPARATION

0-7645-5194-9

0-7645-5325-9

0-7645-5210-4

Also available:

Chemistry For Dummies
(0-7645-5430-1)

English Grammar For Dummies
(0-7645-5322-4)

French For Dummies
(0-7645-5193-0)

The GMAT For Dummies
(0-7645-5251-1)

Inglés Para Dummies
(0-7645-5427-1)

Italian For Dummies
(0-7645-5196-5)

Research Papers For Dummies
(0-7645-5426-3)

The SAT I For Dummies
(0-7645-5472-7)

U.S. History For Dummies
(0-7645-5249-X)

World History For Dummies
(0-7645-5242-2)